# Noxious New York

**Urban and Industrial Environments**
Series editor: Robert Gottlieb, Henry R. Luce Professor of Urban and Environmental Policy, Occidental College

For a complete list of books published in this series, please see the back of the book.

# Noxious New York

## The Racial Politics of Urban Health and Environmental Justice

Julie Sze

The MIT Press
Cambridge, Massachusetts
London, England

MIT Press books may be purchased at special quantity discounts for business or sales promotional use. For information, please e-mail special_sales@mitpress.mit.edu or write to Special Sales Department, The MIT Press, 55 Hayward Street, Cambridge, MA 02142.

This book was set in Sabon by SNP Best-set Typesetter Ltd., Hong Kong, and printed and bound in the United States of America.

Printed on recycled paper.

Library of Congress Cataloging-in-Publication Data
Sze, Julie.
  Noxious New York : the racial politics of urban health and environmental justice / Julie Sze.
     p.   cm.—(Urban and industrial environments)
  Includes bibliographical references and index.
  ISBN-10: 0-262-19554-2   ISBN-13: 978-0-262-19554-6 (alk. paper)
  ISBN-10: 0-262-69342-9   ISBN-13: 978-0-262-69342-4 (pbk : alk. paper)
    1. Environmental justice—New York (State)—New York. 2. Urban health—New York (State)—New York. 3. Minorities—Health aspects—New York (State)—New York. I. Title.
GE235.N7S94   2006
614.4'27471—dc22
                                                                2006049437

10 9 8 7 6 5 4 3

# Contents

# Acknowledgments

New York City is a place I love well. I love the energy and density and the constant stimulation, on the subways and the streets. It's a place my parents came to in the United States not knowing English and with few resources, and made lives for themselves and our family. It's a difficult and exciting place to live. Like so many others before me, New York City both fascinates and frustrates me, and it is the place that I have spent years researching, writing, and thinking about. New York City is also a profoundly personal and geographic space for me. On my way from work from Brooklyn to Harlem, I rode my bicycle through many different neighborhoods. I rode over the Brooklyn Bridge, with the World Trade Center looming in the distance, through Chinatown where I grew up, through the edge of the Village, where I went to school, up Madison Avenue where the Metropolitan Transit Authority and corporate headquarters of many Fortune 500 companies are located, through to Central Park, which I rode straight through to Harlem, where I worked next door to the Apollo Theatre.

In this book, I will take you through four neighborhoods in New York City. These are not the glamorous or glittering sections of the city, although they have been focal points of recent gentrification and intense land use development and real estate speculation. This is the gritty, polluted New York City, where asthma rates and lead poisoning rates are high. These are the places, mostly working-class and minority spaces, where despite a grim physical landscape of despair, community activism flourishes.

This book is shaped by time as well as space. I was supposed to defend this project as a dissertation proposal on September 11, 2001, when the World Trade Center attacks happened. For days afterward when I rode my bike, I felt my lungs constricting from the air pollution from the vast environmental damage of the disaster. For weeks and months, I wondered why my project mattered at all when the world seemed so burdened. I can not claim to answer that particular question, but my book ends with another event: I defended this project as a dissertation when I was eight months pregnant. Sofia was kicking excitedly throughout the defense as my committee members asked a series of difficult and challenging questions. When we emerged from the meeting, held on a hot day in August 2003, we found that massive blackouts had darkened New York City, the rest of the Northeast, and the Midwest. Given that part of this book is on energy deregulation and its effects, the irony was not lost on all who were present. In other words, energy policy became real. This book, researched and written before Sofia was born, is dedicated to her as a testament to the hopes that we can create a world with more justice for all.

I am heavily indebted to many people. First and foremost are the many activists who shared their struggles and their stories with me. These include Peggy Shepard, Cecil Corbin-Mark, Swati Prakash, Eddie Bautista, Carlos Padilla, Elizabeth Yeampierre, Marion Feinberg, Joe Perez, Frances Sturnim, Luis Garden-Acosta, Yolanda Garcia, and Mike Ewall in particular.

I'm continually inspired by the work of California and national environmental justice organizers from Communities from a Better Environment, Silicon Valley Toxics Coalition, Environmental Health Coalition, PODER, and Jose Bravo at Just Transition. Others whose work and commitment to environmental justice helped me along the way include: Michel Gelobter, Lily Lee, Torri Estrada, Na'Taki Osborne, Max Weintraub, Omar Freilla, Emily Chan, Diana Pei Wu, Leslie Lowe, Angela Park, Michele DePass, Tom Angotti, and Eva Hanhardt. My friends and colleagues from the Environmental Leadership Program also helped create and sustain a sense of a national intellectual and environmental community, especially to the class of 2002, (with extra special shout outs to: Max Weintraub, Matt Klingle, Kim Todd and Margo Tamez). Many environmental justice scholars have helped to support and encourage my work along the way, including Sheila Foster, Robert Bullard, Luke Cole, Michael Dorsey, Raquel Morello-Frosch, Rachel Stein, Lisa Park, and Joni Adamson.

I thank my committee members from New York University: Andrew Ross, Arlene Davila, Jack Tchen, Troy Duster, and Harvey Molotch. In particular, my chair, Andrew Ross, was a close reader and editor. His productivity, political commitment, and range and depth of knowledge are inspiring and intimidating. Thanks to other faculty at NYU, especially Lisa Duggan, and Robin Nagle who took us to Fresh Kills where I got to smell, taste, and feel what mounds of garbage actually mean. I also want to thank particular staff members, Alyssa Hepburn, Madala Hilaire, and John and the other security guards in the building for their daily conversation. There are several colleagues and friends from NYU without whom this book could not have been written: Adria Imada, Kim Gilmore, Tanya Erzen, Sujani Reddy, Alondra Nelson, and Thuy Linh Tu. My colleagues at the University of California at Davis have created and fostered a wonderful place to work, teach, and learn. In American studies, these include Jay Mechling, Eric Smoodin, Michael Smith, Carolyn Thomas De La Peña, Grace Wang, Cary Cordova, and Kay Clare Allen. There is an amazing intellectual community at Davis. In particular, I thank Miroslava Chavez-Garcia, Richard Kim, Kimberly Nettles, Jesikah Marie Ross, Laura Grindstaff, Thomas Beamish, Bruce Haynes, Wendy Ho, Bettina Ng'weno, Sergio De La Mora, Gayatri Gopinath, Benjamin Orlove, Judith Newton, Luis Guarnizo, Simon Sadler, Louis Warren, and Ari Kelman (the other one) for their friendship and support. I also thank the U.C. President's Postdoctoral Fellowship Program, which has created another vibrant network of scholars. Thanks also to Williams College, which awarded me a Bolin Fellowship, and the American Association of University Women, which awarded me a dissertation fellowship.

Thanks to series editor Robert Gottlieb and the anonymous reviewers who offered detailed comments that vastly improved the content. Thanks to Roshani Parekh for her research skills. Thanks also to Clay Morgan, Sandra Minkkinen, and the staff at The MIT Press who worked on different aspects of editing, design, production, and marketing.

Books don't get written in a vacuum, and friendship can help us get through the highs and lows of research and writing. In particular, I want to thank Jessica Garrison, Joy Singleton, Dave Colburn, Holly Telerant, Manisha Shah, Eleanor Lai, Jean Ma, Luz Gomez, Omar Jadwat, Susan Falk, Mahtab Habibian, Doug Heller, Danny Espinosa, Julie Maxson,

Ori Tzvieli, Maura McDermott, Ben Gertner, Bita Nazarian, Wells Chen, and Clarence Ting.

Most of all, I thank my parents, Lily and Tony Sze, and my sisters, Betty and Lena. All of them have very little idea of what I do. But they have offered me good food and laughs, and they give me perspective on what really matters in life. Finally, I thank my husband and partner, Sasha Abramsky (three books and counting; maybe someday I'll catch up). His careful editing and labor are embedded in this book. So too is his way of making me think about things in different and better ways. We may not always agree, but what we do agree on is the need to think, argue, and engage with the complex world in which we live in. In the words of Alfred Leavitt, a centenarian he once interviewed, "May we live a long, interesting, and above all—a tempestuous life."

# Introduction: Environmental Justice in a Moment of Danger

*Noxious New York* examines the culture, politics, and history of environmental justice activism in New York City; the intersection of planning and health, especially through the prism of asthma; and changes in garbage and energy systems as a result of privatization, globalization, and deregulation. It tracks urban planning and environmental health activism in four primarily minority and low-income communities in New York City: Sunset Park and Williamsburg in Brooklyn, West Harlem in Manhattan, and the South Bronx in the late 1980s and 1990s. These neighborhoods share racial and poverty demographics, housing stock, and zoning designations, as well as social and political histories as centers for working-class waterfront employment and municipal neglect (or in some cases, active destruction by state policies such as highway building). Historically central to the economic activity of the industrial city, each neighborhood has faced a rough transition to economic marginality in the recent past. Hurt by the decline of manufacturing and constrained by zoning designations that concentrate noxious polluting facilities in specific neighborhoods, these communities are characterized by high rates of despair (high levels of unemployment, disease, exposure to environmental pollutants as well as low levels of income, home ownership and education), an excess concentration of noxious facilities, and a lack of environmental benefits such as open space (see table 1).

During the 1980s and 1990s, a number of environmental justice campaigns emerged in response to proposals to site or expand noxious facilities in predominantly low-income areas and communities of color. These facilities were for sanitary or environmental services, including incinerators (medical waste and municipal), sludge and sewage treatment

**Table 1**
Comparison of the four neighborhoods in my study with the city-wide averages in terms of racial demographics, land for industrial land-use, percentage of the population assisted, and percentage of renters

| | New York City-Wide | Brooklyn Community District 1 Williamsburg/Greenpoint | Brooklyn Community District 7 Sunset Park/Windsor Terrace | Bronx Community District 1 Melrose/Mott Haven | Bronx Community District 2 Hunts Point/Longwood | Manhattan Community District 9 West Harlem |
|---|---|---|---|---|---|---|
| Percentage of population assisted (2001) | 19.8 | 33 | 24.2 | 44.9 | 42.7 | 27.6 |
| Industrial Land Use | 4.2 | 37.7 | 13 | 21.6 | 19.4 | 2.2 |
| Percentage Black or African-American Nonhispanic | 24.5 | 5.5 | 3.5 | 25.9 | 21.4 | 31.3 |
| Percentage Hispanic | 27 | 37.7 | 52.7 | 70.8 | 75.8 | 43.2 |
| Percentage Asian or Pacific Islander Nonhispanic | 9.8 | 3.6 | 17.4 | .5 | .4 | 5.1 |
| Renter occupied | 69.8 | 86.4 | 73.9 | 93.7 | 90.1 | 90.3 |

*Source*: New York Department of City Planning. Based on U.S. Census Bureau 2000 Census PL File and SF 1

plants, solid waste transfer stations, and power plants. The campaigns, which sprang up to oppose the proposals, brought thousands of ordinary citizens of diverse races and backgrounds to demonstrations and public hearings. These included the campaigns against the Brooklyn Navy Yard incinerator, the Bronx-Lebanon medical waste incinerator, the Sunset Park sludge treatment plant, and the North River sewage treatment plant. In addition, campaigns emerged in response to intensifying trends of privatization and deregulation in the solid waste and energy sectors that led to an increase in the number of waste transfer stations and power plants. In two of these neighborhoods, multiracial or multi-ethnic coalitions developed in response to particular controversial land use and environmental disputes (between Puerto Ricans and Hasidic Jews in Williamsburg and between Chinese immigrants and Latinos in Sunset Park). These environmental justice campaigns illustrate how these coalitions proved effective, if only around specific issues. I discuss individual facilities and campaigns, situated against broader and longer-term patterns of urban change, with an emphasis on the racial dimensions of such change.

Despite being geographically dispersed, these four neighborhoods are structurally linked through zoning designations that help construct an imagined political community shaped around a framework that interprets their land use and development struggles in remarkably similar ways (see figure 1). The four areas are mixed-use and waterfront neighborhoods, areas where there is a close proximity of uses on that land. Residents of mixed-use communities live with both the potential negative environmental health implications from proximity to noxious uses at the same time that these communities are a key part of each neighborhood's history and economy, as well as a central component of the city's overall economic diversity (Angotti and Hanhard 2001). These four neighborhoods appear remarkably similar to one another, but that did not guarantee that they would act with shared interests. Borrowing from Benedict Anderson's (1983) analysis of how nations are cultural constructs, my study analyzes how residents in these neighborhoods created a shared sense of place and identity, centered on their belief that they were targeted as victims of environmental racism, and also acted as political agents responsible for bringing environmental justice to their community. In this sense, these four neighborhoods also shared an imagined

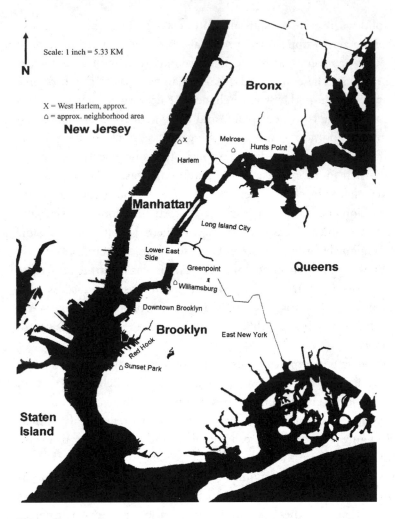

**Figure 1**
Map of New York City and neighborhoods in this study
(Credit: Pratt Center for Community Development)
*Note*: Melrose and Hunts Point approximately comprise the South Bronx

community with other urban localities that used environmental justice as their new language and approach to old problems of race and urban poverty. Although these were neighborhood-specific struggles, they cannot be understood apart from larger movements for environmental justice or the reality that they were being waged in one of the largest and most important cities in the world.

*Noxious New York* provides an overview of how the four neighborhoods and the issues of concern that their campaigns fought are structurally and symbolically linked. In each neighborhood, campaign, and coalition, I identify the main environmental justice organizations, the central community concerns on environmental health and clean air, and the political critique that the campaign developed. In each, leaders argued that the local residents were viable political agents, and they rejected social perceptions and corporate and government policies that characterized the poor and communities of color (both places and people) as dirty, pollutable, and disempowered. Each neighborhood framed its particular dispute as a breakdown in democratic decision making, using the language of environmental racism and environmental justice. They portrayed the polluting facilities as a violation of the human right to clean air in order to demonstrate the dangers of promoting economic interests over public and environmental health.

One of the goals of this book is to give voice to the activists who have been working on environment, health, and justice issues in New York City, some for over three decades. Many of their efforts have gone largely unrecognized and hidden from public view. The voices and stories, anger and eloquence, of people like Carlos Padilla, Elizabeth Yeampierre, Eddie Bautista, Peggy Shepard, and Luis Garden-Acosta are important to share. Some of them, like Yolanda Garcia, lost children to asthma.[1] Asthma is a key concern for activists; its spectre hovers like smog. Environmental justice activists in New York City believed and acted on the belief that child asthma was exacerbated by pollution in their neighborhoods. Environmental justice activism in New York City and nationally is driven largely by concern over high rates of asthma in minority communities, which has increased in the past two decades.[2]

In this history of contemporary activism, I document the ways in which activists in New York City's communities of color have come to ask why their neighborhoods are, in their words, "targeted" and treated

...mental "sacrifice zones," contributing to epidemic rates of
. and other environmentally influenced diseases. In response,
,orations and government agencies (at the local and state levels)
.ave generally brushed aside community assertions about environmental racism and injustices by framing these claims exclusively through the
prism of discriminatory intent. The result has been countless intractable
battles in New York City, suggesting that conflicts over race, land use,
and the environment are a never-ending quagmire. This study seeks to
understand how and why communities of color relate to and engage with
the politics of urban development, environment, and health. This history
of environmental justice activism in New York City thus offers a better
appreciation and explanation of why there are so many kinds of disputes
like these in cities and communities of color in contemporary urban
America.

In the four neighborhoods in this study, community-based organizations used the discourse of the environmental justice movement to frame
their local disputes. This language of inequitable racial distribution of
environmental benefits and pollution burdens is not limited to New York
City. In large cities throughout the United States—Los Angeles, Boston,
San Francisco, Seattle, Oakland, Baltimore, Detroit, and Philadelphia,
among others—environmental justice provided a crucial political and
discursive framework for communities of color to negotiate redevelopment, urban change, and competition over resources broadly defined—
environmental, political, and social. New York City environmental
justice activists seized hold of the national discourse of the environmental justice movement and applied it to the particular conflicts of low-
income and minority communities struggling to negotiate their place and
identity in the face of massive social and economic change: globalization, privatization, and deregulation. This national discourse, coupled
with the assertion of local and racial identity, directly shaped how residents responded to urban redevelopment and change. Discursively and
politically, community-based environmental justice activism challenged
several assumptions. Environmental justice activists focused on the
racially disproportionate ways in which seemingly nonracially specific
environmental, siting decisions, and policy changes were made, especially
on the health effects and impacts on local communities. Their activism
also rejected the notion that professionals, technocrats, and bureaucrats

from private companies and the government necessarily know best in the realm of health, environment, and community development policy that shapes their communities.

## Why New York?

Scholarship by Laura Pulido (2000) and recent work by Raquel Morello-Frosch, Jim Sadd, and Manuel Pastor (2002) have spotlighted how environmental and health inequalities are produced and reproduced in Los Angeles. In contrast, environmental justice campaigns in New York City have largely been neglected in the academic literature, although they have been well tracked by the city's investigative reporters. There are four studies on the Brooklyn Navy Yard campaign in Williamsburg (Gandy 2002, Miller 2000, Shaw 1996, Checker 2001). Yet the focus on that campaign alone omits the diversity and complexity of the "golden age" of New York City environmental justice activism and how these various campaigns are linked, in part because the issues that catalyzed the activism are overlapping. Many of the campaigns over different issues and through distinct time periods take place in the same neighborhoods. To illustrate how complex issues are linked, consider two recent controversies. First, New York City, like most of the East Coast and the Midwest, experienced a widespread blackout in August 2003. During the blackout, 490 million gallons of sewage spilled into the New York's rivers because the city never built generators at key sewage treatment plants to keep the plants functioning during a blackout. At least part of the reason that diesel generators are not currently being built is community concern over the health effects of diesel emissions. As one newspaper reported, "City officials attended meetings and gave presentations describing what the city felt it needed to do, but were met with anger and distrust from people nearby" (Elliot 2003). Here, sewage, energy, and air pollution are interlinked in a complex web of political conflict with environmental dimensions and tied to past controversies that remain unelaborated, clearly shaping the anger and distrust of local residents toward the city (over, in fact, proposed power plants in the area in the context of energy deregulation). Similarly, Oak Point in the South Bronx is the site of a former illegal dump where the city wants to build jails, while some segments of the community want industrial recycling, and what is actually being proposed is a power plant. Dumps, jails, recycling, and power plants are all mixed up in a contentious past and present and over competing visions of the future (Urbina 2004). Neither of these conflicts, or any of the others I examine in this study, can be explained in isolation—of issue or policy (air pollution, energy, garbage), community or neighborhood, or outside a serious analysis of race and urban environment, and environmental justice discourse, analysis and history.

There is no book-length treatment of New York City's environmental justice issues or activism. Therefore, one of the primary goals of *Noxious New York* is to document in detail the key activist campaigns in New York City as a way of better understanding the central features of urban environmental justice activism. This study complements David Pellow's *Garbage Wars: The Struggle for Environmental Justice in Chicago* (2002). I use a similar framework that focuses on the importance of process and history, the role of multiple stakeholders, the effects of social stratification by race and class, and the ability of those with the least access to resources to shape the struggle for environmental justice. But this study focuses not just on garbage; it also explores energy, air pollution, urban planning (zoning), and public health issues within the context of privatization, deregulation and municipal retrenchment. The case studies cover a variety of issues and industries, institutions, and "dirty processes," and they are directed at the links within and between this broad spectrum. This work also builds on Mathew Gandy's environmental history of New York City, *Concrete and Clay: Reworking Nature in New York City* (2002). In his study of the urban environment in New York City, Gandy briefly discusses environmental justice activism in his examination of the relationship among nature, cities, and social power.

New York City is an ideal site to understand the relationship between cities and social power, especially in the context of globalization and the framework of the world-city and local-global processes. It has undergone a well-documented economic transformation from the mid-twentieth century to today, from a solid manufacturing base to an economy based on finance, industry, and real estate (FIRE; Fitch 1993). This transformation has had particularly disastrous impacts on African Americans and Puerto Ricans, many of whom were previously employed in the manufacturing sector. Urbanists have detailed changes in global capitalism and the spatial and psychological impacts of these political and economic changes on global cities like New York.

However, there has been far too little attention paid to how communities of color are affected by global and corporate forces in New York City itself, much less the environmental and health components of recent spatial and political transformations. The privatization of solid waste and energy deregulation has led to radical changes in the local landscape—changes that have potentially negative health and environmental effects in communities of color already devastated by epidemic rates of asthma. Yet these major efforts to increase privatization and deregulation of environmental services in New York City have not been well explored.

The lack of serious scholarly attention to the efforts of the nation's largest city to privatize and deregulate environmental services is surprising given the larger democratic and political issues at stake. The governing ideology underpinning energy deregulation is the belief in the virtues of less government intervention and the free market, and thus must be understood within broader changes in political ideology. Privatization and deregulation, linked through the belief in and rhetoric of free markets, represent complementary policy choices. As a process, privatization denotes reducing the roles of government while increasing those of the private sector in activities such as asset ownership. In turn, to deregulate is to reduce or eliminate specific governmental rules and regulations that apply to private business.

This study is one of the few that analyzes environmental racism and the environmental justice movement as responses to privatization and deregulation and specifically engages world-city and globalization literatures. Environmental justice activists have argued that they are like "canaries in the mine" that face the "front line" of environmental and health risks. Environmental justice activism in New York City is an important example of the racialized and local response to the politics of neoliberalism, defined as a set of particular economic and development policies that favor deregulation, privatization, and free market approaches (Davila 2004).

In "The Environmental Problematic in World Cities" (1995), Roger Keil argues that the "environmental problematic" of world cities refers to "a specific *urban ecology* which emerges from a world city's relationship to the global economy and to other world cities" (288). He advocates taking an urban ecological view of world cities—one that simultaneously pays close attention to local political processes. This environmental policymaking discourse in world cities is global in significance and takes place among larger political transformations. It is through the examination of world cities that the process of understanding economic and ecological transformation, traced through the weakening of manufacturing and production and the increasing importance of financial industry and the information infrastructure (structured by globalization and hierarchies of cities over rural spaces, and between nations), is heightened. Keil notes: "How pollution's effects are distributed internally is a function of the largely racialized, gendered, and class-based divisions created by world city formation. Land use and the cost of growth are equally determined by the world city's international role. . . . The construction of a built environment for global capital in these cities and the transnational pressures on local land use have . . . exacerbated the stress on residential communities, green spaces, and public spaces used by the majority of citizens" (1995, 289). Similarly, Knox (1995) suggests that "world cities have also come to be special kinds of cultural spaces, sites for the construction of new cultural and political identities, for new discourses, texts, and metaphors through which the struggle for place is enacted" (246).

Environmental justice activism is thus important to analyze because racial minority communities are at the front lines of resistance to these policies and discourses valorizing the market and the private sector at the expense of the public and community interests. Environmental justice activism, like nuclear activism in the 1970s, throws a wrench into an arena that corporate polluters and the government want to dominate. As Christopherson (1994) argues, "Issues such as environmental quality, safety and freedom from urban congestion are not conceived of as urban qualities that citizens create, but as commodities. Access to these commodities is to be obtained not through citizen action, but consumer rights" (415). Conversely, environmental justice activism is a critique of the distribution of environmental pollution-as-commodity. Ultimately this activism is intimately tied to larger political factors and ideological transformations, specifically solid waste privatization and energy deregulation, which are disingenuously promoted by their corporate advocates and government allies as race-neutral policies that benefit everyone equally. In their activism against the siting of power plants and the expansion of waste transfer stations, New York City communities of color are intervening in larger debates about the need to protect the environment, public interest, and democracy, in the context of wrenching political and ideological changes that are altering the role of the state in relation to the community. After all, deregulation is a largely ideologically driven attempt by proponents to decrease the power of the state in regulating the private sector and is of direct benefit to corporate interests. Their resistance is of special import given the large scale of the solid waste and energy problem, the changing structure of these industries, and their pollution impacts. These macropolicy changes have local impacts that need to be closely analyzed. New York City's garbage privatization and New York State's energy deregulation offer an excellent opportunity to understand how communities, specifically low-income and communities of color, respond to policy change. In exploring these topics, I follow Weinberg, Pellow, and Schnaiberg's (2002) discussion of the "treadmill of production" in their analysis of the political economy of recycling: that local actions should be understood within larger regional and global processes, the driving action is conflict over scarce resources, and the idea that political and economic processes are not distinct.

The recent history of the impact of pro-development and pro-business ideology on concrete land use development and environmental proposals has also not been well documented. In particular, New York City's mayor Rudolph Giuliani stands out as a villain in this story for his belittling of the health and environmental concerns of local neighborhoods, especially those comprising low-income residents and communities of color. His derisive personality and combative politics were not confined to environmental issues and are perhaps exemplified through his criminal justice policies and lenience toward police brutality (McArdle and Erzen 2001). His response to environmental justice campaigns was just one more salient example of how hostile attitudes and politics toward low-income communities and neighborhoods of color in New York City were managed by city hall in the 1990s. Scholars have linked changes in New York City's garbage policy under Mayor Giuliani (which I detail in chapter 4) with the cultural politics embedded in his "quality of life" agenda. As Cohen (2005) writes, "Changes in the city's landscape during his tenure were tangible: there was less garbage on the sidewalks (including the end of the plague of dog droppings). Gone too were the squeegee men, the embodiment of urban poverty, who cleaned the windows of cars stopped in traffic for spare change; befouling city streets with crimes from drunkenness to public urination was no longer tolerated; and X-rated ('dirty') movie theaters and sex shops were aggressively driven out. . . . The coincidence of municipal garbage, animal feces, social outcasts and social dirt in the cultural and economic capital of a triumphant America is striking, for it illustrated the ways in which filth" remains politically contentious in contemporary culture (vii–viii).

Thus, this study adds to the literature on New York City politics and social movements. It builds on the urban redevelopment literature on New York City that documents the decline of manufacturing since the 1970s and the rise of postindustrialism and the service sector economy, analyzing the spatial and political impacts of these transformations. Some of these studies (Fainstein 1994, Savitch 1988) focus on politicians, planning authorities, and corporate actors, while others (Mele 2000, Abu Lughod 1994, Smith 1996) examine local activism in response to the after-effects of fiscal crisis, such as large-scale arson and planned shrinkage of city services. This study also looks at large-scale actors, though it focuses mainly on local respondents to macropolicies. Understanding the history of New York City's zoning code is crucial to any critique of environmental policy, but policy analysis is incomplete without attending to how real people live through their impacts. New York City's working-class communities have suffered devastating structural changes as a result of uneven development in the postindustrial city. Despite (or perhaps because of) the disproportionate effect of postindustrial change on New York City's black and Latino communities (especially those on the waterfront), activism has flourished in response to these political and social changes.

## Environmental Justice Overview

The approach here uses a broad environmental justice framework that builds on and integrates existing and new methodological, theoretical, and historical perspectives. At the same time, it maintains a political commitment to the urgent conflicts over environmental resources, pollution, and exploitation in communities.

Nationally the environmental justice movement emerged in the 1980s as a result of the confluence of events and reports that brought the terms *environmental racism* and *environmental justice* into the public sphere and into policy discourses.[3] Subsequent reports documented the "unequal protection" from environmental pollution by local, state, and national regulatory agencies.[4] Environmental racism describes the disproportionate effects of environmental pollution on racial minorities, while *environmental justice* is the name of the social movement that emerged in response to this problem. Because it describes the disproportionate balance between high levels of pollution exposure for people of color and the low level of environmental benefits they enjoy, environmental racism can be defined as the unequal distribution of environmental benefits and pollution burdens based on race.

The founding document that catalyzed the environmental justice movement is the Principles of Environmental Justice, adopted at the 1991 First People of Color Environmental Leadership summit and widely circulated. The principles were aimed at combating not only the abuses of corporate polluters, but also neglect by regulatory agencies and class and racial biases in mainstream environmental groups.[5] The environmental justice movement gained mainstream political momentum when President Clinton signed an executive order on environmental justice in 1994 mandating that all federal agencies generate agency-specific strategies to address the disproportionate pollution experienced by minority communities.[6] Issues taken on by the environmental justice movement and defined as exemplifying environmental racism run the gamut, from toxic and chemical pollution (oil refineries and petrochemical facilities in Cancer Alley in Louisiana); to military pollution on Native American lands; occupational exposures (in the garment industry and in Silicon Valley factories staffed by Asian and Latino immigrant women workers); health effects of poor housing such as lead poisoning; and consumption of contaminated fish by poor and immigrant communities.[7] Ideologically, environmental justice expands the concept of environment to include public and human health concerns, in addition to natural resources such as air, land, and water (Di Chiro 1998).

Environmental justice refers to the academic literature and the analytic framework that examine how race and class affect environmental issues. There is a large and growing literature on environmental racism, the environmental justice movement, and environmental equity. Its disciplinary locations are primarily located within sociology, natural resource policy, and environmental law, although environmental justice writings also appear within the disciplines of philosophy and environmental ethics, geography, and radical political economy. Excellent histories of the environmental justice movement have been published in recent years (Cole and Foster 2001, Taylor 2002; as a component of subaltern environmentalism, see Egan 2002), as have critical appraisals of the movement's strengths and weaknesses (Pellow and Brulle 2005). Social movement scholars have identified the key features of the environmental inequality framework and the environmental justice paradigm (Pellow 2000, Taylor 2000). The diverse issues, constituencies, and geography found under the umbrella of environmental justice are linked through a worldview, or environmental justice paradigm, that emphasizes an injustice frame (Taylor 2000, Capek 1993). Pulido and Peña (1998) argue that the distinction between mainstream and environmental justice issues is based not only in issue identification, but on positionality, or a person's location within the larger social formation shaped by factors such as race, class, gender, and sexuality.

The debate that has dominated the first generation of quantitative sociological research on environmental racism has revolved around the question of whether race or class is the primary factor in disparities of environmental exposure.[8] New York City's environmental justice activism contributes to the emergent scholarship on race and class, social movements, land use, and environmental activism in an urban context. Poor health that results from substandard environmental conditions is an important part of the landscape of urban inequity, measurable and comparable to poor education, housing, income, and mobility. Sociologists Cynthia Hamilton and Robert Bullard have suggested that the exposure of African Americans and other minorities in metropolitan areas to high levels of pollution is an outcome of racialized urban development. They argue that urban growth and development exist beside decay and blighted slums (Hamilton 1993). Elevated pollution exposure for people of color is at least in part an outcome of industrial growth and economic development by industrialists and landlords and neglect from regulatory agencies. According to Bullard (1994), "toxic time bombs" are not randomly scattered across the urban landscape, but are in fact concentrated in communities that have a high percentage of poor, elderly, young, and minority residents. Elevated toxics exposure takes a heavy economic and health-related toll in terms of the cost of toxic clean-up in polluted housing units. Environmental health scientists are beginning to document the health effects of disproportionate urban pollution exposures.[9]

This study moves beyond traditional environmental justice studies that draw from quantitative sociology by focusing on discourses of justice and how debates over culture, identity, and place frame the allocation of social, health, and environmental benefits and burdens in a society deeply stratified by race and class. Understanding whether and how environmental racism is real, and why it exists in New York City is, by definition, a complicated set of issues requiring a complex set of methods. One approach is quantitative, although there are few statistical studies of environmental equity in New York City (Fricker and Hengartner 2001). The statistical approach alone is difficult because of the changing demographics of particular neighborhoods and zoning designations and in part because of the problems of documentation and official record keeping by the Department of City Planning (Maantay 2000).

Ultimately I suggest that the why and how questions can best be answered by using an interdisciplinary approach that prioritizes the social, symbolic, and lived meanings of environmental justice activism. Rather than narrowly defining the issue of environmental justice in New York City in relation to the "race versus class" debate and overt discriminatory intent, I examine the histories and effects of particular policies such as zoning in creating problems of overconcentration of polluting facilities and what that pollution means for the affected communities in terms of their racial and community identity.

In doing so, I address and improve upon what Laura Pulido (2000) criticizes in dominant strands of environmental justice research. She argues that environmental justice and racism research has been "estranged from social science discussions of race" and is divorced from concerns of geography, in particular, how racism produces geographic and spatial inequalities. These theoretical deficiencies are built on narrow views of racism. These narrow views limit political claims and ultimately reproduce a racist social order. Pulido echoes political philosopher Iris Marion Young's (2000) call to analyze social movements and analyses that focus on claims for justice through lenses of "social difference" rather than "identity politics." Young suggests that social movements that prioritize the politics of difference reject abstract claims to justice, focusing on differences in social position, structures of power, and cultural affiliation in both political discussion and decision making. She writes, "Processes that produce and reproduce residential racial segregation illustrate how structural relations become inscribed in the physicality of the environment, often without anyone intending this outcome, thereby conditioning future action and interaction" (96).

Thus, this study illuminates the larger social and political meaning of urban environmental justice activism by closely examining the operations of justice, knowledge, and power in the postindustrial global city, drawing from theories on race and discourses of justice (Gelobter 1994). As Young (1990) writes, "Without such a critical stance, many questions about what occurs in a society and why, who benefits and who is harmed, will not be asked, and social theory is liable to reaffirm and reify the given social reality" (5). I use the discourse of fair distribution of benefits and burdens as an organizing principle for understanding environmental justice activism. This framework is particularly useful in understanding how community and racial identity is influenced and shaped by the distribution and consumption of public services ("benefits") in relation to environmentally polluting facilities ("burdens"). As geographer David Harvey (2001) notes, social movements around environmental justice, discrimination in land and housing markets, police violence, social integration, and education are mediators of what he calls "militant particularism," which translates from the personal to a broader terrain of politics that is a vibrant force in city life and political life writ large (207).

Following Pulido's call for a critical analytical approach to race in environmental racism research, I apply Omi and Winant's (1986) concept of racialization as a sociohistorical process to the field of environmental justice studies, especially in understanding the racial meaning of garbage and blight for urban communities of color. In particular, I examine how health, environment, and diseases, especially asthma and air pollution, are racialized through environmental justice activism. Environmental justice activists see themselves as racialized "communities of color" who share histories and perspectives with each other and with other places and peoples outside New York City. Of course, that racialization does not elide the differences among racial groups or mean that environmental justice activists act monolithically. There were several conflicts within specific places and between neighborhoods documented in this book where different environmental justice activists were at odds. Some of those differences were ascribed to racial and ethnic difference (debates about authenticity, who sold out, and who really represented the community). Overall, however, environmental justice activists generally did racialize particular health, land use, and environmental policy debates in remarkably consistent ways—whether the focus of attention was air pollution, garbage, sewage, or energy. The production of environmental racism and the social construction of the environmental justice movement follow similar processes of identity production through the spatialization and racialization of pollution and environmental politics. In this sense, I follow historian Eric Avila's (2004) analysis of the postwar transformation of race and space in Los Angeles and his call for racial and spatial ways of thinking about urban space, although my focus is primarily on health and environment.

### American Studies and the Culture of Environmental Justice Activism

This study is shaped by two key features: my training in American studies and its interdisciplinary character. This book is the first effort to explore environmental justice from an American studies perspective and one of a few that take an interdisciplinary approach to the topic (Pellow and Park 2003). Both features offer useful frameworks for understanding environmental justice that deepen our analysis of environmental racism and the meanings of environmental justice.

In *American Studies in a Moment of Danger* (2001), George Lipsitz argues that American studies is an ideal intellectual field to understand the culture of politics and the politics of culture. In the contemporary moment, characterized by corporate concentration and extreme local and global inequality, older commonsense notions of culture and place have been obliterated. He writes, "We need to appreciate the ways in which new social, cultural, economic, and political practices are rupturing traditional connections between culture and place, making local identities more and less important at the same time" (20). For Lipsitz, American studies is a privileged field to analyze global transformation because culture is key to understanding ideology and hegemony. Additionally, American studies scholarship has been particularly interested in social movements (May 1996, Denning 1996, Mechling 1996). Scholars have suggested that the field needs to be engaged more seriously with social science questions and methods (Lauter 2002), as well as environmental justice topics in particular (Fisher-Fishkin 2005). Elsewhere I have argued that because environmental justice is a cultural field, its articulations and lived meanings should be analyzed as such (Sze 2002). Culture also offers key sites to critique processes of labor, consumption, and culture that are rendered invisible by corporate capital. Similarly, the world city literature suggests that the urban and the local are key analytical sites in the context of globalization. In my study, I analyze the culture and meaning of environmental justice activism and environmental racism through consumption and social practices, which have material and health effects that are unequally distributed by race and class in the preeminent world city, New York. For example, how transportation produces air pollution, the material effluence of contemporary society that produces trash in high volumes, and the need for energy that drives our consumer society are all also cultural issues, although they tend to be framed primarily through environmental or policy lenses.

Environmental justice activism in New York City is about racial, geographic, and local identity at the same time that it is about a specific facility, issue, or campaign because particular social identities are produced and reinforced through the politics of race, place, and the urban environment. Environmental pollution, like risk, is a quantifiable "thing" that can be measured as well as socially reproduced (Beck 1993). I also examine the key role of science and technology in constructing knowledge and practice using discourses of rational urban planning approaches through zoning and in environmental health research.

## Interdisciplinary and Postdisciplinary Approaches to Environmental Justice

I use an interdisciplinary approach to analyze environmental justice activism in New York City. Some of the disciplines I draw on have taken on topics more common in environmental racism research, while in others, my approach is relatively new. I agree with theorists who critique narrow disciplinary approaches to new political formations, especially in the context of globalization and the restructuring of state formations. As Brenner (2004) writes, "Heterodox, postdisciplinary approaches to social analysis have become increasingly relevant in an era in which established divisions between social, economic, political and cultural processes are being undermined" (23). Similarly, Lipsitz (2001) suggests that "the present moment of global social and cultural transformation requires us to develop *trans*national and *post*national as well as national ways of knowing. . . . Industrialization, nationalism and the cold war were not just historical processes and events—they were also ways of knowing and ways of being. . . . Yet, many of the cultural and community crises we face today emanate from the ways in which the sense of place that guided social movements and scholarship in the past has now become obsolete" (4–5).

To presume that environmental racism and environmental justice are best analyzed solely through policy analysis and statistical data analysis begs the question of how best to understand the cultural and ideological roots of this inequality and local and racial resistance to the politics of neoliberalism and globalization. Environmental justice activism demands a more complex way of knowing—one that moves through community studies (which analyze campaigns individually) into a more dynamic analysis that puts campaigns in conversation with one another within a single city or between cities, and between sectors, and within frameworks of globalization and privatization. It should be clear by now that this study is qualitative and interdisciplinary.

Chapter 1 deals with the history of zoning and public health in New York City insofar as this history informs contemporary concern over how race and class affect clean air and urban environmental politics. It thus adds to the emerging literature on environmental justice history (Pellow and Park 2002, Washington 2005). Urban and environmental history offers a deeper historical view of the roots of contemporary problems. Historical links between planning and public health (and their divergence) are significant because urban environmental justice activism seeks to reconnect the fields of public health and urban planning through its concern with health disparities in environmentally influenced diseases such as asthma. Beginning with the nineteenth-century sanitary movement, I demonstrate how urban planning and public health were linked through the planning and building of sanitary services and infrastructure by experts, grounded in a shared history and concern with the problems of the modern city.

Chapter 2 continues a historical focus, looking at garbage, sewage development, and sludge management in New York City. In describing the history of environmental justice campaigns, this chapter highlights the larger macropolitical and historical forces, including federal legislation that shaped the spate of facility building in the metropolitan region in the 1980s and 1990s, within the framework of race, stigma, and pollution. I build on Cohen's (2005) notion that garbage policy is tied to a larger cultural politics of morality and filth, broadly defined. The need to find solutions to dispose of New York City's garbage, sewage, and sludge, often as a result of federal mandates, is the main reason for the extraordinary confluence of facility building in the past two decades. This chapter continues by outlining recent activism—specifically, the four campaigns that served as opening salvos for two decades of environmental justice activism. One of these, the campaign in Sunset Park, is a rare study of an Asian-Latino (new immigrant) coalition working on an environmental justice campaign. When successful, local environmental justice campaigns show that communities can effectively organize against corporate and governmental power by using a combination of politics, law, and science.

In chapter 3, I focus on how gender, race, and youth shape the politics of asthma activism in New York City. Race has been the primary frame for understanding environmental justice activism, but this chapter foregrounds gender and the politics of the family as important factors (Krauss 1994, Epstein 1992, 1997, Di Chiro 1998). Children are highly susceptible to the harmful effects of environmental pollutants, in particular, the health risks associated with high rates of air pollution. Environmental justice activists in New York focus on the outdoor air pollution risks as exacerbating already poor health conditions in their communities. Despite the centrality of asthma as an urban, racial, and environmental justice problem, it is just beginning to garner attention outside the field of public health and the sociology of health (Brown et al. 2005, Loh et al. 2002).

Not long after the launching of these campaigns, activists responded to New York City's proposal to radically restructure the solid waste disposal system that sought to privatize the residential solid waste stream, as well as New York State's deregulation of the energy industry. Chapter 4 examines the racial geography of environmental justice activism on garbage, drawing theoretically from geographers who write specifically on race and environmental racism (Laura Pulido and Ruth Gilmore), as well as Marxist geographers who analyze uneven development (Neil Smith and David Harvey). In other words, I analyze the actual spaces of neoliberalism and global capitalism, using garbage as the focal point (Brenner and Theodore 2003). In focusing on the racial and cultural politics of urban neoliberalism in New York City, I build on Davila's study of Latinos in East Harlem (2004). I show how citywide coalitions built on the foundation of early campaigns by mobilizing around the policy shifts on garbage and power: the Organization of Waterfront Neighborhoods and Communities United for Responsible Energy. Comprising members of communities hardest hit by industrial decline on the waterfront, these coalitions responded with particular ire to proposals to increase the number of waste transfer stations and power plants run by corporate polluters. The coalition's leaders, veterans of the earlier campaigns, applied the lessons they had learned about community mobilization, coalition building, and the importance of political strategizing and research. I analyze the local coalitions closely while connecting this activism to global problems associated with garbage. In chapter 5, I examine environmental justice activism against an energy deregulation plan in New York City. Land and environment are the means through which capital extracts profit in an increasingly privatized and corporate city. These changes were the outcome of the general ideological shift to the right at the city level, which mirrored larger changes at the state, national, and global levels.

The last chapter analyzes how environmental justice groups engage with the politics of urban planning and public health. I look at how activist groups have shifted their focus from fighting siting proposals of individual noxious polluting facilities to actively engaging in community planning and community-based environmental health research processes. Community-based planning responses to environmental racism in New York City are significant steps forward from years of environmental justice organizing against particular land use and siting disputes. Community-based initiatives are necessary to the democratization of science and health research, in part because science and technology are key factors in producing environmental problems. This chapter adds detail and geographic scope to Jason Corburn's excellent *Street Science: Community Knowledge and Environmental Health Justice* (2005), which focuses on Williamsburg. Indeed, the environmental justice movement's engagement with community-based science and research is part of the tradition of community science, which challenges conventional practices of health research and environmental risk assessment. Critics of traditional risk assessment methods tacitly call for an environmentalist epidemiology—one that sees the world in terms of a broad network of intricate interconnections. Such a science, they imply, would be more in keeping with reality and therefore would be a better instrument for documenting and remediating the health problems caused by exposure to toxic substances. New York City environmental justice organizing has produced some of the most innovative community-based environmental health research partnerships around the issues of air pollution and asthma nationally, as well as community-based planning that seeks to improve a number of local problems. Although not unique to environmental justice organizations, these activists hold values and worldviews that tend to privilege everyday knowledge and lived experience in engaging with expert and scientific knowledge (Corburn 2005, Tesh 2000). An example of environmental justice activists' worldview on health is in their embrace of the concept of cumulative risk and the precautionary principle. Cumulative risk looks at risks in combination, thereby rejecting the dominant risk assessment methodologies that look at factors in isolation, in laboratory conditions, and truncated from social factors. They also advance the principle of precautionary action, which calls for preventing harm to the environment and to human health. Both are key factors in environmental justice activism in New York City in terms of how activists engage with the politics and epistemology of asthma and air pollution.

## Methodology and Sources

This book, which began when I worked at an environmental justice organization, is based on seven years of participant observation research involving regular attendance at demonstrations and organizing meetings, public hearings, and community meetings. My work for this organization established levels of trust and personal connections that enabled a greater access to the participants in this study than I would otherwise have had.

I chose to focus on West Harlem, Sunset Park, Williamsburg, and the South Bronx because in each of these neighborhoods activist organizations explicitly used the language of environmental racism and the environmental justice movement to frame their politics. Although I acknowledge that I could have included East and Central Harlem, Red Hook, and Greenpoint, where many of the same health and environmental concerns prevail, I limited the study to these four neighborhoods because in each, there was a strong community-based organization that saw environmental justice at the core, rather than the periphery, of its identity as a community group involved in a land use or development struggle. These groups are West Harlem Environmental Action, UPROSE, El Puente, and the South Bronx Clean Air Coalition. However, I am not suggesting that either the neighborhoods or the community organizations are equivalent. The organizations have different political and financial resources and employ different tactics. Nor am I discounting the central role of other mainstream environmental or grassroots support groups and the multitude of local civic organizations and community boards. My goal is not to overstate the role of environmental justice organizations in policy disputes and to deemphasize mainstream consumer interest or environmental organizations, but rather to highlight how these organizations had a distinct perspective and activist trajectory.

The groups I focus on are not necessarily representative of their community. Indeed, there were complex internal conflicts during these campaigns, especially in the South Bronx. I have tried to avoid a simplified or teleological narrative of environmental justice activism, which might have focused on the seamless move from individual campaigns to successful citywide coalitions, or from dispersed interests to harmonic convergence. Instead, my focus on environmental justice organizations seeks to show how effectively these groups were able to use a discourse of environmental justice despite their conflicts and contradictions.

From the vantage point of these environmental justice organizations, I examine how they share a politics of racial identity, with all its faults, limits, and contradictions, and a politics of knowledge, especially in relation to scientific and experiential knowledge (Fischer 2001). Environmental justice activists prioritized racialized discourses through which to understand land use and environmental disputes in their communities. Finally, issues of racial disproportionality and distributive and procedural justice are central to New York City's environmental justice campaigns. Thus, I look at how distributive justice can be achieved in urban environmental and land use policy while also considering questions of procedural justice. The distributive effects (or outcomes) of urban environmental policy and the questions of who benefits from and who is burdened by public policy are shaped by social relations. The starting point for environmental justice claims in New York City and nationally is that communities of color face an elevated exposure to health hazards due to the distribution of toxic exposures. Complementing the focus on distributive outcomes are questions and concerns for procedural justice in the political process (Fletcher 2004, Shrader-Frechette 2002, Young 1990). In each of the four neighborhoods, the existing industrial and polluting infrastructure explains the context in which health and environmental issues in these campaigns were defined. The concerns expressed by environmental justice organizations were never simply reducible to health and environmental issues. Rather, the questions of a fair decision-making process and the entitlement to equal protection by the state in the form of regulatory action buttressed each neighborhood's (and later, citywide coalition's) claims for health and environmental justice.

I conducted extensive interviews with activists, and consulted publicly available demographic data and legal and historical records. I drew on activist profiles, personal biographies, and personal narratives. Because these campaigns were relatively recent, I also relied on national, citywide, and local community newspapers. Much can be learned from any community meeting in the South Bronx, Williamsburg, Sunset Park, or Harlem and public hearings. When ordinary people talk about their daily lives or when children testify about their asthma, people's agency and self-understanding about race, history, science, and environmental risk are highlighted (Gregory 1998). My use of fieldwork and interviews draws from urban anthropology and critical science and technology studies, alongside environmental sociology, in order to make sense of environmental justice activism at the level of individuals and personalities, as well as from structural perspectives (organizational dynamics, competing notions of acceptable risk). Ethnography in environmental justice research provides a complementary framework to quantitative sociology in the understanding of constructions of race, gender, urban land use, pollution and risk. This emphasis on stories echoes Barbara Allen's (2003), study of environmental justice activism in Louisiana. One of her key points is that who tells what stories is central to understanding the politics of and stakes for her informants. Thus, this book tells several environmental narratives of individual activists and neighborhoods and within a city, state, and nation where the litany of environmental injustices seems to grow daily.

# 1

## What's Old Is New: Public Health and Planning as Historical Antecedents to New York City's Environmental Justice Activism

The loveliness of the urban sunset, when the dust and smoke-laden air throbs with rich color. . . . The American City of the Future . . . is the most splendid city of the world.
—Charles Mulford Robinson, *The Call of the City* (1908)

In journalist Charles Robinson's 1908 paean to urban life, *The Call of the City*, he offered a rejoinder to Jack London's *The Call of the Wild*. Robinson celebrated the energy of the city over that of the countryside and thus stands as an emblem of Progressive enthusiasm for the city as an ideal expression of modern life. In the early twentieth century, Progressive reformers sought to improve urban conditions of life and labor, especially for the working-class and immigrant masses, and to simultaneously envision and create an urban ideal. Reformers in the fields of public health, urban planning, social work, housing, and education worked zealously to solve the multitude of problems of industrial life that reached a zenith in the nineteenth-century "City Pathological" (Hall 1988). These conditions included high rates of disease and labor exploitation. Robinson's celebration of dust and smoke was echoed by American and European industrialists who largely saw smoke and other symbols of industrial effluence as an exemplification of productive labor, full employment, and social progress. Such perceptions of smoke changed during the course of the twentieth century, in large part because of the increasing associations of smoke with poor health, through the problems associated with smog and a degraded urban quality of life. Yet despite such change, the Progressive era and its nineteenth-century antecedents remain crucially important to understand in providing a historical basis for contemporary environmental justice activism, for it was during this period that separate trajectories in public health and urban planning developed as a result of changing ideologies of reform and professionalism.

It is precisely this joining of public health and urban planning that contemporary environmental justice activism seeks to reintegrate. Analyzing New York City's planning and public health history helps to explain the historical roots of many of the current problems. This history illuminates how race and class have historically inflected the politics of urban land use development that have coalesced under the banner of environmental racism and attempts to remediate these conditions through environmental justice activism. Primary among these concerns are the health effects of air pollution from noxious facilities, especially from environmental or sanitary services such as garbage, sludge, sewage, and water systems. The neutral answer to the question of why noxious facilities are concentrated in areas with high populations of working-class and nonwhite populations is that zoning allows such uses. However, this answer in isolation ignores the complexity of how health and illness have historically been stratified in New York City by race and class through the spatial organization of the urban environment.

This chapter provides the historical context for environmental justice issues and activism in New York City by explaining how and why certain neighborhoods—Sunset Park, South Bronx, Williamsburg, and West Harlem—are home to such a large concentration of polluting facilities and the health effects of such concentration. It is thus a contribution to an emerging literature on environmental justice history.[1] Environmental historians have documented how mainstream environmentalism's wilderness and preservationist conceptions of the environment as a pristine green space devoid of people were derived from romantic and transcendentalist ideals and reflected class and racial biases (Dowie 1995, Gottlieb 1993, Taylor 2002). This bias of what constitutes the environment shapes what historian Sylvia Hood Washington (2005) calls "the environmental 'veil'" in environmental history that masks the "historical perspectives of socially marginalized communities who have experienced environmental inequalities from their own perspectives" (7). Environmental studies and environmental history have also, until relatively recently, tended to neglect the city, which was defined in opposition to wilderness, and questions of race and class, although this is rapidly changing (important exceptions include Colten 2004, Kelman 2003, Hurley 1995, Cronon 1992).

My contribution to unmasking that environmental veil in understanding New York City's environmental history is to situate contemporary activism within two historical frameworks: land use development and urban planning, particularly through the lenses of race, class, and zoning; and public health, specifically race and disease politics. The vast literature on race and disease, specifically tuberculosis (Wailoo 2001, Gamble 1989, Roberts 2002), and race and urban planning (Sandercock 1998, Goings and Mohl 1996) suggests the important nexus between the urban environment and its negative effects on the life chances of racial minorities. The focus on the meaning and the remedies of health disparities of disease based on race spans well over a century. For example, black public health activists during the Progressive era intervened in discussions of disproportionate rates of disease (such as infant mortality and tuberculosis) by focusing on structural racism as opposed to individual approaches, which stood simultaneously for group and racial pathology.

The literature on race and planning highlights the enormous impact of planning policy, such as zoning and midcentury federal urban renewal policy, on black communities. Recent planning histories, especially from African American urban historians, have moved away from the celebration of modernist planning and a race-neutral approach to these policies. Yet while the urban planning literature and history has used these examples to examine the impact of planning policies on African American and other nonwhite communities, there are still significant gaps (Gregory 1998, Thomas and Ritzdorf 1997, Thomas 1997, Sugrue 1996). Aside from the important literature on urban renewal (Schwartz 1993, Caro 1975), there is a surprising dearth in writings about the historical impact of urban planning on communities of color in New York City.

Urban planning and public health, and the role of sanitary services in the urban environment, have a long and closely interlinked history (Greenberg et al. 1994). New York City holds a special role in the development of both modern American city planning and public health as the site of the first sanitary survey in the United States in 1864 and through its historic citywide zoning resolution of 1916 when the Board of

Estimate (the city's governing body) passed the first comprehensive city-wide zoning ordinance in the United States. This chapter focuses on zoning because of its importance in explaining and justifying the siting of contemporary noxious facilities. New York City's zoning history and the discourse of scientific zoning are key to understanding the importance of race, class, and real estate values to this supposedly neutral tool. I focus on two pivotal moments in New York City's zoning history: the 1916 zoning resolution and the 1961 zoning resolution.

Urban planning and public health as areas of reformist concern were historically linked through a shared concern with the problems of the city and the urban environment. They developed expressly to remediate these social problems. Theories of disease causation are important to the development of the modern city because these theories, specifically the miasma theory, justified and enabled the building of large urban environmental systems.

Advocates of miasma theory believed there was a relationship between weather and atmosphere (in other words, climate), and disease. Contemporary environmental justice activism, especially through its belief in the relationship between air pollution and poor health, echoes nineteenth- and early twentieth-century claims made in highly contested and politicized debates about disease causation in the urban environment. It also shares with its antecedents a concern with the problem of high disease and illness rates in disenfranchised urban communities.

Looking closely at environmental justice activism in New York City reveals the larger meaning of debates about environmental racism and urban environmental problems, which are tied to factors other than the particular facilities in question. Political debates about controversial facilities stand simultaneously for broader controversies about the relationship of race, poverty, health, and the environment, which have a longer historical scope. These are conflicts that raged in, and continue to envelop, professional public health and urban planning circles. They are, in other words, about the larger question of what constitutes the proper solutions to these problems. Some commentators have derisively suggested that contemporary environmental justice activism represents a "return to miasma" since activists maintain that there is a direct link between noxious facilities and high disease rates, particularly in respiratory diseases such as asthma (Miller 2000). The implication by these critics is that the science that undergirds environmental justice activism is incorrect. But this simplification of the science and the politics draws the wrong lesson from public health history. First, it is possible that the lack of scientific corroboration of environmental activists' claim may be an artifact of the slow incorporation of environmentalism into science rather than a conclusive judgment about the actual effect of pollution on health (Tesh 2000). Second, the building of urban infrastructure in practice as a result of the sanitary movement did indeed improve the environment and the health conditions of low-income urban populations, even if the scientific understanding of the mechanism of disease causality was flawed in theory.

## Public Health and Urban Planning: Historical Links

The founding of both modern urban planning and public health was grounded in a shared history and concern with the problems of the modern city and by using scientific tools such as health or sanitary surveys. The costs of urbanization that social reformers sought to remedy stemmed from the rapid, often chaotic, and unplanned physical growth characteristic of mid-nineteenth-century cities. Historians describe a landscape of extreme pollution and poor health. Unpaved or poorly paved streets and inefficient or nonexistent collection of garbage (including offal, excrement from thousands of horses and hogs, and vast amounts of city dust) were common (Schultz and McShane 1978). The rapid population increase in urban industrial centers such as London and New York, alongside devastating Asiatic cholera, yellow fever, smallpox, typhus, typhoid, dysentery, diphtheria, and scarlet fever epidemics, which claimed thousands of lives throughout the nineteenth century, made palpably clear the health problems in cities in the context of massive immigration and industrialization. For example, New York City was struck by yellow fever in 1803, cholera epidemics in 1834 and 1849, and typhus and cholera in 1892 (Markel 1999).

The shared connection between urban planning and public health evolved from the nineteenth-century sanitary movement to early twentieth-century Progressive era reforms to clean up food, water, and air and to create urban parks, reforms known more generally as "moral" or civic environmentalism, although they would not have been known as such at the time (Boyer 1978, Greenberg et al. 1994). The divergence between city planning and public health widened during the Progressive era due to a number of complex factors. Most obviously, the "natural limit" of health gains due to engineering interventions (the building of water supply, sewage, and waste disposal systems) was a factor. But equally significant were shifting ideologies and political agendas that affected the fields of planning and public health, specifically trends toward professionalism and bureaucratization (Kirschner 1986).

## Theories of Disease Causation

The history of nineteenth-century public health debates has been well documented (Rosen 1993, Duffy 1990). Competing theories of disease causation included four main paradigms: contagion theory (which held that illness is contagious and quarantine is the answer), supernatural theory (based on the belief that diseases are caused by supernatural or divine forces), personal behavior theory (which argued that disease results from improper conduct), and miasma theory (which advocated for a relationship between weather, atmosphere, and disease). Miasma theory differs from the other three because it separates the source of the disease from the victims of the disease (Tesh 1996).

These theories competed for influence for many years. Supernatural, contagion, and personal behavior theory were older theories that preceded the nineteenth century. Miasma theory was championed by Edwin Chadwick, an acolyte (and personal secretary) of Jeremy Bentham, the English utilitarian philosopher. Chadwick, the secretary of Britain's Poor Law Commission, wrote the 1842 *Report on the Sanitary Conditions of the Labouring Population of Great Britain,* which led to the passage of the Public Health Act and the creation of the General Board of Health in England. The major debate in the latter half of the nineteenth century was between proponents of miasma theory and contagion theory.[2] Chadwick's influential sanitary reform in London advocated an environmental approach to disease control. This approach suggested that economic class and living conditions, rather than character or morality, were the sources of disease. Its basic lesson was that diseases are caused by environmental factors, although debates on what these environmental factors were, and what sorts of diseases they caused and what prevention policies they called for, continued. The radical change that this view of disease causation entailed was that personal morality was not the issue because the problems were physical. Thus, their solutions would be physical and technological (Schultz and McShane 1978). But at the same time that miasma theory was gaining influence, it was challenged by new knowledge. In 1850, bacteria were added to a list of possible pathogenic microorganisms. The theory that infectious diseases were due to the growth of germs in the body remained controversial until Robert Koch's discovery in 1876 of the anthrax bacillus, which ushered in the "bacteriological revolution" and the "germ theory of disease."

## The Emerging Divide in Public Health and Planning

The *sanitary movement* is the umbrella term for English and American efforts to improve public health through sanitary reforms. Its intellectual basis was the miasma theory. The sanitarians believed that cleanliness, fresh air, and pure water were essential to community health and espoused the notion that diseases were caused by miasma. Although the theory proved to be wrong, the sanitarians' reforms contributed greatly to the general improvements of community health in the nineteenth century through the rapid growth of sanitary (or environmental) services (Duffy 1990). The growth of sanitary services systematically lowered disease mortality rates with the construction of efficient water supply and sewage systems. For example, in the nineteenth century, water supplies were by and large privately held; by 1910 more than 70 percent of cities with over 30,000 people owned their waterworks. By 1907, nearly every city in the United States had sewers. The filtration of water and sewerage brought a dramatic drop in typhoid mortality rates, a drop that averaged 65 percent in major cities (Schultz and McShane 1978).

In addition to specific technical engineering interventions, the sanitary movement proffered a theory of the city and a concrete agenda for city improvement. More than just clean water and the development of sewage and garbage systems, the early sanitary reform movement acted on the theory that "a clean city is a healthy city" (Rosen 1993). From the early utopian and fanciful vision of Hygeia, a city of health developed by the British sanitarian B. W. Richardson, the relationship between cities and health was intimately tied in the sanitarian agenda.[3] Concretely, sanitarians sought to improve housing and the physical environment. They called for decent living conditions and making clean water, food, and milk available, especially to the urban immigrant poor (Duffy 1990). The physical environment encompassed rapid transit systems and parks, since landscape architects believed that the physical solutions to health problems rested on the construction of large urban parks as lungs for the city.

These reformist ideas, while linked to contemporary concerns, also clearly differ from modern conceptions and tools of city planning. Historian John Peterson argues that the sanitary environment, not the urban environment, represented the root concern, and sanitarians were applying the same survey techniques to rural areas, estates, and the nation as they were to cities.[4] Therefore, these developments should not be equated with city planning as conceived and advocated in the twentieth century. Rather, they should be viewed as responses to urbanization peculiar to the nineteenth century, made possible by new understandings of environment and health. Nevertheless, Peterson concurs that the city planning inspired by sanitary reform anticipated certain broad features of nineteenth-century planning practice at the same time that it anticipated its failure due to professional specialization and lack of political power.[5]

Sanitary improvements could not have happened without particular political ideologies and methodologies, chiefly the belief that technological expertise could transcend political corruption. One key method was the sanitary survey, which proceeded from a rigorous application of sanitary principles and reflected the special nature of the planning impulse within sanitary reform. The first American survey that resembled the planning process occurred in New York City in 1865 when the Citizens' Association, a municipal reform group led by some of the city's wealthiest merchants, sponsored and published a report entitled *Sanitary Condition of the City*. Following Chadwick's report, that survey offered a building-by-building investigation of the entire city by collaborating physicians, engineers, and chemists. In the introductory statement, the report claims that "a vast proportion of the sickness in our city is produced by causes that are positively *preventable*, or that may be removed" (Citizens' Association 1970, xiv). The report set out its concerns for the social conditions of strife that had beset New York during the 1863 draft riots when Irish immigrants rioted for three days in response to Lincoln's announcement of the Enrollment Act of Conscription. The riots, which targeted blacks, caused numerous deaths and $1.5 million of damage (Frost 2005). The report read: "It was difficult to believe that so much misery, disease and wretchedness can be huddled together and hidden by high walls, unvisited and unthought of, so near our own abodes. . . . What numbers of these poorer classes are deformed! What numbers are made hideous by self-neglect and infirmity! Alas! Human faces look so hideous with hope and self-respect all gone! And female forms and features are made so frightful by sin, squalor and debasement!" (xv). The report divided the city into sanitary districts, where sanitary inspectors collected a wealth of data about the living conditions and disease and death rates in those districts. The inspectors were particularly concerned about diseases connected with "conditions of insalubrity"—consumption, typhus, cholera, dysentery, and diarrhea. The report called for an increase in conditions of cleanliness and clean air and made a number of recommendations for improved housing and sanitation.

Although sanitary surveys and methods were not unique to cities generally or New York specifically, it was in urban spaces that the most concrete gains in public health were achieved. Additionally, it was in the realm of city administration that the sanitary movement made its most far-reaching political intervention. Evolving doctrines and practices of municipal administration and city planning developed in the context of extreme political corruption, exemplified by the notoriously corrupt Tammany Hall in New York City. At the beginning of the era, Progressive reformers shared a language, a sense of common purpose and cross-pollination, and an obsession with professionalism. Leading public health officials and city planners used metaphors of bacteria and disease to attack the ill effects of population congestion. The new professionals in housing reform, settlement houses, social work, planning, and public health preached a "gospel of cooperation" across the boundaries of expertise. These fields were linked by their concern with the problems of the modern city and the application of scientific methods to urban problems (Kirschner 1986). In each of these fields, debates about the role of individual versus community, and how to weigh the rights of the individual versus state power, were of active concern. Professionalism defined itself at least implicitly against a generalist reformist passion for urban or social problems. The trends of professionalism, already burgeoning in the sanitary movement, became solidified during the Progressive era, in no small part due to sanitary reform itself. Professionalism was both a product of and a process in the division between public health and city planning.[6] The professional identities that people held dear became even more sacrosanct with time, particularly as burgeoning fields of public health and city planning sought to establish their respective domains through professional associations and credentializing processes.[7]

This emphasis on professionalism over politics, and different professional identities and methodologies, served to widen the gap between planning and public health. By the turn of the century, health departments were beginning to spin off many of the former responsibilities of nineteenth-century health boards. Garbage collection, water supply and sewage, nuisance removal, and tenement housing were now handled by separate municipal departments (Duffy 1990). The transformation of public administration was a result of the growth of specific fields of knowledge and the importance of centralized administration, which led to the emergence of a permanent bureaucracy and a "strategic elite" (Schultz and McShane 1978). The trends toward specialization and professionalism tended to lessen the passion for social justice that had inspired the creation of these movements. By the 1920s, the reformers had lost the sense of crisis that had bound them together as the turn inward manifested in many ways: health workers focused on individual pathology, social workers discovered casework, and city planners focused on zoning. This turn had larger ideological implications, as professionals turned from their passionate concerns for social causes to professional obsessions with social function (Kirschner 1986). The changing ideologies in reform movements were also tied to larger political shifts in the meaning of democracy at the turn of the century. As one historian describes the ideological transformation, "Democracy at the end of the 19th century was a product of agrarian values and fear of centralized power. However, 'the new professionals' . . . were the product of an urban crisis. In a society that believed that democratic politics depended upon democratic information, they trafficked in knowledge that was inscrutable to the general public (such as invisible germs or mathematical formula to calculate open space)" (Kirschner 1986, 72).

In the field of public health, the turn inward was a result of the ascendance of the germ theory of disease. This turn into the body and into the laboratory shaped the trajectory of public health research and intervention. Medicine and public health underwent a fundamental transformation and paradigm shift at the end of the nineteenth and beginning of the twentieth centuries. Advances in medicine—pathology, histology, physiology, chemistry, and other fields—provided a new view of disease causation and set the stage for the bacteriological era. By 1900, a good many pathogenic organisms had been identified, and other factors in the spread of disease had been discovered. Vaccines were beginning to appear in a large enough scale to protect entire populations. While the hegemony of the germ theory of disease did not mean that environmentalist approaches ceased to exist, they tended to lose the contest for legitimacy and funding (Kirschner 1978). Tesh (1996), in her study of the political ideology of disease causation and prevention, suggests that the germ theory of disease kept the problem of disease prevention in the laboratory, thereby ensuring that its focus on health was technical, medical, and scientific.

A similar trend emerged in urban planning. The fragmentation of planning practice and the emphasis on scientific planning ensured that the field turned away from questions of health and living conditions. The origins of American city planning, in sharp contrast to European experiences, rejected the strong hand of the state, preferring instead that private benevolence such as settlement houses take primary responsibility in planning issues, especially housing (Hall 1988). Marcuse (1980) suggests that American city planning was almost entirely removed from the kind of social concern that characterized planning in Europe. Elsewhere, planning historians date the beginning of city planning by its professional and institutional form to 1909, the year of the first National Conference on City Planning and Congestion (Hall 1988). In the early days of the profession, planning shifted from an emphasis on beautification to the science of city planning. By 1916, the discourse of the science of planning and rational zoning had gained hegemony.

## Race and Health in the Urban Environment in the Progressive Era

Much of the history of public health and urban planning thus far recounted is primarily concerned with how class operates in the urban environment in the context of industrialization. The discussion of the urban problem and the solutions advanced during the Progressive era were concerned chiefly with the immigrant poor. But the general problems that Americans faced as they collectively transformed from an agrarian to an urban populace were even more acutely felt by African Americans in the midst of the Great Migration. In the first decades of the twentieth century, the black population in the United States transformed from an overwhelmingly rural and southern people to urban and midwestern and northeastern populations. The scope and magnitude of this transition has been well documented, including the focus on the problems associated with high rates of poor health in black communities. For example W. E. B. DuBois, in his landmark study, *The Philadelphia Negro* (1899), commented on this problem. In his 1906 *The Health and the Physique of the Negro*, DuBois further observed that "even in consumption [tuberculosis], all the evidence goes to show that it is not a racial disease but a social disease" (89). Tuberculosis is an excellent example of the complex nature of historical debates about disease causation and evolving interpretations of the relationship between race, class, and disease. It is also linked with the history of the sanitary movement because tuberculosis is closely related to housing conditions and access to clean air as a cure (Gandy 2003). Samuel Roberts's *Infectious Fear: Tuberculosis, Public Health and the Politics of Color and Illness in Baltimore, Maryland, 1880–1940* (2002) illuminates how the history of tuberculosis is intertwined with racial politics in urban space, shaping the future contours of urban renewal and the later development of public housing through the stigmatization of African Americans and their neighborhoods as diseased.

At the beginning of the Great Migration, the health of blacks and the reason for their high disease rates was seen as both a medical and a moral issue (Wailoo 2001). The increasing numbers of racial minorities in the city threatened the social order as racist explanations of degraded black housing and living environments began to flourish. In some cities, black tuberculosis mortality rates were up to seven times higher than those of whites. Thus, these higher rates of disease "amplified middle-class antipathy towards the 'lower classes' and heightened anxieties over immigration and racial mixing. . . . Anxieties over class, race and disease flowed from fears that these stigmatized groups would act as reservoirs for the contagion of wider society" (Gandy 2003). Racist commentators argued that blacks were actually healthier under slavery because the system of slavery produced an economic incentive to keep slaves in "good health" and "free from disease" (Gamble 1989). This perspective, associated primarily with southern physicians, argued that the "natural proclivities" of blacks emerged when they attained freedom from slavery (McBride 1991).

Were blacks in the cities experiencing similar gains in public health as white and immigrant populations at the turn of the century? Based on census data, Haines (2001; Preston and Haines 1991) shows that life expectancy at birth for African Americans in 1900 was ten years shorter than the life expectancy for whites. The black-white gap continued to increase, peaking at twelve years in 1930. Thus, the general answer was that African Americans still suffered poorer health outcomes.[8]

In sharp contrast to racist explanations of poor health, black public health activists during the Progressive era intervened in discussions of disproportionate rates of black disease. The gains being made to reduce immigrant and white infant mortality were not being translated to blacks in the South and the North. This disparity became a key concern for black health activists, who understood that campaigns for improved health were not race neutral (Smith 1995, Gamble 1995). Black health activists focused on structural racism as opposed to individual analyses to answer the question of why blacks suffered ill health in greater numbers, because they understood that such an individual focus was also always a question of group and racial pathology. The Tuskegee Institute, the research institution led by Booker T. Washington, proclaimed that the "three graces of health" were "pure food, pure air and pure water," echoing the mantra of Progressive health reformers. Washington also instituted and sponsored National Negro Health Week (Brown 1937). And he shrewdly used the contact between the races as a way to manipulate white fear of black disease as a catalyst for increased funding and to leverage resources.[9]

The discursive logic of black health activism during the Progressive era emphasized institutional factors and social structures to explain disproportionate rates of black disease in the context of scientific racism and a widespread acceptance of eugenic thought and policy. Environments were changeable, whereas genetics and biology (in other words, race) were not. These explanations were contrasted with individual behavior, as well as genetic and biological inferiority arguments, which tended to focus on black behavioral pathology and innate genetic inferiority as the source of higher rates of disease among blacks. Black activists' notions of health and the environment were both structured by and resistant to dominant eugenic assumptions that the disproportionate disease rates that blacks faced were due to a "natural" decline of black health conditions in a postslavery context. "Race" and the "environment" were represented as opposites. While eugenicists and hereditarians argued that the racially unfit were genetically inferior, black health activists privileged environmental factors and environmental reform in explaining why blacks were generally unhealthier. These activists, particularly black women, focused on developing public health programs for their constituents (Smith 1995).

These debates about the racial disparity in disease rates in the urban environment persisted throughout the twentieth century, regaining significant attention in the post–civil rights era, although under different rubrics—health disparities research and social epidemiology (Nelson 2003). As an example of contemporary concern over a similar set of issues, I show in chapter 3 how disproportionately high rates of minority asthma served as a catalyst for environmental justice activism in New York City. Mainstream and traditional public health and policy approaches to overcoming racial disparities in health largely interpret these disparities as the function of qualities inherent in or intrinsic to particular minority groups—such as genetic susceptibility, decreased participation in screening programs, or ambiguous "cultural factors"—or as the function of personal behavior, such as diet, smoking, exercise, or parenting skills. The discourse of health disparities research and social epidemiology counters individualistic and depoliticized views of human health and disease causality, focusing on "extrinsic" factors such as class, race, and power dynamics (Berkman and Kawachi 2000). I show how the politics of race and gender shape the debates about asthma causation and treatment, including the home visits approach, which echo Progressive antitubercular and other social reformist public health practices.

## Zoning Matters, 1916–1975

At the same time that planning and public health diverged widely, they were paradoxically fused through the mechanism of zoning. In 1913, the

New York City Board of Estimate established the Committee on City Planning to consider the question of building control. Two reports over the next three years recommended that such control be adopted. The Board of Estimate approved the 1916 New York City Zoning Ordinance on July 25, 1916 (R. Platt 1991). The 1916 regulations established three types of zoning districts addressing use, height, and area. Use districts governed whether land was used for residence, business, or unrestricted (mostly industrial) use. Height districts controlled the shape of the buildings. And area districts governed the requirements for yards, courts, and other open space. The differences of protection for use districts varied greatly: residential areas enjoyed the greatest protection, while unrestricted areas were those places with low levels of urbanization where future development was assumed to be largely industrial (Makielski 1966).

Following New York City's 1916 comprehensive zoning ordinance (the first in the nation), hundreds of other localities followed suit. By 1932, there were 766 comprehensive zoning ordinances across the nation regulating uses and bulk of entire cities (Feagin 1989).

Zoning emerged in the late nineteenth century and hit its zenith in the early twentieth century with the reform zeal of Progressives who believed that the urban environment could be improved by technical expertise, scientific knowledge, and rational city planning (Babcock and Bosselman 1973). The emergence of zoning as city policy during the Progressive era exemplified these beliefs in rational planning and good government, particularly in solving the conflict between local land uses and perceptions of neighborhood life. Zoning boosters saw local uses as "irrational," representing narrow political or geographic interests, while they supported rational, disinterested, "objective," and professional views on land use through methods like citywide mapping (Makielski 1966).

Zoning was upheld by the landmark U.S. Supreme Court case *Village of Euclid* v. *Ambler Realty Company*, which established the constitutionality of zoning through the mechanism of the police power in 1926, after considerable debate about whether zoning was "scientific" or "political" (Brooks 1989). The segregation of land uses was primarily seen as protecting residences from the noxious effects of industry. But segregation of land, usages, and populations was also explicitly linked by David Westenhaver, federal district court judge, in the *Euclid* case. He wrote that "the blighting of property values and the congestion of population, whenever . . . certain foreign races invade a residential section . . . was so well-known as to be within judicial cognizance" (Murphy 1989). Zoning acted to protect property values, and those property values affected the population that inhabited a particular area.

The New York City zoning resolution preamble states, "This Resolution is adopted in order to promote and protect public health, safety and general welfare." Zoning depended on a complex umbrella term, *congestion*, which referred to both population density and building overconcentration of skyscrapers. Fears of congestion consciously drew on health fears in terms of both epidemics and fire safety issues. As expressed by the Manhattan borough president, George McAneny, in 1913 in a resolution before the Board of Estimate and Apportionment, there was "a growing sentiment in the community that the time has come when an effort should be made to regulate the height, size and arrangement of buildings . . . in order to arrest the seriously increasing evil of the shutting off of light and air . . . to prevent unwholesome and dangerous congestion . . . and to reduce the hazards of fire and peril to life" (Makielski 1966, 14). Congestion was thought to "breed disease by inhibiting sunlight and ventilation in offices," in addition to exacerbating difficulties for fire control (Willis 1993, 6). One of the primary rationales for zoning was for public health purposes to ensure adequate light and air for an increasingly congested urban population (Ward and Zunz 1992). The link between congestion and disease was a primary concern, especially in densely populated urban immigrant neighborhoods. Zoning governs not only permitted uses, but development within districts governed by use, bulk, and parking requirements. Use regulations designate the terms of uses for an area of land (commercial, residential, manufacturing), while bulk regulations set a limit on size and distribution of uses, such as the "intensity of development . . . including limitations on the shape and location of buildings to protect light, air . . . and privacy and open space" (Harrison, Ballard, and Allen 1950). In theory, bulk and use zoning are complementary, and planners could designate an area for use and control its bulk by setting height limitations on the building and mandating spaces between buildings (Kirschner 1986).

Zoning designations both reflect land use patterns created by the real estate market and determine the proposed location of noxious and polluting facilities. New York City's zoning practice is not inherently discriminatory. It can provide beneficial effects in response to urgent social and environmental problems, and it was justified historically as a method to improve public health in the context of increased population density and extreme conditions of congestion. Yet the shape that New York City's zoning policy took mirrored and magnified social stratification based on race and class. Zoning in New York City was never explicitly racial or discriminatory, characterized by housing covenants.[10] Rather than explicit de jure racism and segregation, zoning regulations contributed to implicit de facto discrimination through the application of land use policies.

Despite the rhetoric about rationalizing a chaotic environment through scientific (and objective) zoning, politics and class relations have been central to New York City's zoning policy and history. How areas were classified was a social and a political process from its inception. For example, large areas of the Bronx, Brooklyn, and Queens were classified as unrestricted (with less protection than residential areas), including many poor and working-class areas in New York City. This history set the stage for later land use and development conflicts, as battles over uses of space and between different groups of people who occupied them intensified.

Despite the public health rationale for zoning, the primary factor for the rise of zoning in New York City was economic. The overbuilding of Manhattan and real estate speculation in the period immediately preceding the 1916 regulations had led to a steep decline of land values and a depressed real estate market (Makielski 1966, Revell 1992). Zoning was used as a way to stabilize the city's real estate economy by creating incentives for new investment by preventing overbuilding and real estate speculation (Weiss 1992). Real estate developers and elite interests such as the Fifth Avenue Association were major supporters of zoning. The association, an alliance composed of upscale retail merchants and real estate owners located on Fifth Avenue, grew increasingly alarmed at the "prestige problem" involved in the mingling of elite shoppers with immigrant workers and of the "best stores" being encroached by garment factories and loft "invasions" on Fifth Avenue (Makielski 1966). Through the mechanism of zoning, the association ultimately succeeded in defining Fifth Avenue and the midtown area as an upscale office and retail district rather than as an expanding area for garment manufacturing.

The 1916 zoning resolution stood relatively unchanged until 1961, when the city underwent a laborious process to update it. It was clear to many by the 1960s that the existing resolution was inadequate and needed an upgrade. Zoning was the mechanism for addressing new social contexts. Transformations in the economy and population addressed included increasing trends of deindustrialization. The city justified the 1961 changes by the need to manage these new realities, especially the need to maintain industrial growth areas. However, the resolution did little to stem deindustrialization (Waldinger 1996). Some of the other economic and cultural imperatives that influenced the 1961 version included urban renewal and redevelopment policy; the decline in the port economy; a significant increase in the white-collar, finance, industry, and real estate sectors; and increasing populations of poor people of color, especially African Americans and Puerto Ricans.[11]

There were several major changes to the original resolution. New York City was divided into three basic zoning districts—residential (R), commercial (C), and manufacturing (M)—which changed the categories from residence, business, and unrestricted. The three basic categories were further subdivided by the intensity of use, whether for retail or manufacturing categories, parking, building, bulk, or residential density. Key features included the floor-area ratios (an index to calculate the total permitted area), new requirements for open space and plaza provisions, permissive zoning for "community facilities" (which serve the "general welfare" of the city), economic incentives for developers who would build "in the public interest," recognition of large-scale projects, performance standards for industry, and "recognition of the automobile and its off-street storage in all districts" (Strickland 1993). The concept of incentive zoning—offering a bonus of extra floor area to encourage developers of office buildings and apartment towers to provide public spaces—was also introduced.

The key concepts behind the 1961 updates to the 1916 resolution were the themes of order and protection. In the report by the consultant contracted to produce the blueprint for the 1961 resolution, *Plan for Rezoning the City of New York*, the first reason given for the need to update the resolution is that the existing regulations "fail to provide the protection which the greatest city in the world deserves. . . . Half of the inhabitants of the City lived in non-residential districts; and at present over half of the area of the Commercial District is actually used by residences" (Harrison, Ballard, and Allen 1950). The report assumed a strong preference for the ideal of people living only in protected residential districts.

This assumption of people and uses in their proper place denied the reality that low-income and racial minority populations have always been overrepresented in what became designated by city agencies as non-residential districts. In fact, in many cases, the zoning designation was imposed onto a residential, mixed, commercial, or manufacturing district. People lived in areas designated as unrestricted before the 1961 changes and continued to live in heavy manufacturing districts despite what their zoning designation indicated. In addition, the zoning resolution allowed for "nonconforming uses." The governing concept of nonconforming uses is that regulations generally do not affect existing land uses or buildings that were legal when built under former codes or different classifications. Zoning regulations do not protect residences within manufacturing zones, requiring only a buffer around districts zoned as residential, rather than residential areas within districts zoned for manufacturing.

This problem of nonconformance and its impact on local neighborhoods in New York City was recognized at the time of the 1961 resolution. As Louis Winnick (1990) documents in his history of Sunset Park, the zoning changes accelerated trends of abandonment and housing decline in the neighborhood. In one fell swoop, over 2,000 residences, containing an estimated 10,000 people, were thrust into nonconforming status. The marketability of the housing stock was thus undermined by limiting permissible repairs and improvements and placing the houses outside appropriate codes of protection. This lack of protection continues to be a major source of contention in Sunset Park, as in Williamsburg, West Harlem, and the South Bronx. As one resident in the South Bronx said in the context of the campaign against the Bronx-Lebanon medical waste incinerator: "They say this is an industrial area, that there are no people here. Aren't we people?"(Carlos Padilla, personal communication, April 15, 1999).

In the only exhaustive analysis of industrial zoning changes and environmental justice in New York City, geographer Juliana Maantay (2000) outlines the relationship between demographics and industrial rezoning in New York City from the 1961 changes to 1998. Her study tracked 409 zoning changes involving manufacturing areas. Since the city has rezoned major manufacturing zones from manufacturing to other uses at three times the rate that areas have been rezoned to manufacturing, the remaining manufacturing zones have experienced an intensifying concentration of noxious uses. Her major finding was that zoning and race are connected in terms of neighborhood demographics and transition of zoning uses. The most manufacturing zone increases occurred in the Bronx, the borough with the most minority and low-income population, while Manhattan experienced the most decreases in manufacturing zones. Maantay demonstrates how rezoning has concentrated industrial uses and the concomitant health hazards into an ever-shrinking number of neighborhoods, and thus argues that the siting of polluting facilities has never been a simple matter of race-neutral zoning designations and policy. She shows that the overall effect, if not intent, of zoning changes is to distribute and concentrate manufacturing and industry in neighborhoods with fewer financial and social resources to organize politically, particularly communities of color and low-income neighborhoods outside Manhattan. The populations in these areas also tend to carry less political clout than those in more affluent areas with heavy percentages of home ownership. Zoning changes take place in neighborhoods deemed by the city to be "marginal" or "deteriorated" as opposed to "stable" (Maantay 2001). What these terms mean, and how they are assigned and designated, is shaped by racial and class assumptions and biases.

Maantay's findings are confirmed by looking at the neighborhoods examined in this book. The South Bronx, West Harlem, Williamsburg, and Sunset Park are all mixed-use districts on the industrial waterfront. Many subareas of these communities are zoned for M3, or heavy manufacturing, which affords the least protection from the effects of industrial use. The lowest levels of regulatory protection are in M3 (as opposed to M2 or M1 districts), which have lower levels of protection compared to commercial and residential districts. At the same time, these communities face a higher concentration of pollution from noxious facilities. According to the resolution, M3 districts cannot reasonably be expected to conform to those performance standards that are appropriate for most other types of industrial development. They meet the lowest level of performance standards, where heavy industry with maximum noise, traffic, and pollution is allowed. In the 1980s and 1990s, environmental justice activist concern with the negative health effects of pollution increased with the proposal of additional polluting facilities in their communities, which I detail in the next chapter. Their feeling and concern of being targeted is borne out, in part because of the zoning changes that concentrate noxious uses for citywide needs in fewer and fewer communities.

## Conclusion

The health and environmental politics of class, race, and gender in the city are by definition complicated and intersectional. The history of urban planning and public health sheds light on contemporary concerns, demands, and the logic of urban environmental justice activism. Environmental justice activism did not emerge ex nihilo in the 1980s. Rather, the conditions that produce the problems that environmental justice activism responds to have a much longer and complicated history. The example of tuberculosis suggests that what is old is new and highlights the persistence of old race- and class-inflected anxieties, albeit cloaked in new forms. A tuberculosis epidemic in New York City in the 1990s hit poor neighborhoods and people of color hardest, in part because of poor housing conditions, the influence of AIDS, growing resistance to anti-TB drugs, and the explosion of TB in prisons (which formed a revolving door because a high concentration of those involved in the criminal justice system come from poor urban communities, where they return after the end of their sentences; Wallace and Wallace 2003).

I close by returning to the suggestion that environmental justice activism signifies a return to miasma because activists make certain assumptions about the relationship between air pollution and disease causality that echo earlier beliefs about disease causation. It is, I believe, inconclusive and preliminary to suggest that environmental justice activists "get it wrong" regarding disease causation and the urban environment. These debates are still evolving and highly contested. As I show in chapter 3 on asthma and community-based health research, environmental justice activists are asking some of the right questions and helping to find the answers to complex questions about the relationship between race, class, place, and disease. Also, the valuable lesson from public health and urban planning history that contemporary environmental justice activism represents is that there is a crucial link between urban place and disease, as well as the importance of activism and policy in improving health and environmental conditions. The next chapter looks more closely at particular environmental justice campaigns and how they are linked through their concern with disproportionate exposure to environmental pollution based on race and class.

# 2

# New York City Environmental Justice Campaigns: Stigma, Blight, and the Politics of Race and Pollution

When you go to sleep as a child, and foul odors and smells are the norm, the inability to excel becomes a problem. This problem is physical, it's medical, it's emotional. You begin to understand that you are less. Multinational corporations don't know the fine quality of the people here. They only see the Latin Kings. They have a preset notion of who we are. We need to attack this kind of mentality, this pollution of the mind. For us here in the South Bronx, there *is* no acceptable level of toxins.

—Carlos Padilla, South Bronx Clean Air Coalition, April 27, 1999

The United States is a country of contradictions. On the one hand, we expend time, energy and effort building up the world's most impressive supply of garbage. Then we consign it to unsightly dumps, burn it up to form air pollution, or use it to fill in what some people consider scenic wonders. Mostly, however, we do one of two things; we forget about it. Or we bitch about it. It smells, it's ugly, it's depressing. Garbage, truly, is one of our misunderstood majorities. A shabby apartment is considered a "dump"; our prisons, schools, and armed forces are considered "dumping grounds" for misfits and misbreeds. A person said to be maligned is said to be "dumped on." A defecating dog is said to be "taking a dump." A handy and current pejorative is to call something disagreed with "garbage."

—Katie Kelley, *Garbage*

In 1860, New York City residents became outraged by the garbage problem when a newborn baby was devoured by a rat in Bellevue Hospital. The incident showed how the lack of systemic garbage collection contributed to an out-of-control vermin problem, since rats grew larger and emboldened by constant feeding from street garbage (Kelly 1973). Ever since, garbage historians have charted the ebb and flow of municipal and popular concern with garbage and sanitary facilities, particularly on the part of the poor and oppressed, who tend to suffer most from substandard services. A century later, in 1962, the Brooklyn chapter of the Congress of Racial Equality (CORE) staged a symbolic operation "clean sweep" of Bedford-Stuyvesant, a predominantly black neighborhood. Members dumped collected debris on the steps of city hall, charging that the Sanitation Department practiced discrimination by providing unequal services: three pick-ups each week in black areas but five days in predominantly white communities (Corey 1994). Six years later in the same neighborhood, during the summer of 1968, black youths burned garbage as an expression of their rage and anger. In response, sanitation men regularly removed litter baskets from "trouble spots" in order to reduce potential ammunition for urban warfare. In 1969, the Puerto Rican nationalist Young Lords followed their Brooklyn brethren by throwing and burning garbage in East Harlem to protest the lack of garbage collection services (Gandy 2002). As one leader recounted, "It launched us as a group. At the time, we used it as a strategy, an overall campaign issue to mobilize the community. . . . Whenever we rapped with our people on the stoops, we'd bring it up. We could all relate to garbage. They got rid of their frustration by throwing garbage" (Kelly 1973, 139–140).

While today, there may be fewer popular uprisings that employ garbage in this way, many of the seething frustrations about political and racial neglect persist, even as this discourse has been channeled into other forms of activism, specifically environmental justice activism. In this chapter, I survey four campaigns concerned with sanitary services—colloquially known as noxious or "garbage" facilities—sewage and sludge treatment plants, and incinerators in the late 1980s and early 1990s. These campaigns were waged, in turn, against the Bronx-Lebanon medical waste incinerator, the North River sewage treatment plant, the Brooklyn Navy Yard incinerator, and the Sunset Park sludge treatment plant. In each instance, a diverse set of constituencies was involved from elected officials, from the local level (city council members) to state and U.S. congressional representatives; local community organizations and block associations (including the local community board); and city, state, and national political advocacy organizations.[1] My focus is on the community-based organization in each campaign that promoted the idea of environmental racism as the reason that the facility was in or proposed for their neighborhood and that used the language of environmental justice to stop, or at the very least improve, its operations. These

are the South Bronx Clean Air Coalition, West Harlem Environmental
Action, the Community Alliance for the Environment (organized by El
Puente in Williamsburg), and UPROSE (formerly known as United
Puerto Rican Organization). Race played a significant role in their interpretation of the politics of clean air and land use development. These
organizations would later work in citywide environmental justice coalitions in response to changing city and state policies on garbage and
energy.

In each of these campaigns, leaders of environmental justice organizations challenged the disjuncture between the invisibility of crucial
municipal service operations—garbage, energy, sewage, and sludge—and
the visibility of the public perception that these neighborhoods were
racially marked sites of blight, pollution, and decay. The energetic nature
of their challenge belied the assumption that low-income neighborhoods
of color hosted compliant populations with insufficient intellectual and
political resources to fight for their health and environment. Community
leaders used the language of the national environmental justice movement to frame their local disputes as examples of environmental racism.
The leadership of these campaigns was primarily focused on their immediate political goals: closing the Bronx-Lebanon incinerator, preventing
the building of the Sunset Park sewage treatment plant and the Brooklyn Navy Yard incinerator, and seeking remediation of the effects of the
North River sewage treatment plant. At the same time, environmental
justice organizations used these campaigns to educate their neighborhoods on a whole host of scientific and political issues, hold elected
officials and public agencies accountable, and strengthen community
resources through the development of their respective organizations. In
that sense, New York City environmental justice organizations shared
certain features with other postindustrial communities involved in clear
air issues. These include a deep sense of connection to the politics of local
place and community, as well as a commitment to developing the social
capital and resources through which to engage in political action over
residents' concern with issues of environmental risk, air quality and
health (Wakefield et al. 2001). This chapter elucidates the particular
timing of these campaigns by answering the question of why they all
emerged at roughly the same time. I examine the external factors behind
the extraordinary confluence of facility building, as well as the larger

structural and racial issues that shaped land use development in New York City, using an analysis of the politics of stigma, blight, and pollution.

In the annals of garbage lore, New York City is king due to the notoriously corrupt control of the local waste industry. New York City is also unique because of the extreme density of people, the amount of garbage produced, and its regional impact. New York State is the third largest state producer of garbage (31.1 millions tons per year) after California (66.1) and Texas (44.8).[2] Benjamin Miller's *Fat of the Land: Garbage in New York: The Last Two Hundred Years* (2000) opens with an account of the notorious 1987 "garbage barge" incident, in which a ship named the *Mobro* left Long Island with 3,000 tons of New York–area garbage and sailed, in turn, to Louisiana, North Carolina, Mexico, and Belize in a fruitless search of a dumping destination and returned intact after four months. Although the garbage was not from the city, it was widely reported and understood in the media to be New York City's garbage. The garbage was finally incinerated a few months later and its ashes deposited in a Long Island landfill. Miller writes: "The 'barge heard round the world' was generally perceived as a warning of an impending nationwide garbage crisis that could threaten our environment, economy and public health. It was not. It was just a bit of garbage that got away— out of the usually closed orbit of municipal-operations-as-usual into a spotlight that cast intense embarrassment on the hapless actors who once again had failed to fulfill the essential public task entrusted to them" (13). Despite opening with this tale, Miller rejects the idea of garbage as symbol and focuses instead on the political economy of garbage.[3] He examines how garbage policy shapes transportation systems and land use patterns (in that landfilled garbage created the site of the World's Fair and in describing how Fresh Kills landfill has dominated the landscape of western Staten Island). In contrast, anthropologist Steven Gregory (1998) analyzes the *Mobro* incident and garbage on a broader symbolic level of social and racial meaning. He sees garbage as a complex cultural symbol that is tied to ideas of social pollution, poverty, and urban disorder. In his account of a youth garbage clean-up campaign in Lefrak City, a predominantly African American housing development in Queens, he argues that garbage was rendered significant by how local African American community activists drew on and reworked historical and mass-mediated discourses about the interrelation of race, place, and urban blight in Corona, Queens. The particular symbolism of a youth garbage clean-up campaign, which took place in the summer of the "garbage barge," represented both a local response to the "garbage problem" and a rejection of the association of black youth with crime in this neighborhood, by emphasizing their positive contributions to community improvement.

This account of the four campaigns integrates both emphases, attending to issues of political economy and the role of federal laws in creating new environmental demands (Miller), while also analyzing the relationship between garbage and community identity (Gregory). This view accepts the idea of garbage as a culturally and politically loaded symbol representing larger trends of social or municipal neglect. In questioning why particular communities are being "dumped on," metaphors and perceptions of neglect are central. But despite their centrality to activists and local residents, these metaphors tend to be ignored in the academic literature and by state and corporate interests that back the construction or operation of particular facilities. Far too often environmental justice campaigns are shoehorned by competing interests into a paradigm of the "not-in-my-backyard" syndrome, caricatured and better known as NIMBYism. Nevertheless, these environmental justice campaigns engage a different, though related, set of concerns and issues. While it is unwise to ignore the role of self-interest as a catalyzing factor for environmental justice activism, the particular race and class composition of these communities ensures that issues of race, land, power, and health take precedence over the protection of property values, a key feature associated primarily with NIMBYism.

The four waste facilities examined here were presented by supporters as necessary for the city good and discussed within a rhetoric of the larger necessity, inevitability, and progress. In fact, these projects were a result of poor public planning (sometimes generations in the making). Ultimately two of these projects were never built, and one was closed. The one exception to the larger-necessity argument was the medical waste incinerator, which was not proposed to handle local demand but as a for-profit facility to deal with regional medical waste. I have included it nonetheless because as an incinerator (albeit one that burned medical as opposed to municipal waste), the Bronx campaign to close it was linked closely to the Navy Yard incinerator campaign. The environmental justice campaigns foregrounded and made public the argument about racial disparities and inequity of distribution of public services and noxious facilities.

Residents in these four neighborhoods also shared an active historical memory of the consequences of top-down planning and the worst excesses of urban renewal in creating, facilitating, or accelerating the conditions of neighborhood decay. All four are mixed-use industrial communities, particularly vulnerable to the city's zoning and land use policy. As Schwartz (1993) documents, the city, through its Committee on Slum Clearance and urban renewal policy, "moved against" industrial districts in the mid-twentieth century. The legacy of Robert Moses's race-inflected highway, housing, and open space projects is important to understanding the visceral community response to the city's plans to site noxious facilities in these same neighborhoods. The role that this historical memory played in environmental justice organizing ensures that race and racism form a primary framework through which to understand contemporary planning and land use development struggles (Gregory 1998). The history of redevelopment policy and urban renewal in facilitating blight, at the same time it was aiming (in theory) to destroy it, as well as the role of this blight in exacerbating social, geographic, and health stigmas of racialized neighborhoods, will also be discussed.

## Risk, Stigma, and Racial Pollution

Perhaps it is stating the obvious to suggest that there is a relationship between physical waste (garbage), stratification based on race or class, and public health. However, it bears repeating that the association of people of color and low-income populations with garbage and the ascription of value to that metaphor has a long, fascinating, and sordid history (Melosi 1981, Gandy 2002). Similarly, environmental philosopher Robert Higgins (1994) identifies the cultural sources of meanings of racial and social pollution, in that minority environments are seen as "appropriately polluted" space. Racial segregation at work and at home, insofar as it generates perceptions of populations as pollutants, facilitates the environmental burden placed on those communities because, he writes, "environmental pollution is fittingly relegated to 'socially polluted spaces.'"

In organizing against the health impact of garbage facilities, racialized communities in New York City are recent additions to a long history that links garbage with social stigma and pollution. By stigma, I follow Gregory, Slovic, and Flynn's (1996) definition of five features of geographic stigma in their study of risk perception, environmental stigma, and health policy. First, they stipulate that the source of stigma is a hazard. Second, the standard of what is right or natural is violated or overturned. Third, the impacts are perceived to be inequitably distributed. Fourth, the possible outcomes are unbounded (meaning that there is scientific uncertainty over health and environmental consequences). Last, the management of the hazard is brought into question through questions of competence or corruption. Bush, Moffatt, and Dunn (2001) build on this notion of geographic stigma by offering a complex analysis of social, economic, and historical contexts. In their study of Teeside, the largest steel and petrochemical complex in the United Kingdom, the authors identify place images and symbols associated with the region and describe how these are negotiated and contested by different social actors. Economic decline and environmental pollution are intertwined, and the stigmatization of Teeside as a geographic place is related to its industrial character, air pollution, and the poor health of its residents. Residents understand "dirty" neighborhoods as "unhealthy" places. Four types of stigma are concurrently operating: technological (industry), air pollution (or dirt), health, and social stigma. The role of political neglect is also a key factor in social stigma.

In contrast to earlier associations of garbage, filth, and disease with the stigmatization of people based on their poverty, race, or ethnicity, late-twentieth-century environmental justice campaigns in New York understand the stigmatization of places, people, and garbage as a catalyst for social movement mobilization and community organizing. Similar to Teeside residents, environmental justice activists in the four neighborhoods clearly perceived a relationship between economic decline, environmental and air pollution, and health and social stigma. In New York City, these stigmas became a mobilizing force for residents, especially through the identification of increased risk due to air pollution. The prominence of concerns about air pollution and its impact on levels of asthma reflected the real epidemiological fact of high rates of child asthma. At the same time, the centrality of child asthma as a feature of environmental justice activism revealed how residents used their increased risk of asthma as a catalyst for social change. This social construction of asthma and air pollution activism shows how the meaning of social and geographic stigma in urban industrial contexts currently operates. Thus, increased exposure to pollution has become the primary channel through which residents have learned to reject the stigmatization of places where low-income and people of color coexist with garbage facilities.

The symbolic meaning of garbage has changed over time and place. Rather than representing disease and health in the nineteenth-century sense, garbage now represents political neglect, broadly defined to encompass, at different times, the local community board, elected officials, citywide politicians, and larger institutions, including mainstream environmental groups. Residents in these four neighborhoods questioned the reasons for locating the noxious facilities for waste in their communities and challenged the assumptions harbored by the relevant authority or agency in choosing their neighborhoods as appropriate sites. In each case, environmental justice organizations questioned the official reason for the choice of location, as well as the bureaucratic promise that the facility would produce no environmental or health impact. Moreover, these campaigns emerged in direct response to the city's changing garbage policy, under three different mayoral administrations (Ed Koch, David Dinkins, and Rudolph Giuliani), each of whom sought to anticipate the closure of Fresh Kills Landfill in Staten Island or changing federal policy regarding wastewater treatment and ocean dumping of sludge—or both. The politics of location and site selection is by no means straightforward, as the social and political history of zoning in New York City indicated. While there may be unclear evidence for deliberate targeting, what is reasonably certain is that race and class dynamics citywide, as they related to the composition of these particular neighborhoods, ensured that these communities believed that they were bearing the brunt of the burden of sanitary services and the environmental pollution these facilities create. It is not by random happenstance that they emerged as the circumstantial victims of bad planning, lack of vision, and poor decision making on issues relating to garbage, sludge, and sewage.

## External Pressures: Local Impacts

New York City, like all other cities, is not an ecosystem unto itself. Thus, it is important to understand how external pressures such as federal laws and commodity markets for garbage and medical waste have affected the building or proposal for sanitary facilities. Too often studies of environmental campaigns omit the legislative context for why facility siting occurs in a particular time or place. Before exploring the four environmental justice campaigns responding to municipal and medical waste incinerators, a sludge treatment, and a sewage treatment plant, I take a brief detour through the history of sanitary and environmental policy to provide a better understanding of where the proposals for these facilities came from and what kinds of needs they responded to. The proposal for the Brooklyn Navy Yard incinerator and the Sunset Park sludge treatment plant and the actual construction of the North River sewage treatment plant in West Harlem and the Bronx-Lebanon medical waste incinerator were all clearly shaped by larger legislative or commercial directives. This section spotlights these trends in order to contextualize the history of these facilities, and thus the environmental justice activism that emerged in response to them.

City managers have never developed a satisfactory way of handling New York City's effluence, from solid waste disposal to sewage. Through its history, different methods tended to dominate at specific periods, but garbage service has always highlighted political problems, such as the conflict between individual and government control, and the nature of municipal government (Corey 1994, Melosi 1981). Consumption and urbanism are identified by several theorists as emblematic forms of modernity under a specific mode of industrial development, linked by their final material product: garbage.[4] By the end of the nineteenth century, a separate and highly organized industry existed to sort and reuse urban waste. Wholesalers and waste dealers depended on scavenging children and women from the poorest strata of society to sort and forage for food, fuel, and marketable scraps. This industry represented the "first time in human history that disposal became separated from production, consumption and use" (Strasser 1999, 109). In general, the main categories of residential garbage handled by New York City government were ashes (from coal), animal and vegetable scraps, and rubbish (paper, rags, bottles, and metals).[5] Urban change in the late nineteenth and early twentieth centuries had given rise to the emerging garbage problem (Melosi 1981). The growing production and consumption of goods made the scale and magnitude of the waste problem much greater than that encountered by previous cultures and in earlier historical periods.

In the latter half of the nineteenth century in New York City (as nationally), the primary debate by city managers about proper methods of garbage policy was between incineration and reduction. (Reduction is the process by which profitable grease and waste are frugally squeezed from garbage to produce glycerin, grease, and fertilizer through heat or with chemical solvents. Incineration is the burning of garbage, sometimes with energy as a useful by-product.) There was a good deal of public discussion about whether garbage was best insulated from corruption as a private or public matter; whether street cleaning was best undertaken by the city inspector, police, or board of health, and how this issue was affected by the city's consolidation in 1898, when all five boroughs joined to make modern New York City. Before 1878, New York City had paid for trash sorting but realized that contractors were making money by selling the recovered materials. By 1882, the city required contractors to pay for "picking privileges," for a fee of more than $100,000 for those rights in Manhattan and the Bronx.

The first permanent garbage incinerator in the United States was built in 1885 on Governors Island, off the tip of Lower Manhattan, by Frederick Morse, a relative of the telegraph inventor Samuel Morse. By 1892, there were more than a dozen incinerators operating in the United States. A decade later, 15 percent of the largest American cities were using incineration, and 10 percent were using reduction. From 1849 to 1918, Barren Island in Jamaica Bay was New York City's primary waste processing site. In 1894, Mayor Thomas Gilroy set up a committee to make recommendations on the latest and most scientific principles of waste management. The committee's final recommendations called for an end to ocean dumping of garbage and expressed a preference for reduction over incineration. It also suggested that in order to best accomplish this reduction, householders should separate refuse into separate receptacles for kitchen waste and dry trash. In 1895, Colonel George Waring was named commissioner of the department of street cleaning, the predecessor to the department of sanitation. Although he held the position for just a few years, until 1897, he was the most influential person ever to hold the job (Corey 1994). It was under his tenure that an efficient garbage and rubbish recycling system was established that succeeded in temporarily ending ocean dumping. But in violation of the 1888 Marine and Harbor Protection Act, the city resumed ocean dumping of garbage in 1918. This stopped only when New Jersey successfully sued New York in a case that went to the U.S. Supreme Court in 1934.[6]

After 1917, reduction and other resource recovery efforts faltered due to an unfavorable reclamation market and the changing composition of waste in the 1920s, characterized by increased packaging and synthetic materials. By one estimate, municipal waste increased at a rate five times that of the population increase between 1920 and 1970, largely due to increased affluence and consumption. The largest culprit is packaging.[7] In 1933, the New York City Board of Estimate purchased Brooklyn Ash and its network of twenty-two incinerators. By 1924, the proportion of waste incinerated had nearly doubled.[8] Under the tenure of Sanitation Commissioner William Carey from 1938 to 1940, landfills became the favored method of disposal in New York City, following national trends (Miller 2001, Melosi 1981). But the pendulum quickly swung back to incineration. In 1948, the board of estimate approved an ambitious $44 million construction program for five new destructors (another name given to incinerators) and to upgrade existing disposal facilities (Corey 1994). Despite the ambitious building agenda, the city constructed only three of the five proposed destructors: at Betts Avenue in Queens, Gansevoort in Manhattan, and South Shore in Brooklyn. At the same time, New York City's waste stream increased 78 percent in one decade, from 1955 to 1965. In the decades after World War II, the number of incinerators in the United States plummeted from a high of 300 to a low of 67 in 1979 due to expensive labor and fuel, and abundant land for landfills, as well as the changing negative perceptions of smoke.[9] In 1958, the city assumed operations of all private dumps as part of a larger restructuring of solid waste management in response to complaints of extortion by private carters from businesses and buildings throughout the city (Corey 1994). By 1970, there were eleven landfills dotted across every borough but Manhattan.[10]

By the 1970s, the federal government, through the newly created Environmental Protection Agency (EPA), promoted solid waste incineration as a means of energy self-sufficiency in the context of the oil crisis.[11] In response to the exhaustion of landfill space and changing national trends that favored incineration, Mayor John Lindsay proposed the Brooklyn Navy Yard incinerator in 1967. This incinerator proposal languished until it was revived by the Koch administration, which called for mega-incinerators to handle the volume of landfilled garbage. There would be one in each borough, with Wards Island designated for Manhattan: in Baretto Point in the South Bronx, Maspeth in Queens, the Arthur Kill landfill in Staten Island, Wards Island, and the Brooklyn Navy Yard. The project stalled through the 1980s for a variety of political and economic reasons until it was revived in the 1990s under Mayor Dinkins. In 1991, the department of sanitation declared incineration to be its preferred waste management strategy (Miller 2001).

Local New York City communities were also affected by federal policy regarding wastewater treatment of sewage and ocean dumping of sludge. In 1972, Congress enacted the first comprehensive national clean water legislation in response to growing public concern about serious and widespread water pollution.[12] The Clean Water Act required of communities that by 1977, sewage plants were to remove at least 85 percent of the pollutants passing through them, and it allocated funds to help communities reach this goal. Sewage is a mixture of whatever is flushed down toilets, runs through showers and roads, and enters one of the nation's 16,000 publicly owned treatment plants. The sewage waste disposal system combines human and chemical waste into a single product (sewage) that collects, mixes, and concentrates a wide range of noxious and toxic chemicals that are difficult, if not impossible, to separate and detoxify (Harrison and Eaton 2001, Stauber and Rampton 1995). After treatment, there are two separate components: liquid wastewater (discharged into the nearest body of water) and sludge, the semisolid residual leftover, which may include heavy metals, synthetic chemicals, and radioactive waste (the industrial waste discharge is the major source of heavy metals and harmful compounds).[13]

Another federal law with a direct impact on sewage issues is the Marine Protection, Research and Sanctuaries Act. Permit and enforcement provisions of the law are often referred to as the Ocean Dumping Act.[14] In 1977, Congress amended the act to require that dumping of municipal sewage sludge or industrial wastes that unreasonably degraded the environment cease by December 1981. In 1981, New York City filed a lawsuit in federal court arguing that ocean dumping of sludge was environmentally preferable to land-based alternatives. A federal judge ruled in the city's favor. In 1985, EPA found that New York's ocean dumping site (12 miles offshore) was heavily degraded, with bacterially contaminated shellfish, elevated levels of toxic metals, and accumulations of metals and toxic chemicals.[15] In 1986 amendments, Congress directed that ocean disposal of all wastes cease at the traditional 12-mile site off the New York–New Jersey coast and be moved to a new site 106 miles offshore. Amendments passed in 1988 extended the deadline for ocean dumping to December 1991. The legislation was passed in response to the notorious "syringe summer," when soiled gauze, medical waste, scrubs, and 20 million gallons of untreated, raw sewage spilled into New York Harbor and washed up and down the Atlantic Coast (Maeder 1988). A year after ocean dumping was banned, the EPA rewrote the rules governing disposal for sewage sludge, reclassifying it from a hazardous material to a "safe" fertilizer. In part, the agency change was in response to the practical question of where the millions of tons of sludge that had been previously dumped in the ocean could go. Sludge also underwent a marketing campaign and a controversial name change to "biosolids," to be used as fertilizer.[16] Over 60,000 toxic substances and chemical compounds can be found in sewage sludge, although EPA regulates only a fraction of the pollutants in sludge (Stauber and Raupton 1995). Sludge can contain toxins such as polychlorinated biphenyls (PCBs), chorinated pesticides (such as DDT), chorinated compounds (such as dioxin), heavy metals (arsenic, cadmium, lead, and mercury), microbial pathogens, and others (asbestos, petroleum products, and industrial solvents).[17] Federal regulations divide sludge into two types: Class A (more stringent cleaning) and Class B (which follows less stringent standards that leaves more pathogens).[18] Critics of EPA's sludge policy suggest that sludge causes severe health problems, leading even to death in some cases.[19]

In 1979, the U.S. EPA sued the City of New York for violations of the Clean Water Act when it allowed millions of gallons of raw sewage to flow into the Hudson River. As a result of the Clean Water Act and the Ocean Dumping Act, fourteen water pollution control plants were built to treat the city's sewage. According to the New York City Department of Environmental Protection (NYCDEP), three of the plants, including the controversial North River facility in West Harlem, lack dewatering equipment to treat the by-product, so barges carry it to three other facilities for reprocessing. In 1991, the Dinkins administration proposed building eight sludge treatment plants around the city in order to treat the sludge that had previously been dumped into the ocean, at an estimated cost of $1 billion in construction costs and $25 million annually in operating expenses.[20]

Every day, 1,200 tons of sludge is produced from the city's fourteen sewage treatment plants.[21] From 1992 to 2002, New York City's sludge was managed under private contract, costing over $2.5 billion. The first sludge contracts had a notoriously corrupt history, given on a controversial no-bid process, where cost was not the only criterion used to award the contract.[22] Under the first ten years of the sludge contracts, 40 percent of New York City's sludge was handled and converted into pellets of fertilizer at the New York Organizer Fertilizer Company's (NYOFCO) facility in the South Bronx under a $468 million contract (one of the largest contracts ever awarded in New York City) (Egbert 2002). Norman Steisel worked at NYOFCO before joining the city as deputy mayor and did not recuse himself for ethical considerations under the city's conflict of interest board (Flynn and Calderone 1991; Reiss 1991). Another of Steisel's former employers, investment bank Lazard Freres, financed the NYOFCO contract (as well as other controversial incinerator projects, such as the Brooklyn Navy Yard incinerator).

For a decade, approximately a fifth of New York City's sludge was handled by Merco, which won a $169 million six-year contract in 1992. Merco tried to put the sludge in Oklahoma and Arizona, but without success. Finally, it began dumping 400 tons per day of sludge in Sierra Blanca, a poor town near the Texas–Mexico border, without an environmental impact statement or public process. The town, two-thirds Latino with a per capita income of $8,000, was at one time also a proposed site to store low-level nuclear waste from Texas, Vermont, and Maine. Merco applied for an extension of its sludge permit, hiring Governor George Bush's former legislative director as its lobbyist. The citizens of Sierra Blanca, suffering from a number of health maladies, including blisters, asthma, allergies, and skin diseases, filed a civil rights complaint with the EPA, which was later dismissed. The dump in Sierra

Blanca finally closed when New York City canceled its contract for cost reasons (Yardley 2001).

The need to find solutions to dispose of New York City's garbage, sewage, and sludge, often as a result of federal mandates, is the main reason for the extraordinary confluence of facility building in the past two decades. The main purpose of this summary is to show how federal law puts pressure on New York City, which in turn shapes the landscape of local neighborhoods. What is also clear is that in certain instances, the potential for massive profit, from garbage or sludge, is also a factor in the anger and critique by neighborhood activists. These residents are offended that their communities are rendered less habitable through association with visible stigma symbols, such as smokestacks and garbage trucks, and invisible symbols, such as bad smells. At the same time, environmental justice activists are particularly outraged by the increase of air pollution and negative health effects and the profits that private companies make off the effluence of the city.

## The Bronx-Lebanon Medical Waste Incinerator

The history of the siting of the Bronx-Lebanon incinerator in the South Bronx begins elsewhere. The original facility was proposed for a Rockland County location in suburban New York (Hennelly 1994), but the facility was abandoned at that site because the developer had not obtained the correct permits. The incinerator was then proposed for downtown Manhattan, to be built by Beth Israel Hospital, but community opposition rendered that proposal politically impossible. The Bronx-Lebanon medical waste incinerator opened in 1991 and immediately catalyzed a vibrant multiyear organizing campaign to shut it down. It was finally closed in 1998, and the smokestacks that released its fumes were torn down in 1999. The incinerator, which cost almost $20 million to build, was intended to burn 48 tons of medical waste per day from fifteen hospitals throughout the region. It was first owned by Remtech and then sold to Browning Ferris Industries (BFI), a large multinational waste corporation. The facility was subsidized by $15.1 million of publicly financed tax-exempt New York industrial development bonds as well as the waiver of millions of dollars in sales and property taxes. The incinerator was sited just blocks away from 2,300 units of public housing, three public schools, and several parochial schools (Stein 1992). By the time that the incinerator closed, the facility had been cited for over five hundred violations of toxic releases (Sugarman 1997). The campaign itself was a textbook example of environmental justice activism. It combined relentless citizen pressure on elected officials and regulatory agencies; creative public actions and press strategies; research on the public health issues and the finances of the incinerator operator; and the building of successful coalitions, mobilized around deriving and creating meaning from the facts—in particular, that from highways to waste transfer stations, the South Bronx handles more of the city's total volume of effluence, such as traffic and waste, than it generates itself.

In the early years of the campaign, the opposition was organized by an alliance of groups: the South Bronx Clean Air Coalition, the Riverdale Committee for Clean Air, and the North Bronx Clean Air Coalition.[23] By 1994, the leadership was almost exclusively from the South Bronx Clean Air Coalition (SBCAC), composed of sixty schools, churches, and community groups. Its coordinating committee met weekly for several years, and all members either lived or worked in the community and were long-time community and civil rights activists. For example, Panama Alba and Richie Perez were affiliated with the National Congress of Puerto Rican Rights and were activists in the sixty-year struggle (ultimately successful) to stop the U.S. Navy from using Vieques Island in Puerto Rico as a military training ground. Marian Feinberg, another leader, was a blue-collar health worker and occupational health specialist of Jewish descent and fluent in Spanish, who grew up in a heavily polluted part of New Jersey.

The residents of the South Bronx are extremely poor and predominantly Puerto Rican. The campaign against the incinerator was strongest in the South Bronx neighborhoods of Melrose, Port Morris, and Mott Haven (in Bronx Community District 1) and Hunts Point (in Bronx Community District 2). Over 90 percent of the population in both community district rent. According to the 2000 census, approximately 96 percent of the population are Hispanic or African American (in both community districts). In 2004, 63.6 percent and 58 percent of the population received public assistance, in Community Districts 1 and 2 respectively (data from the New York City Department of City Planning

Community District Profiles, 2006). The South Bronx is one of the poorest congressional districts in the nation and houses the largest concentration of New York City Housing Authority projects in the Bronx, with over 44,000 people in public housing out of a total population in the community district of approximately 82,000.

The SBCAC was run by a coordinating committee of, at any given time, approximately seven to ten community leaders. The coordinating committee was the public face of the coalition at community events. It successfully engaged large segments of the community, especially elementary schools, through a culture of confrontation combined with a language of morality, religion, and righteousness. One early and important supporter of the coalition was Reverend Earl Kooperkamp who held church services in front of the incinerator at one action (Carlos Padilla, personal communication, April 15, 1999). Another religious supporter of the campaign was Father Luis Barrios of St. Ann's who was one of the nineteen people arrested at the campaign kick-off event for blocking commuter traffic for hours on the Bruckner Expressway during rush hour in 1992 (Burger 1997).

By naming themselves the "Clean Air Coalition," they pushed the issues of air pollution, asthma, and community health to the fore. The campaign also helped dramatize the human face behind alarming health statistics, particularly relating to levels of asthma. For example, the principal of St. Luke's School came to the coalition for help, citing the rising absentee student rate to the asthma epidemic, and estimated that 40 percent of children in pre–K to eighth grade in her school had asthma (Marian Feinberg, personal communication, June 25, 2002). Many of the key spokespeople in the coalition highlighted child asthma rates in explaining their opposition to the facility. The past chairperson of the coalition, Carlos Padilla, has a daughter with asthma. According to Padilla, "What angers me is that some want to get the better of life at the expense of others, including their health. Profit at my children's expense makes me angry. These people from the incinerator are not from the community. They don't employ the community. But they take the resources and health of the community" (personal communication, April 15, 1999). Many of the students attended rallies wearing gas masks and surgical masks to dramatize how the air had become their enemy. Entire schools attended rallies, and buses were chartered to press conferences at city hall to dramatize the human and social costs of the incinerator to the community.

The coalition used asthma to creatively structure its political demonstrations. Themes for SBCAC-sponsored events included a "Hit a Home Run for a Breath of Fresh Air" day, and President's Day rally and march where two demonstrators, costumed as Abraham Lincoln and George Washington, called for the closure of the incinerator. About three major public rallies and demonstrations were held every year (for a total of twenty-two over the eight-year campaign), with attendance varying from twenty protesters up to a thousand. SBCAC was media savvy, understanding what kind of events attracted media attention (See figures 2.1 and 2.2). For example, the symbolism of the Bruckner Expressway sit-in was deliberate. The Bruckner was the primary highway trucks used in hauling medical waste to the facility (Medzon 1992). The action forced suburban commuters to stop and look at the communities underneath the highway, with a large banner visible from the road. The press release for the action reasoned that this "inconvenience" to motorists was justified since "political motorcades constantly disrupt traffic to accommodate the political purposes of elected officials. Since they have failed in their responsibilities, and we have had to take the responsibility for protecting our own communities, we assume the same right—for a much more important reason. The preservation of human life."

The particular reality of the South Bronx is central to this campaign. The racial and poverty shifts in the 1960s were sudden and extreme and have been recounted by many others. In 1960, 50 percent of the population was white, 10 percent black, and 40 percent Puerto Rican. By 1970, the black and Puerto Rican population was over 90 percent, and almost 44 percent of the adult population had no higher than a seventh-grade education (New York City Department of City Planning, 1977). The media stereotype of the South Bronx as an "urban jungle" emerged in the 1970s as devastating cycles of arson, abandonment, and divestment eviscerated the physical landscape, and gang warfare ravaged the social environment (Jonnes 1986). In the national imagination, the South Bronx exemplified the urban crisis, a place where the media liberally used rhetoric about slums, urban decay, devastation, ruin, and blight to exemplify the horrors of abandoned inner cities across the

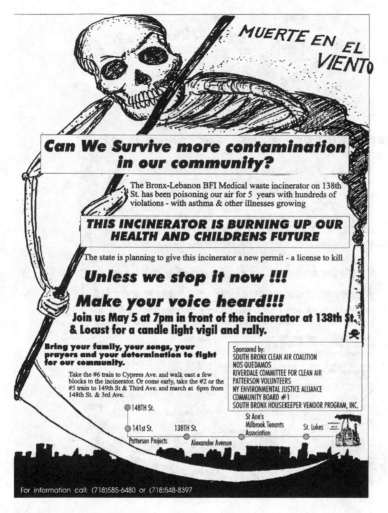

**Figure 2.1**
South Bronx Clean Air Coalition flier in English

**Figure 2.2**
South Bronx Clean Air Coalition flier in Spanish

United States. President Jimmy Carter made a historic appearance on Charlotte Street in the South Bronx in October 1977 with promises of federal aid to rebuild the city (this after the infamous *Daily News* headline describing President Ford's urban policy, described as "Ford to City: Drop Dead," in response to its fiscal crisis).

The grim reality of the South Bronx in the 1970s was a result of many well-documented factors. Deindustrialization, city policy on housing welfare recipients, redlining, tax delinquencies, and the uneven impact of an economic recession are just some of the factors (Rose 1994, Birch 2001; Fitch 1993, Caro 1975). Analysts at the time, and historians and critics since, have focused on government's active creation of the "problem," especially through overt and covert policies of planned shrinkage and benign neglect. Roger Starr, New York City's housing commissioner under Mayor Abe Beame, declared to the *New York Times* in 1976 that the city should engage in a policy of "planned shrinkage," or the idea that services should be moved out of "unviable" slum neighborhoods and directed instead to neighborhoods where there was a "continued willingness to live." Starr's remarks caused an uproar, and he was forced out of his position even though he was articulating a policy the city had already begun years earlier (Wallace and Wallace 1999). In addition, the construction of new housing developments such as Co-op City drew many middle-class residents to the northeast corner of the borough. The poverty and despair in the South Bronx only worsened in the second half of the 1970s.

The South Bronx community is also burdened with a punishing transportation and polluting infrastructure as a result of geography and the not-so-invisible hand of master planner Robert Moses (Freilla 2004). As the only borough linked to the mainland of the United States, it is bounded by the city's most concentrated transportation infrastructure: the Bruckner Expressway, the Major Deegan Expressway, the Sheridan Expressway, the Cross-Bronx Expressway, the Willis Avenue Bridge, and the Third Avenue Bridge. That infrastructure translates into thousands of vehicles crossing through the area daily.

Marshall Berman writes about the social dislocation of transportation on community life in his classic study of modernity, *All That Is Solid Melts into Air* (1982). Here is what he says about the impact of one road, the Cross-Bronx Expressway, on his childhood home:

The Bronx's dreadful fate is experienced, though probably not understood, by hundreds of thousands of motorists every day, as they negotiate the Cross-Bronx Expressway, which cuts through the borough's center. This road, although jammed with heavy traffic day and night, is fast, deadly fast; speed limits are routinely transgressed, even at the dangerously curved and graded entrance and exit ramps; constant convoys of huge trucks, with grimly aggressive drivers, dominate the sight lines; cars weave wildly in and out among the trucks: it is as if everyone on this road is seized with a desperate, uncontrollable urge to get out of the Bronx as fast as wheels can take him. A glance at the cityscape to the north and south—it is hard to get more than quick glances, because much of the road is below ground level and bounded by brick walls ten feet high—will suggest why: hundreds of boarded-up buildings; dozens of blocks covered with nothing at all but shattered bricks and waste. . . . Ten minutes on this road, an ordeal for anyone, is especially dreadful for people who remember the Bronx as it used to be: who remember these neighborhoods as they once lived and thrived, until this road itself cut through their heart and made the Bronx, above all, a place to get out of. (291)

In his account, Berman describes the acute ambivalence of old-time white ethnic South Bronx residents toward the destruction of their community by highway building. They acknowledged that Moses was destroying the fabric of their neighborhood at the same time that this intrusion was hastening their social and economic climb into the middle classes and suburbs.

But what of those left behind, or those who replaced Berman and his generation, now largely poor, working class, and black and Puerto Rican? Like Berman's cohort, the leadership of the SBCAC also carries a strong and visible attachment to place. These activists both embraced and rejected the iconography of destruction of the South Bronx. However, rather than leave the neighborhood, community leaders mobilized the imagery of destruction as a rationale to stop further development that is perceived to deter the South Bronx from its community-based revitalization efforts. In recent years, environmental justice activists have critiqued the legacies of what they call transportation racism, highway construction, and their health and social impacts in the South Bronx (Freilla 2004).

Thus, the siting of the incinerator was held in particular disdain because it was perceived to be a result of institutional neglect and political corruption in the wake of the community's attempt to reinvent and remake itself. Padilla draws attention to the inequity in siting dangerous facilities in poor neighborhoods and communities of color: "The issue is the selection process. . . . When something's good, it's theirs, and when it's bad, it's ours" (personal communication, April 15, 1999). Such ire led to a multipronged strategy against the incinerator, including legal action. When, for instance, the New York State Department of Environmental Conservation (DEC) did not issue an environmental impact statement, the coalition filed a lawsuit in the state supreme court against the incinerator in 1991. It argued that city and state environmental agencies had abused their discretion in granting a "nonsignificance" claim of no environmental impact. The case also claimed that the agencies failed to notify the public, citing the fact that the 1989 notice of the construction permit was advertised at only two newsstands in the Bronx and only in English, despite the fact that the majority of the population in the area around the incinerator was Spanish speaking. The second lawsuit, filed in 1992 on behalf of a number of politicians and community residents, charged that the DEC acted in an arbitrary and capricious manner in directing and advising the incinerator proponents to represent false ownership. The suit contended that the "Bronx-Lebanon" incinerator was not truly owned and operated by the Bronx Lebanon Hospital, which had sold its name to bypass a law limiting medical waste incinerator ownership to hospitals. This suit was dismissed on the grounds that the statute of limitations had expired (Levin 1999). Additionally, the character of medical waste was deemed by community activists to be hazardous in terms of air quality.[24] The plastics content in plastic disposables is dangerous to burn, and both plastic and paper products contain significant amounts of trace metals (Green 1992).

These legal strategies were not the sole avenue for action that the SBCAC pursued. Another key component was the strategic use of scientific language and terms through which the coalition was able to garner political support. As one leader explained, "We were David against Goliath, and science was the slingshot we used to finish up the incinerator" (Carlos Padilla, personal communication, April 15, 1999). They transformed their own knowledge base through their protest to demonopolize knowledge from the hands of technical experts and regulatory agencies. According to another member of the coalition, Joe Perez:

When we started the campaign, the community didn't know anything about incinerators. The company figured that they could put it here, and nobody would know or care. We are Black and Latino, we are vulnerable. They didn't care about us. They told us the incinerator was "state of the art," and we didn't know any better. And that we wouldn't question them. When we started the Campaign, writing fliers, we'd just list diseases and say that the incinerator would make them worse. We didn't know for sure. But then we hooked up with allies, like Lois Gibbs' group and their campaign "Health Care Without Harm." And we found out we were right. In those early days, we didn't know. But then it became second nature to us. And it became second nature to the kids who grew up going to rallies. They'd use words like "particulate pollution" and "environmental racism" and explain it to their parents. (personal communication, March 1, 1999)[25]

The coalition challenged the opposition between "rational" experts, who saw themselves as above the community, and community members, who were assumed to be lacking knowledge and to be confrontational and irrational in their responses. The consultant employed by the incinerator owner declared that the facility was "state of the art" at community hearings. The consultant was, in the words of SBCAC activists, "arrogant." Perez goes even further to critique the experts who worked with the coalition: "They were very valuable, and helped us a lot. But sometimes, they get arrogant too. They use big words, and don't let us do anything by ourselves. They don't understand that people in the community are falling asleep when they talked. It was awful" (Perez, personal communication, March 1, 1999).

In response, and by contrast, the coalition, in its fact sheets for community members, emphasized their "facts," which were based on the "commonsense" perception of risk and on knowledge based from other sources. For example, one flier read, "What rational person could believe either that this particular incinerator was 'state of the art,' given the well-publicized releases of toxic smoke, or that the burning of radioactive waste could have benign effects" (SBCAC Fact Sheet, n.d.). In fliers with headlines like: "Facts about the Bronx Lebanon Incinerator," the coalition argued that "state of the art" is a "misnomer" and that burning of dangerous medical waste would lead to elevated pollution exposures. As one leader said early in the campaign, "I'm sure they told the people in Chernobyl the same sort of thing" (Joe Perez, personal communication, March 1, 1999). At an even more basic level of communication, the coalition fought to get Spanish translation at meetings and to have hearings scheduled at night so more community members could attend. They tried to upturn the culture of the environmental policy decision-making process into a more multilingual and community-friendly one than the business-as-usual model.

The coalition also suspected that the scientific claims of the incinerator operators were spurious. The leadership acknowledged that such claims were inherently political and could be used tactically in support of their position. The coalition successfully pressured the incinerator owner to pay for an independent report, which ultimately found that the incinerator had a high propensity for excessive pollutant emissions and that on multiple occasions, toxins had been released directly into the air. This was ultimately a major factor in the closure of the incinerator (Kappstatter 1997). The report verified the coalition's claim that the incinerator was a faulty operation, and it did so through a scientific and objective sphere of authority. The coalition had previously relied on personal stories about the rise of asthma rates after the facility opened in the community through the assistance of emergency medical doctors at Lincoln Hospital. However, the coalition's claim was seen as tainted by their advocacy position. Getting the independent consultant to document the faulty operations at the facility legitimized the coalition's chief arguments.

Finally, the group focused on political strategies. Francis Sturim, another coalition organizer, remembers, "We'd go to any meeting where a politician would be at, and we'd yell questions on the incinerator. We became experts at rattling people" (personal communication, July 7, 1999). The logic of the leadership was that since it was politics that had allowed the facility to be built, those were the best terms through which the campaign would be won. Public pressure from the coalition forced regulatory agencies and politicians to acknowledge the problem. According to Padilla, "The agencies knew all along the facility stank. They just waited to see how long they can get by before we'd get to them. They didn't know that we'd be like a pit bull at their tail, never giving up, telling them to do their damn job" (personal communication, April 27 1999). Part of the political strategy was to highlight the money and people behind the corporations that ran and owned the incinerator (tracing it back to the British royal family). The original company that operated the incinerator had filed for bankruptcy in 1993. A major rally and march took place on May 5, 1997, Cinco de Mayo day, and drew over one thousand participants. Cinco de Mayo (celebrated on May 5), is a date of great importance for the Mexican and Chicano communities. Cinco De Mayo

**Figure 2.3**
South Bronx Clean Air Victory flier

marks the victory of the Mexican Army over the French at the Battle of Puebla in 1862. Although the Mexican army was eventually defeated when the French sent more troops, it came to represent a symbol of Mexican unity, patriotism, and resistance to foreign occupation. For SBCAC, Cinco De Mayo was chosen as a symbol of pan-Latino resistance to occupation—in their case, against corporate polluters.

This rally was a turning point in the campaign and is credited by those inside and outside the coalition as providing a major impetus for Senator Alfonse D'Amato and Governor George Pataki to take a stand (Sturim, personal communication, July 7, 1999). The governor, with the support of other prominent Republicans such as Mayor Giuliani, negotiated the incinerator shutdown soon after (see figure 2.3). With more than 200 children in attendance singing songs, the incinerator stacks were torn down in 1999, bringing to a close the era of incineration in New York City that had begun with the first incinerator on Governors Island in 1885 and had peaked at twenty two municipal waste incinerators in the 1960s (Martin 1999).

## The Brooklyn Navy Yard Incinerator

The Brooklyn Navy Yard waste-to-energy (WTE) incinerator near Williamsburg was proposed to be fifty-five stories tall and built at the cost of $550 million.[26] It was supposed to generate 465 million kilowatt hours of electricity per year by burning 3,000 tons of trash daily. This incineration was projected to emit 800 pounds of lead a year, nitrogen oxide (a key component of smog), as well as mercury and dioxin, and to produce hazardous ash. The organizing against the incinerator is one of the better-documented environmental justice campaigns nationally, in large part because of the number of people involved, the press attention that the campaign received, the unique multiracial and multiethnic coalition between Puerto Ricans and Hasidic Jews that developed, and the victory that the defeat of the building of the incinerator represented.

From the time it was the center of New York City's defense industry in World War II, the Brooklyn Navy Yard has long been a symbol of racial exclusion and discrimination.[27] Williamsburg has the largest amount of land, 12 percent, devoted to industrial uses of any of New York City's fifty-nine community districts, ten times the citywide average (Perris and Chait 1998). In 1999, 34 percent of the population was on public assistance, and 86 percent of the population rented their housing (U.S. Census Bureau, SF1, 2002). The majority of the residents of this neighborhood who were involved in the campaign were from two deeply divided ethnic groups: the Satmar sect of Hasidic Jews, and Latinos, primarily Puerto Rican and Dominican Catholics. The Orthodox Jews and Latinos had competed in the past for limited resources in the community, especially around public housing. However, around this issue, representatives from both the Hasidic and Latino populations organized in tandem against the incinerator. (For a detailed analysis of this campaign and Latino-Orthodox relations and perspectives on the campaign, see Checker 2001.) Orthodox anger over the facility had been simmering for years. In 1985, the Satmars turned out 15,000 people for a march across the Brooklyn Bridge in order to pressure the city to pull out of signing a contract for the incinerator. The effort failed at the time but laid the groundwork for the later coalition. In 1991, El Puente, a progressive Latino organization focused on youth empowerment, the United Jewish Organization, and the New York Public Interest Group (NYPIRG) led the fight for their respective constituencies in a coalition called Community Alliance for the Environment, also known as CAFE (Shaw 1996). El Puente's charismatic founder and leader, Luis Garden-Acosta, came out of the faith-based progressive movement and was also an activist with the Young Lords, a student at a Catholic seminary, a Lindsay mayoral aide, and a founder (and later public critic of) the Woodhull Medical Center.

The Brooklyn Navy Yard incinerator campaign was extraordinarily long and complex, with a number of procedural and administrative hearings that spanned a decade and a number of diverse interests and organizations involved.[28] The New York City Department of Sanitation (DOS) needed the city's final approval of the project, a vote on the proposed contract itself, as well as approval from the state DEC. The public campaign kicked off in earnest in 1991 when Mayor Dinkins announced that the city was going ahead with its plan to build an incinerator at the Brooklyn Navy Yard, despite a campaign pledge that he had made for an incinerator moratorium, which had won him the endorsement of the Satmar Hasidic community.

Residents became active around the issue, especially because there was a long-standing awareness of the neighborhood's fragile environmental health (Anderson 1994). Williamsburg, long a haven for artists, has undergone a fairly intense period of gentrification, but it remains highly polluted. Williamsburg and its neighbor, Greenpoint, are home to 30 solid-waste transfer stations, the Newtown Creek sewage treatment plant, 30 facilities that store extremely hazardous waste, 17 petroleum and natural gas storage facilities, and 96 above-ground oil storage tanks. The area also houses 60 facilities storing, using, or manufacturing 10,000 pounds or more of hazardous substances, 161 facilities reporting hazardous substances in the citywide facility inventory database, 21 Toxic Release Inventory facilities,[29] and 11 facilities using or storing extremely hazardous materials with risk management plans, as well as Radiac Corp., a storage and transfer facility for toxic, flammable, and radioactive wastes, which is adjacent to homes and businesses and less than a block away from a public school (Corburn 2002). It is also home to a 17 million gallon oil spill in its aquifers as well as hazardous waste remediation sites at the Brooklyn Navy Yard. Additionally, the neighborhood is part of the city's "lead belt," an area of high concentration of childhood lead poisoning from household sources and from sandblasting from the Williamsburg Bridge, and high asthma rates (Corburn 2005). This infrastructure is why residents were opposed to the emissions from the incinerator. Gaseous emissions from solid waste incineration can be grouped into three categories: carcinogenic, non-carcinogenic, and acidic gases. There are also environmental and health risks associated with incinerator ash disposal.[30]

The Brooklyn Navy Yard incinerator project was first proposed in 1979 as a result of mounting pressure to close Fresh Kills on Staten Island. The first environmental impact statement for the facility was prepared in 1984, and its projections were based on data taken during the Ford administration in the 1970s. In March 1989, the city asked the state DEC commissioner, Thomas Jorling, to initiate the Navy Yard permit process.

The incinerator was supported by Wall Street, the Koch and Dinkins administrations, the mainstream media (particularly the *New York Times*), and the governor. A large component of CAFE's campaign was research directed at uncovering the money trail behind the incinerator. Wall Street investment firms such as Lazard Freres had a direct stake through the issuance of municipal bonds to pay for the construction of the incinerator (Shaw 1996). Local educational meetings, press conferences and large public events put pressure on the Dinkins administration to delay the building of the incinerator. The anti-incinerator coalition lobbied for legislation in the city council requiring prior approval of the solid waste management plan (a comprehensive plan to deal with its garbage) by the council. The legislation transferred certain decision-making authority away from the mayor to the city council. The mayor agreed to close down smaller incinerators in other communities, upgrade others, and increase citywide recycling in exchange for city council votes to approve the Brooklyn Navy yard incinerator. In August 1992, the city council approved an "SWMP" (solid waste management plan) that included the incinerator project, in exchange for closing two of three existing highly polluting old incinerators and upgrading the third (environmentalists later sued to keep the third facility in Southwest Brooklyn closed).

CAFE mobilized thousands to the city hall hearings to protest and give public testimony (figures 2.4 and 2.5). The Latino youth of El Puente were vocal critics of the incinerators and gave speeches at large public events. They also organized around a "recycle first" agenda that promoted the economic development potential of recycling. In particular, the dumping of the toxic incinerator ash became a hot issue. The DEC

**Figure 2.4**
Brooklyn Navy Yard incinerator flier in English

**Figure 2.5**
Brooklyn Navy Yard incinerator flier in Spanish

commissioner had devised a solution to the toxic ash problem when he produced a signed agreement to send the ash to a landfill in Pennsylvania. However, the landfill did not exist yet and no permits had been approved (Miller 2000).

CAFE then turned to electoral politics, specifically the 1993 mayoral election. Rudolph Giuliani ran as an "incinerator skeptic" to distinguish himself from David Dinkins. Upon taking office, Giuliani became more inconsistent on the issue of the incinerator. He first asked the DOS whether it would be more cost-effective to haul garbage to out-of-state landfills or build the incinerator. In the time since CAFE had started its protests, the costs of landfilling garbage had fallen far below those of incineration. The incinerator was further derailed after samples taken from the Navy Yard showed levels of toxic chemicals in the soil and groundwater high enough for potential inclusion in the federal Superfund program. Incinerator opponents discovered that DOS had known about the contamination of the site since 1988 but had not informed the New York State DEC. The incinerator has never been built, and it is unlikely to ever be constructed.

In his account of CAFE as an exemplary case study in coalition activism, long-time activist Randy Shaw (1996) writes:

The coalition's ability to delay for so long, perhaps even to prevent the construction of the Navy Yard incinerator is one of the great social change success stories of the past decade. To understand the magnitude of the achievement, consider the massive gentrification and development boom that swept New York City through most of the 1980's. The Koch administration was accustomed to getting what it wanted, particularly when its opponents were predominantly low-income, minority people. Wall Street also expected to obtain what it desired (in this case, the lucrative bond contracts that were part of the incinerator project); Felix Rohatyn[31] and his colleagues were not accustomed to being stymied by the likes of Williamsburg's Latinos and Hasidim. (103)[32]

Describing the history of the campaign is not to overstate its long-term impact in terms of the long-standing conflict between the deeply divided Hasidic and Latino populations. As Luis Garden-Acosta states, "The campaign showed that we can work together when it suits our mutual interests. At the same time, El Puente continues to work on protecting our particular land and development interests in Williamsburg, even if they come into conflict with past partners" (personal communication, October 24, 2002). Rather than a simplistic feel-good example of multiracial and multi-ethnic organizing, the Brooklyn Navy Yard campaign exemplifies how environmental justice campaigns offer an opportunity for deeply divided populations to work together on short-term issues and interests that they may share, particularly on health and environmental issues.

## North River Sewage Treatment Plant

In 1986, community outrage erupted in response to the start of operations at a $1.3 billion North River sewage treatment plant located at 137th Street along the Hudson River in West Harlem (Gonzalez 1992). Community concerns were centered on air quality issues and persistent complaints of rancid odors that smelled like rotten eggs (later found to be related to higher-than-permitted levels of hydrogen sulfide) (Purnick 1989). After the facility opened, community discontent crystallized into action and became an emerging community-based organization engaged with health and environmental issues in West Harlem. On the symbolically chosen Martin Luther King Day in 1988, "The Sewage Seven"—West Harlem District leaders Peggy Shepard and Chuck Sutton, state senator David Paterson, former city council member Hilton Clark, and three others—were arrested for holding up traffic at 7:00 A.M. on the West Side Highway in front of the North River plant. Gas-masked and placard carrying, they held up traffic across from the plant on Riverside Drive to dramatize the unbearable situation.

Air quality is a significant concern for the West Harlem community because of the epidemic and rising rates of asthma. Estimates are that asthma rates are five times the national average, with 31.4 percent of those under age thirteen with the disease, compared to a national average of 6.3 percent (Santora 2005). Six of the seven diesel bus depots in Manhattan are located above 125th Street in predominantly black and Latino communities. West Harlem is 75 percent African American and Latino. As of 2004, 40 percent of the population receives public assistance; 90 percent of the population rents (data from the New York City Department of City Planning, Community District Profiles, 2006).

The community concern over the facility stretches two decades back to when it was first announced. The North River sewage treatment plant was proposed in the 1960s on the river between West 70th and West

72nd Street in the more affluent, primarily white community of the Upper West Side. Vernice Miller (1994), in her account of the siting history of the facility, describes the poor planning process that led to the construction of North River at its present location. First proposed in 1914 by the New York City Department of Public Works (DPW) as one of seven plants on the Hudson River to treat sewage, it was intended to deal with sewage from the West Side, which would then be moved by tunnel to be processed at the Wards Island facility on the East Side. In 1953, the department decided that the cost of tunneling was too high and instead decided to construct a single primary treatment plant on the West Side. This decision guaranteed that the plant would need to be large enough to meet the needs of sewage treatment for about 1 million people. At the request of the city planning commission (CPC), the DPW moved the plant from the proposed site to 137th Street; the original site was too small unless the plant was double-decked, and it was deemed "incompatible" with development plans for the West Side. Robert Moses refused to cede land for the sewage facility to be built on the West 70th–72nd Street site, and was deeply invested in the massive West Side improvement plan, which he promoted as a member of the CPC (Caro 1975, Miller 1994). Implicit in this decision was the political weight given to the development plans for the Upper West Side over the interests of the residents of West Harlem. When plans for the facility reemerged in the 1960s, local residents and prominent black politicians from Harlem immediately registered their displeasure. For example, Manhattan Borough president (and Harlem resident) Percy Sutton testified at a public hearing that the facility would "stigmatize" West Harlem. He called the facility an "indignity" and charged that "these are the indignities that make people feel they are not equal . . . I am hurt, deeply hurt, that you do not understand what you are doing to Harlem."[33] This social and racial stigmatization is a theme that remained constant over three decades of community opposition to the facility.

In 1968, the board of estimate voted to permit the initiation of this site, despite protests from West Harlem residents who had not been adequately informed about the proposal. Construction of the facility began in 1972. The design of the plant had been adjusted in the 1970s and early 1980s to save money, when state and federal contributions dipped for construction costs. The city decided not to enclose the plant in its entirety and to lower its capacity from 225 million to 180 million gallons.[34] In 1979, the EPA issued a finding of no significant impact for the facility, meaning that no environmental impact statement would have to be done.

But the facility turned out to have a number of design and construction flaws (Egbert 2002).[35] Whatever the specific technical reason, the nearby community objected to living atop what was essentially a "toilet bowl" for the West Side of Manhattan. The state DEC's testing found that the plant was producing 28 percent higher-than-allowed levels of hydrogen sulfide, which, in excessive quantities, deprives human cells of oxygen. Community leaders cited a particular sensitivity to this effect, since many local residents suffered from sickle cell anemia, a condition where cells have insufficient oxygen (Severo 1989).

Harlem has a severe lack of open space and parks due to a legacy of institutional neglect in open space planning, exemplified through the actions of Robert Moses (Dunlap 1989). In his capacity as commissioner of the New York City Department of Parks and Recreation, Moses built 255 parks; only 1 was in Harlem. The racial effect of Moses's building projects in housing, transportation, and open space has been well documented (Caro 1975). He spent millions to build, enlarge and improve Riverside Park but neglected the area between 125th and 155th streets in West Harlem. His investments in the Upper West Side were directly related to his underinvestment in Harlem. The state attempted to remediate the effects of the facility and the lack of recreation space that was a product of his policies through the construction of Riverbank State Park on top of the facility, the only state park in Manhattan (Dunlap 1989).

Despite this attempted community benefit of open space, local anger continued. This anger was channeled into the founding and development of West Harlem Environmental Action (WE ACT), a community-based organization to spearhead an organizing and legal campaign, as well as to act as a community watchdog to monitor the operations of the plant (the acronym dropped the "H" so that it spells out "we act" to represent community action). The organization was founded with three main objectives: to force the city to fix the North River sewage treatment plant, participate in future siting and planning decisions in West Harlem, and affect the public policy agenda by positioning environmental justice as a major political issue (Shepard 1994). One of the founders described the social and environmental ills that her community faced: "The spaces in which we live affect our spirit and our actions. Oppressive physical surroundings perpetuate and reinforce their residents' oppression. The processes by which our habitat is planned and built keeps people isolated, disempowered and depressed" (Shepard 1994, 745).

In 1992, WE ACT, along with the Natural Resources Defense Council (NRDC), a major national environmental group, sued the city and its DEP in state court in response to numerous water quality and air pollution violations. Lawyers from the city argued that the suit was unnecessary because the DEP was acting in the community's best interest. However, a state supreme court judge ruled that WE ACT could sue because there was no public hearing or opportunity for local groups to intervene in agreements made between city DEP and state DEC. The lawsuit was the first in the city's history in which it had been sued for creating a nuisance from smells. It charged that the smells were a result of "intentional, unreasonable, negligent, reckless and abnormally dangerous siting, design, construction and operation of the plant." In 1993, the parties reached a settlement agreement that called for strict enforcement of corrective actions by the state and the city at the facility, required monitoring, and held that $1.1 million must be given to WE ACT and NRDC toward the establishment of the North River Fund to address a range of community, environmental, and public health issues. The settlement agreement forced the city to carry out a $55 million program to reduce odors from the plant. This lawsuit was significant because it decreed that local government may not always have the last word on citizens' interests, it showed how external action could be taken to improve the operations of a facility, and it created new legal obligations for cities for community-targeted resources (Anderson 1994). WE ACT continues to use legal advocacy to press for its environmental health and political goals.

### Sunset Park Sludge Treatment Plant

In the early 1990s, a multiracial, multiethnic organizing campaign took place in Sunset Park against a proposed sludge treatment plant. This case study is unique in New York City and nationally because coalition members were from Asian immigrant and Latino communities. It is a significant example of how diverse communities can mobilize around common concerns for health and the environment. Environmental justice concerns acted as a bridge issue for Asians and Latinos in Sunset Park, although, as in the Navy Yard incinerator campaign, it was a temporary coalition formed in response to a specific issue rather than a longer-term alliance of interests. As in Williamsburg, the Sunset Park campaign represents the generally unrealized potential of multiracial and multiethnic community organizing on environmental justice and community health issues.

Sunset Park is located on the Brooklyn waterfront. The neighborhood, historically made up of a Scandinavian population, now hosts large Asian (mostly Chinese) and Latino (primarily, but not exclusively, Puerto Rican) communities, with a growing population from the Middle East (Winnick, 1990, Muñiz 1998). Seventy-four percent of the population are renters, 53 percent are of Hispanic origin, and 17 percent are Asian. By 2000, the Asian population had doubled from the 1990 census (All data from the New York City Department of City Planning community district profiles 2006). The neighborhood suffered from decline as a result of macro and micro shifts in population, in particular, the emergence of Sunset Park as a Puerto Rican barrio, and changes in employment and industry. Policy changes and other urban trends such as zoning designations, the building of the Gowanus Expressway, redlining, and blockbusting also played a major role in the development of the neighborhood (Muñiz 1998). Its revitalization in the 1980s and 1990s has been credited to the vibrancy of new immigrant communities (Winnick 1990), and it is often cited as an emblematic immigrant global neighborhood in New York City (Hum 2004).

Through the first part of the twentieth century, the Brooklyn waterfront was the main port of entry for goods coming into New York (it is the waterfront of *On the Waterfront* fame, with its longshoreman and mob influence). The South Brooklyn waterfront is distinguished by two large facilities: Bush Terminal and the Brooklyn Army Terminal. The former, constructed in 1890, consists of eight-story industrial and warehouse buildings that run from 28th to 50th streets. Bush Terminal housed a mix of manufacturing, warehousing, and distribution firms. Promoted as an "industrial city within New York City," Bush Terminal was recognized as one of the first industrial parks in the nation and became a model for other urban industrial centers. On Second Avenue between Fifty-Eighth and Sixty-Fifth streets are the warehouses of the Brooklyn Army Terminal, a military ocean supply facility designed in 1918 by Cass Gilbert.

With the economic decline of the Brooklyn waterfront as a result of containerization (cargo is sent in large metal containers, which facilitate the transfer of goods from sea-based to land-based transportation), Sunset Park suffered. This global move to containerization hurt the Brooklyn port because of its geography since containers are unloaded and then put directly on trains or connected to trucks (the policies of the Port Authority also favored Port Elizabeth in New Jersey). Containers coming into Brooklyn by sea have little train access, and trucks must travel through Brooklyn and Queens to get onto the mainland of the United States through the Bronx.

Additionally, Sunset Park already bore the scar of one of the worst planning decisions of the twentieth century in New York City: the building of the Gowanus Expressway. The highway, which opened in 1941, killed the thriving Third Avenue commercial corridor and split the neighborhood in half. It is a 6.1-mile-long elevated highway that is the southern extension of the Brooklyn-Queens Expressway, connecting the Brooklyn–Battery Tunnel approach, the Prospect Expressway, the Belt Parkway, and the Verrazano-Narrows Bridge. In *The Power Broker* (1975), Robert Caro describes the vibrant community in Sunset Park, segments of which begged Robert Moses to move his Gowanus highway to Second Avenue instead of the heart of the neighborhood on Third Avenue. Moses refused (as was typical), and the community shriveled as stores closed, crime increased, and street traffic decreased. Caro writes, "Once the avenue had been a place for people; Robert Moses made it a place for cars. . . . With its heart gone, the neighborhood had no will to resist the invasion [of blight]" (523–524). The memory of the Gowanus Expressway was actively invoked during the sludge plant campaign, as well as in contemporary land use and development struggles, including the debate over how to repair the crumbling road (Freilla 2004).

According to prominent community leaders, contemporary Sunset Park is divided along ethnic, linguistic, geographic, and other lines, such as citizenship and political culture. Muñiz (1994) documents the development of the barrio, poverty and poor housing conditions, the social geography of Sunset Park, and the central role of displacement, urban rehabilitation, and urban renewal on the lives of Sunset Park's Puerto Rican community. UPROSE, formerly known as United Puerto Rican Organization, was founded in 1966 as the first Latino social services agency in Brooklyn. It was reorganized in the 1990s and redefined its mission to focus on environmental justice issues as a result of the executive director's experience and knowledge on these issues through her civil rights litigation (Elizabeth Yeampierre, personal communication, April 1999). The focus on environmental justice was primarily done through UPROSE's youth contingent, Environmental Enforcers, who regularly attended public hearings on controversial development proposals and testified at public hearing about the effects of the proposed facilities.

Interviews with Chinese organizational leaders reveal the high number of problems for the burgeoning Chinese community that act as barriers to civic participation. Reverend Wong, of the Chinese Promise Baptist Church, cited residents' fears of political participation because of their immigration status (if undocumented), concerns about economic survival, language problems, residential overcrowding and high rent, and lack of services for elderly, disabled, and youth, (personal communication, April 12, 2000). Zantonio Hung of the Chinese-American Planning Council agreed that lack of funding for services for Asian seniors, youth, and disabled people, along with racial violence are key problems for the community (personal communication, March 29, 2000). According to Paul Mak, the director of the Brooklyn Chinese American Association, "The Chinese community in Sunset Park is not a stable one. It is a stomping ground for new immigrants who try to establish a foothold and then move" (personal communication, May 5, 2000). These problems and characteristics generally act as effective barriers to community participation.

These factors make it all the more remarkable that the deeply fractured Latino and Asian communities worked in coalition in response to Dinkins's 1991 announcement for a sludge treatment plant in Sunset Park proposed at Bush Terminal. The main arguments made by the Sunset Park community against this facility were based on health risks and increased air pollution emissions. Concern over elevated asthma rates suffered by Latinos on the waterfront was particularly salient, because of the excessive pollution from the thousands of vehicles traveling on the Gowanus Expressway. "It's unconscionable to place a site so close to the hospital," said Robert Walsh, vice president of Lutheran Medical Center, who added that "the hospital receives 6,000 asthma-related visits yearly" (English 1992).

The primary impetus behind environmental justice organizing in Sunset Park came from the Latino community, particularly UPROSE.[36] Part of this development is a result of geography: the Latino population was located closer to the waterfront. The Chinese community is farther away from the waterfront, concentrated on Eighth Avenue. The Sunset Park community formed a coalition around issues of empowerment and community quality-of-life issues. It was facilitated by Sunset United, a coalition that formed in response to incidents of racial violence.[37] Activists highlighted the contradiction between Dinkins's election as the first nonwhite mayor of New York City, centered on his image of the city as a racially diverse "gorgeous mosaic," and his policies, which, opponents argued, nonetheless contributed to the uneven allocation of environmental burdens and risks, construed by Sunset Park residents as environmental racism (Bennet 1993).

Dinkins's strategy of appointing people of color to his administration contributed to the successful organizing strategy against the sludge treatment plant. Asian Americans who lived in the area pressed James Jao, one of the seven mayoral appointees on the thirteen-member city planning commission, to vote against the proposal. According to Paul Mak, a face-to-face meeting with Jao and a "toxic tour" of the community, along with a protest by approximately 200 Chinese community members, tipped Jao's vote against the facility. Similarly, the Latino appointees to the city planning commission received extensive community pressure to reject the proposal, representing what some observers called a political coming of age for the Latino communities citywide (Bennet 1993). Ultimately, the Dinkins administration withdrew the Sunset Park sludge treatment plan proposal in February 1993 (Fried 1992).

### Conclusion

In the late 1980s and 1990s, there was a brief golden age of environmental justice activism in New York City. Collectively, thousands of low-income and minority residents were mobilized to protest a wide range of noxious facilities. In the heat of each individual campaign, there was little opportunity to reflect on how these various issues were linked, as activists delved into the particular issues they faced (medical waste, municipal waste, sludge, and sewage) as well as the complex political terrain (local, state, and federal policy). At the same time, community activists did recognize that their individual campaigns were linked through the discourse of environmental racism. Leaders of these campaigns networked and formed the New York City Environmental Justice Alliance in 1994. These campaigns are largely undocumented in the academic literature. When they are, the campaigns are analyzed primarily in isolation, separate from the other issues unfolding in the same time frame (Gandy 2002, Shaw 1996).

This singular analytical frame makes some sense because of the degree of complexity and myriad of factors and political players involved in each campaign. However, this framing loses track of other examples of environmental justice activism that were taking place in New York City and misses the larger story of the interrelated politics of race, urban blight, and pollution. Thus, I opened this chapter with a discussion of stigma in order to highlight how community organizations used and transformed associations of race, urban blight, and geography in environmental justice campaigns. In discussing these campaigns, I also showed that race and history played a central role in local and community consciousness of land use and development. The role of memory was a key factor in how environmental justice activism developed in New York City.

There are many lessons learned from looking at this history of environmental justice activism in New York City. These include the problems and challenges of tracing the history of race and urban planning; the legacy of top-down planning as embodied by Robert Moses, who left his mark in all four neighborhoods; and the potential for unusual, multiethnic and multiracial alliances (in Williamsburg and Sunset Park). In the South Bronx and in Williamsburg, we see examples of how communities used the discourse of truth in science and methods such as soil sampling and verification through air and ground testing to strategically support their campaign goals. In West Harlem, we witness the importance of lawsuits in developing community assets and resources, as well as the complex interplay of open space, waste, and race.

It is also important to understand how these separate neighborhoods already had significant experience with land use development battles, common concerns over air quality, expertise in using science and law, and community organizing in constructing distinct environmental justice campaigns on a wide range of noxious facilities. Concern over air quality and the facilities' effects on childhood asthma was a major factor. In the next chapter, I discuss the gender, family, and racial dynamics of asthma activism. What is also clear is that without these individual campaigns, there could not have been the citywide coalitions that emerged in response to changing city and state policies on solid waste and energy, the subjects of chapters 4 and 5.

# 3

# Childhood Asthma in New York City: The Politics of Gender, Race, and Recognition

Asthma, particularly childhood asthma, was an important organizing issue in the South Bronx Clean Air Coalition's campaign against the Bronx-Lebanon medical waste incinerator, West Harlem Environmental Action's campaign against the North River sewage treatment Plant, El Puente's activism against the Brooklyn Navy Yard incinerator, and organizing against the proposed sludge treatment plant in Sunset Park. In other words, the facilities themselves were not the problem. Rather, what mattered were the health effects of these on particular communities and what that pollution represented to these neighborhoods. These campaigns asserted that the communities were already exposed to disproportionate levels of outdoor air pollution and that the addition of another polluting facility was unjust and potentially racially discriminatory. Combating *fatigo*, as asthma is known in Spanish, became a way of life for many low-income youth of color and a defining feature of environmental justice activism in the 1980s and 1990s.

Under circumstances of oversaturation of polluting facilities, campaigning against a new polluting facility is a natural mobilizing step for local communities. Two of the environmental justice campaigns I examine took place in the South Bronx and Upper Manhattan, which have the highest hospitalization rates for asthma in all of New York City. Previously, I suggested that environmental justice activists in New York City used and transformed geographic and social stigmas of their neighborhoods as polluted as a mobilizing force for residents. Their identification of increased air pollution risk was shaped through a discourse of environmental racism.

This chapter analyzes why and how issues of power, racial, and gender identity intersect in contemporary asthma politics. In particular, I examine how race and gender shape asthma politics in New York City, especially through the framework of the family and the child. Issues of race, gender, and authority (moral and scientific) define the terrain of urban air pollution debates. Community concern by parents, school administrators, and religious leaders over high rates of childhood asthma and the disproportionate racial impact of asthma in low-income communities drive urban environmental justice activism.

The growth of asthma activism is not surprising. Asthma has become a major public health problem affecting Americans of all ages, races, and ethnic groups. Children have been particularly severely affected, and the epidemic is most severe among lower-income and minority children (Mitchell 1991). Children of color in low-income neighborhoods have shown the highest increase in rates of asthma in recent years, and the racial disparity has grown steadily since 1980 (Centers for Disease Control 2000).

Environmental justice asthma activism is not unique to New York City. For example, in Boston, asthma has served as a gateway to community action at various levels (Loh and Sugarman-Brozen 2002). But New York does offer an ideal staging ground for analyzing environmental justice approaches to asthma, which focus on a different set of issues from traditional public health views, using a "politicized illness" approach that emphasizes collective identity instead of individual pathways, as well as outdoor air pollution triggers (Brown et al. 2005). New York City is a good place to examine these dynamics because asthma has been a central feature of different environmental justice activist campaigns there and because its community-based organizations have been at the forefront of these scientific and medical debates and in creating new knowledge on asthma in the health and scientific research (which I detail later in this chapter and more extensively in chapter 6). In part, the focus on childhood health risks is a result of increasing scientific evidence indicating that children are more susceptible to the effects of environmental pollution than adults because of fundamental differences in their physiology, metabolism, absorption, and exposure patterns. This greater understanding was exemplified by Executive Order 13045, issued in 1997, which directed federal agencies to consider the vulnerability of children to environmental health risks.[1]

By prioritizing the health of poor urban children of color in their activist campaigns, environmental justice asthma activists are centrally engaged with the politics of race, gender, recognition, and visibility, as well as deeply politicized debates about the causes of and solutions to urban environmental problems and illness. This politics of race and recognition works in two key and interlinked ways: in foregrounding the images and voices of low-income children of color with asthma in political campaigns to change specific public policies, especially on transportation issues, and in inserting these same voices into environmental health research programs. While the problem of high rates of childhood asthma in minority communities is understood in public health circles, the larger social meanings of this community-based activism in the context of the larger politics of asthma have been largely underexplored, especially in terms of how gender and race shape the perception of the problem and the activism to remediate it. The centrality of childhood asthma as a political issue is simultaneously a response to the increased incidence of the disease, as well as an affirmation by environmental justice activists of the importance of the lives of poor children of color who have been historically marginalized.

In focusing on outdoor air pollution as a primary factor in why their communities face high asthma rates, environmental justice activists are involved in larger public health debates about the nature of disease causation. Children with asthma are sensitive to outdoor air pollution since common air pollutants, such as ozone, sulfur dioxide, and particulate matter, are respiratory irritants and can exacerbate asthma (Koren 1995). A number of studies suggest potential short- and long-term health effects among children from outdoor and indoor air pollutants (Morello-Frosch, Pastor, and Sadd 2002; Gilliland et al. 1999). A central theme is how New York City environmental justice asthma activists seek to make childhood asthma a political and structural issue and to emphasize what is known as the precautionary principle in public health. This framing rejects countervailing pressures to individualize and personalize the problem of why and how particular people suffer from disease and illness, an approach not unique to asthma but central to debates about cancer and other diseases (Hubbard and Wald 1993, Steingraber 1997).

I address two main issues in asthma politics: why so many children have asthma and the clinical literature on management interested in how best to treat it. In West Harlem, South Bronx, Williamsburg, and Sunset Park, supporters of controversial noxious facilities (from either the state or corporate sector) argued that there was no proof that a particular facility contributed to high asthma rates. Community activists countered that the science of risk assessment was inadequate to deal with the cumulative exposure that their residents faced, and instead advocated a politics based on the precautionary principle.[2] It is indeed nearly impossible to scientifically prove the impact of a specific new facility manifesting in increased asthma rates on the health of a community. But environmental justice activists argued that the extra burden that these neighborhoods already face due to the higher rates of pollution exposure and the fragile health status that they already display, particularly in the young and old, demanded special protective precautions. This debate about risk factors and etiological frameworks is not, as facility proponents suggested, between "rational science" and "emotional politics," but about the politics of science, specifically the politics of air pollution and asthma, internally debated within public health and medical communities (Mayo and Hollander 1991). This focus on external air pollution explicitly rejects trends in environmental health research that look inward: at both the genetic susceptibility of people of color to asthma and the almost exclusive focus on the internal home environment.

## Childhood Asthma: Race and Gender Dimensions

Since the early 1980s, what has been described by the Centers for Disease Control (CDC) and medical, public health communities and health activists as an epidemic of asthma has been occurring in the United States.[3] In particular, it is a disease that has risen in spectacular numbers for children. The CDC reports that more than 4.8 million children under age eighteen in the United States, or upwards of 6.9 percent, have asthma, making it one of the most common chronic health conditions of childhood. Its prevalence increased by 52 percent for those ages five to thirty-four between 1982 and 1996 (American Lung Association 2003; Wilson et al. 1998). The costs of asthma are numerous and multidimensional, negatively affecting work and school attendance, social life and recreation, emotional well-being, and personal and financial relationships (Nocon and Booth 1989–1999, Kozriskyj and O'Neil 1999). It is the leading cause of childhood hospitalizations and absenteeism. In 1998 in the United States, the National Heart, Lung and Blood Institute

(NHLBI) estimated that the annual costs of asthma were $11.3 billion (President's Task Force on Environmental Health Risks and Safety Risks to Children 1999).

Asthma prevalence is higher in poorer populations and among urban as opposed to rural dwellers (Wilson et al. 1998) and in low-income children in particular (Crain et al. 1994). The racial disparity of rising asthma rates is a very real problem. According to the American Lung Association, asthma attack prevalence rates are 32 percent higher in African Americans than the rates in whites. African Americans also make up a disproportionate percentage of all asthma-related deaths. Black children are four times more likely to die from asthma than white children and three times as likely to be hospitalized for asthma. The prevalence of asthma among Hispanic children overall has also risen sharply (CDC 2000). There is also great variation among Hispanic ethnic groups that has not yet been adequately explained.[4]

Asthma is not a female health problem, nor is it a race disease in the sense that it strikes only a particular group of people. It is a disease that affects a wide array of populations. Nevertheless, diseases can be called racialized and gendered in how they are "defined, characterized, and dramatized," which provides a window on social relations and values (Wailoo 2001). Asthma is a racialized and gendered disease in the sense that the environmental justice activism around asthma is shaped by the racially disproportionate rates in terms of who suffers from it. Asthma activism is gendered insofar as parents in general and mothers in particular occupy a dominant discursive place in terms of beliefs in illness causation and management (Mailick, Holden, and Walther 1994; Prout, Hayes, and Gelder 1999; Marteau and Johnston 1986). Historically, mothers of asthmatics were thought to be ambivalent, overprotective, and rejecting toward their children, thereby contributing to the development of childhood asthma (Gabbay 1982, Guyer 2000). Although this notion of maternal causation has been largely discarded, asthma management remains heavily gendered. Because childhood asthma is a chronic condition, parents and other caretakers of children are heavily involved with the management of childhood asthma. Asthma is also closely associated with urban poverty and illness and with facets of community psychology, particularly in terms of control (or lack thereof) of one's environment.

### Living with Asthma: Implications for Urban Poverty and Health

Individual children with asthma are not generally activists, although they may become the focal point of environmental justice activist concern. In New York City and other cities, parents of asthmatics and administrators of schools with large asthma problems tend to speak for the children of asthmatics out of serious concern for their physical and mental health.[5] Here is how one journalist wrote about the asthma epidemic in the South Bronx:

> The gasping and wheezing exist on such a wide scale that asthma has taken a psychological toll on a community already facing substantial burdens. Men talk of not being able to work, mothers of constantly worrying whether their children might be playing too hard, and youngsters of the moment when their hearts start to thump if they run too fast. . . . "People are so depressed; their children are sick. It's another thing that weighs heavily on them that's out of control," said Chris Norwood, executive director of Health Force, a South Bronx community health education group. "It leads to family-wide, communitywide depression. It prevents people from feeling secure. They live in terror that they're going to collapse any moment." (Nossiter 1995)

In many ways, young people are especially vulnerable to the adverse impacts of damaged environments from physical, mental, and emotional health perspectives. They tend to lack the right of full participation in decisions about their environment that can seriously affect their lives. One consequence is a sense of alienation from an environment that young people feel no sense of control over, which can manifest in adulthood on a communitywide scale.

Popular media have also focused on the rise of asthma as one part of a complex landscape of poor health and poverty, particularly in low-income urban areas with high concentrations of nonwhite populations (Alpert 1999; Stolberg 1999). As journalist David Shipler documents in *The Working Poor: Invisible in America* (2004), "Every problem magnifies the impact of the others, and all are so tightly interlocked that one reversal can produce a chain reaction with results far distant from the original cause. A run-down apartment can exacerbate a child's asthma, which leads to a call for an ambulance, which generates a medical bill that cannot be paid, which ruins a credit record, which hikes the interest rate on an auto loan, which forces the purchase of an unreliable used car, which jeopardizes a mother's punctuality at work, which limits her promotions and earning capacity, which confines her to poor housing" (11). Similarly, a cover story in the *New York Times* magazine, "The Ghetto Miasma: Enough to Make You Sick?" describes: "Something is killing America's urban poor, but this is no ordinary epidemic. . . . Even teenagers are afflicted with numerous health problems, including asthma, diabetes and high blood pressure. Poor urban blacks have the worst health of any ethnic group in America, with the possible exception of Native Americans. . . . It makes you wonder whether there is something deadly in the American experience of urban poverty itself" (Epstein 2003, 75). The author chronicles the network of diseases, exacerbated by poverty, stress, and racism. In addition to asthma, diabetes, and high blood pressure, these include strokes, kidney disease, and certain types of cancer. The use of the language of miasma should be unsurprising, given the public health history outlined in chapter 1 regarding the genealogy of contemporary environmental justice and health activism.

## Environmental Justice Asthma Activism in New York City

New York City is often described as the epicenter of the nation's asthma epidemic, and in many ways, it is at the forefront of environmental justice asthma activism. A 1990 geographic analysis of asthma mortality identified New York City as one of four metropolitan areas in the country whose excessive asthma mortality alone may have driven the overall U.S. trend in the early 1980s (Weiss and Wagener 1990). A New York City Department of Health (2003) estimate was that over 700,000 adults and 300,000 children in the city had been diagnosed with asthma at some time in their lives. Within the city, asthma hospitalization rates in 2000 averaged 33.6 per 10,000 residents, more than twice the national average of 16.7 per 10,000 residents (Garg et al. 2003). It is the leading cause of hospitalizations for children. Children inhale more air on a per kilogram basis than adults and may spend a larger proportion of their time outdoors than adults. Overall, asthma hospitalization rates in New York City increased by 22 percent from 1988 to 1997. Low-income children have a rate 3.5 times greater than higher-income children (Stevenson, Garg, and Leighton 2000). Asthma hospitalization rates among African American and Latinos were five times greater than those of whites (De Palo et al. 1994), and the factors that shape the racially and socially disproportionate ways in which asthma is experienced in New York City have been the subject of intense public health and medical research for well over a decade (Carr, Zeitel, and Weiss 1992; Claudio, Tulton, Coucette, and Landrigan 1999). One in four children in Central Harlem has asthma, double the expected rate and among the highest rates ever recorded anywhere (Pérez-Peña 2003). The overwhelmingly African American and Latino populations of East Harlem and South Bronx have the highest asthma hospitalization rates in the city. East Harlem heads the list at 170.2 hospitalizations per 10,000 population for children aged fourteen years and younger in the year 2000. This compares to a citywide average of 64 and a national average for children of 33.6 per 10,000 people (American Lung Association 2003).

The main contributions that environmental justice activists make are in highlighting the recognition of asthma as a pervasive problem in their communities. Their symbolic intervention is not incidental but central to the politics of environmental justice asthma activism in New York City. As Shipler's title suggests (*Working Poor: Invisible in America*), to be poor is in many ways to be invisible, and conditions of poverty are so interconnected that they seem all-encompassing, even natural. Environmental justice asthma activists foreground their voices and perspectives on asthma through their experience of illness, which they link to particular pollution sources. By naming these sources of pollution as problems, they thus believe in the possibility of remediation. In essence, they reject the ways in which urban pollution is concentrated and experienced in communities of color. They believe, in other words, that particular problems can be addressed and health and environmental justice achieved through community activism.

In New York City, particulate pollution from diesel sources—in particular, buses in West Harlem and trucks in the South Bronx—have been a flash point for environmental justice activism. The problem of diesel forms the base on which new or proposed facilities provide the extra layer of pollution (the sewage plant, the medical waste incinerator, the sludge treatment plant, and the municipal waste incinerator). Diesel burns hydrocarbons, releasing particulate emissions into the air. Fine particulate pollution is particularly dangerous because small particles lodge in the lungs of the young, the elderly, and the sick. Particulate matter includes a wide range of pollutants—road dust, diesel soot, fly ash, wood smoke, and sulfate aerosols—that are suspended as particles in the air. These particles are a mixture of visible and microscopic solid particles and minute liquid droplets known as aerosols.[6] Particulate pollution is classified by size, with finer particles (PM 2.5) considered by health scientists to be more dangerous than coarser material (PM 10) because they are small enough to evade the body's respiratory defense mechanisms and lodge deep in lung tissue.[7]

Northern Manhattan is home to a diesel-fueled Amtrak rail line, six of the seven of Manhattan's Metropolitan Transportation Authority (MTA) diesel bus depots, and a large New York/New Jersey Port Authority bus station. WE ACT, which formed in response to the North River sewage treatment plant, became increasingly active on air pollution and environmental health issues generally in northern Manhattan and their impact on children and youth throughout the 1990s. Of special concern was the diesel exhaust pollution from the five operational MTA bus depots in northern Manhattan, which garaged an estimated 1,200 buses out of the MTA's five borough fleet of 4,400 buses.

Challenging the disproportionate number of diesel buses garaged in northern Manhattan became a priority for WE ACT in 1988 when the MTA built the sixth diesel bus depot in the area. This facility was built on a site adjacent to a middle school and a 1,200-unit subsidized housing development and was of particular concern because of the additional exposure of diesel exhaust that the 240 buses garaged in this facility would create. In 1997 as a culmination of much research and education on air pollution and respiratory health, WE ACT conducted a massive bilingual publicity campaign: If You Live Uptown: Breathe at Your Own Risk. This campaign placed bilingual ads in seventy-five bus shelters throughout northern Manhattan and produced a television public service announcement, brochures, and mail-in postcards designed to mobilize community residents. WE ACT sponsored a major advertisement campaign on bus shelters to pressure the MTA to convert its buses to natural gas. It read: "If you live uptown breathe at your own risk. Diesel bus fumes can kill" (see figure 3.1). Another version of the ad continued: "6 out of 7 of Manhattan's diesel bus depots are located uptown. This puts the health of a half million mostly African-Americans and Latinos at risk. Don't just breathe this all in. Do something. Because clean air is a right, not a privilege, even if you live above 96th St." The text accompanied

**Figure 3.1**
WE ACT Dirty Diesel Campaign image (Credit: Marc Baptiste)

a dramatic photograph of two adults and a child wearing large gas masks.

The campaign, conducted alongside the Natural Resources Defense Council (with which it worked on the North River sewage treatment plant) was aimed at getting the MTA to switch to less polluting natural gas for its city bus fleet (its Long Island fleet already ran on natural gas, a point of ire for Harlem environmental justice activists). The Dirty Diesel campaign was created, publicized, and displayed on the very buses and at the bus shelters that were the source of the controversy. WE ACT received a great deal of media coverage with this campaign, and residents of northern Manhattan sent the New York State governor (who appoints the majority of the MTA board of directors) and the head of the MTA thousands of postcards asking them to pursue less toxic alternatives to diesel fuel. The community achieved a victory in 2000 when the governor required the MTA to agree that all new bus depots constructed in New York City would be designed to house compressed natural gas buses rather than diesel buses. The MTA also included in its five-year capital plan the decision to convert three existing depots, including the Manhattanville depot in West Harlem, to compressed natural gas.

### Engaging the Politics of Asthma Causation and Treatment

Asthma politics encompasses highly contested debates on disease causation, in which environmental justice activists are deeply involved and invested. Asthma results not from a single cause but from a complex interaction of genetic and environmental factors. Although there is no known biological reason for the greater prevalence of asthma among racial minorities, some suggest that higher asthma rates may be a surrogate for lower quality of health care, limited health care access, lack of access to culturally appropriate medical care (for example, as a result of a lack of Spanish translation), and the higher number of minorities living in low-income neighborhoods with substandard housing, which exposes them to cockroaches, peeling paint, and the resulting dust, as well as higher rates of exposure to smokers, all of which can trigger attacks among asthmatics.[8]

Environmental justice activists in New York focus on the outdoor air pollution risks as exacerbating already poor health conditions in their communities. This connection is not accidental; national studies have connected air pollution and mortality and asthma, and domestic air quality (Dockery et al. 1993, Jones 1998). Air pollution risks are also distributed unequally. Air quality has not improved evenly across the board in terms of pollutants reduced or the geographic and demographic distribution in air quality improvements. In 2002, 71 percent of African Americans lived in counties that violated federal air pollution standards, compared to 58 percent of the white population (Black Leadership Forum 2002). A 2003 national study found that Hispanic, African

American, and Asian/Pacific Islander mothers are more than twice as likely to live in the most air-polluted counties as white mothers after controlling for maternal risk factors, region, and educational status (Woodruff et al. 2003). One study of air pollution in New York City found that nonwhites were more adversely affected by air pollution and that the nonwhite risk estimates were generally larger than those of whites, although not to a statistically significant degree (Gwynn and Thurston 2001).

Corporate and state supporters of the noxious facilities in West Harlem, the South Bronx, Williamsburg, and Sunset Park consistently argued that there was no scientific proof that a particular facility contributed to rising asthma rates. This point was rejected by environmental justice activists with other narratives. Community activists, predominantly women of color, testified at public hearings and public events, citing their own asthma or their child's asthma. They countered that the increase of childhood asthma rates must have something to do with outdoor air pollution, and the science of risk assessment was inadequate to deal with the cumulative exposure that their residents faced as a result of the multiple pollution exposures in their neighborhoods (as opposed to single sources in conventional risk assessment analysis).

Environmental justice approaches to asthma draw heavily from the precautionary principle, which is being advanced by public health and cancer activists (Steingraber 1997). This notion, also known as the principle of precautionary action, calls for preventing harm to the environment and to human health. The 1998 Wingspread Statement on the Precautionary Principle, formulated by an international group of scientists, government officials, lawyers, and labor and grassroots environmental activists, defined the principle as follows:

• The release and use of toxic substances, the exploitation of resources, and physical alterations of the environment have had substantial unintended consequences affecting human health and the environment. Some of these concerns are high rates of learning deficiencies, asthma, cancer, birth defects and species extinctions, along with global climate change, stratospheric ozone depletion and worldwide contamination with toxic substances and nuclear materials.
• We believe existing environmental regulations and other decisions, particularly those based on risk assessment, have failed to protect adequately human health and the environment—the larger system of which humans are but a part.
• We believe there is compelling evidence that damage to humans and the worldwide environment is of such magnitude and seriousness that new principles for conducting human activities are necessary.

• While we realize that human activities may involve hazards, people must proceed more carefully than has been the case in recent history. Corporations, government entities, organizations, communities, scientists and other individuals must adopt a precautionary approach to all human endeavors.

• Therefore, it is necessary to implement the Precautionary Principle: When an activity raises threats of harm to human health or the environment, precautionary measures should be taken even if some cause and effect relationships are not fully established scientifically. In this context the proponent of an activity, rather than the public, should bear the burden of proof. (Steingraber 1997, 284)

Environmental justice activists are a major health activist constituency that supports the precautionary principle (Morello-Frosch, Pastor, and Sadd 2002). Significantly, in the Wingspread statement, asthma is identified as one of the key health problems that need this approach. Also, the statements of New York City environmental justice advocates on the issues of causality, proof, and outdoor air pollution and its impact on asthma reflect the importance of the precautionary principle to their asthma activism, even if not defined explicitly as such, and is tied to the scientific uncertainty attached to asthma causation in particular.

One major source of triggers for asthmatics is the indoor environment (Jones 1998). Home environment exposures include tobacco, mold, poor ventilation, water damage, heat irritants (electric, gas, oil, wood), chemical irritants (air fresheners, ammonia, and other chemicals), dust (carpet, cloth-covered furniture, drapes or curtains), pets, dust mites, and bed covers (comforters, wool, cotton, or acrylic blankets). The most controversial of indoor triggers is cockroaches, or the cockroach theory. The National Institute of Allergy and Infectious Diseases (NIAID) and the National Institute for Environmental Health Science (NIEHS) conducted the National Cooperative Inner City Asthma Study, a national study of children with asthma in eight U.S. cities that tested the effects of interventions that reduce children's exposure to indoor allergens and sought to improve communication with their primary care physicians. The study compared the effects of various allergens on asthmatic children living in poor urban areas. The results, published in 1997 in the *New England Journal of Medicine*, suggested that cockroaches may be the chief culprit in childhood asthma. Nearly 40 percent of the asthmatic children were found to be allergic to the insects' droppings and body parts (Rosenstreich et al. 1997).

However, community leaders in New York City questioned the emphasis on indoor air pollution, pointing out that dirt, dust mites, cockroaches, mouse and rat urine, poor housing, and conditions of poverty are not new phenomena. Also, the focus on housekeeping, as opposed to poor housing conditions (such as mold in public housing, an endemic problem), represents this conflict between individualized and systemic approaches to the childhood asthma epidemic. As Marian Feinberg, from the South Bronx Clean Coalition, commented: "The problem with the National Inner City Asthma Study is how it was manipulated in the media. Two bad things happened: the emphasis on cockroaches implied that bad moms caused asthma, and it focused on cockroaches as the main factor" (personal communication, May 2002). She points out the particularly cruel irony is that after this media attention, pesticide companies started marketing their products on Spanish-language and black radio stations with a child gasping for air. These commercials ran despite the fact that pesticide sprays themselves can function as an asthma trigger. In contrast, Feinberg, like other environmental justice activists, prefers to focus on a multidimensional approach to asthma causation and management, exemplified by the campaign slogan: "Cleaner Air, Cleaner Housing, Cleaner Lungs," prominently displayed in the SBCAC offices.

The main aspects of asthma management are taking medication properly, taking care of the home, monitoring air flow, and reducing exposure to common indoor household triggers. Asthma medicines keep the air tubes in the lungs open. The main treatment regimen is the correct taking of preventative medication. This process has grown increasingly complex with the advent of more sophisticated medication, with some children taking up to eight different medications a day. Taking care of the home environment involves recognizing the indoor triggers for asthma and taking steps to remediate these conditions. Home inspection of household exposures is a common approach to asthma management programs. Typically in this approach, representatives of a Healthy Homes project inspect the home, measure the caregiver's knowledge about asthma triggers, and suggest steps to reduce exposures (Krieger et al. 2000). These homes are usually chosen in poor households with asthmatic children. Community health workers can be a valuable tool in efforts to improve the health and environment of particular populations while promoting female and professional identities (Ramirez-Valles 1998). But one lingering question is how to choose which homes to visit. This question is significant given that most homes in the developed world probably have at least one of the household exposures.[9] Community-based asthma education, through churches and community-based organizations, is also being recognized as an effective tool to deal with asthma in low-income and minority populations (Ford et al. 1996, Wilson et al. 1998). However, some environmental justice activists view the home visits approach to asthma with caution for this very reason of where the burden of blame ends up. As Feinberg explained, the emphasis on indoor allergens and housekeeping practices tends to privilege an individualistic versus a systematic approach to the problem: "I understand that it can help some individuals, and that if it helps even one household or child, then it's valuable. But aren't we then accepting the basic conditions of poor housing and outdoor air pollution by this approach, instead of systemically trying to improve housing and the external environment?" (personal communication, May 2002).

WE ACT's asthma program and activism further exemplifies a balanced and complex approach that emphasizes activism and political mobilization alongside legal strategies and community-based health research. WE ACT closely monitors the MTA's promises to reduce diesel in its fleet, which came about in large part as a result of their organizing.[10] WE ACT continues to organize around diesel bus issues, using the strategy of making the experiences and voices of community residents heard in broader political and social arenas. In November 2000, WE ACT filed a Title VI civil rights complaint against the MTA with the U.S. Department of Transportation (DOT), focusing on the MTA's use of public funding to administer its diesel bus facilities in a racially discriminatory manner in New York City.[11] By filing a civil rights complaint, WE ACT focused on race as a central factor in the bus depot problem and its health impacts. The complaint looked at the disproportionate number of diesel bus depots and parking lots in northern Manhattan neighborhoods and the fact that the MTA continued to systematically expand these facilities. These actions, WE ACT claimed, had the effect of discriminating against the predominantly African American and Latino residents of northern Manhattan by disproportionately exposing them to the health risks of diesel exhaust. WE ACT jointly filed the complaint with several of the area's residents, incorporating their testimony directly into the complaint. The complaint asked that the MTA take action to reduce this burden, including halting any further expansion of bus depots and parking lots, closing one of the depots, and accelerating the conversion of the bus fleet to clean alternative fuels. Although the U.S. D.O.T. did find the MTA partially at fault per the complaint, the community did not get the relief they sought due to larger political and bureaucratic considerations (Cecil Corbin-Mark, personal communication, March 30, 2006).

The testimony provided by community residents in this civil rights complaint is a key tactic WE ACT uses to communicate with regulatory agencies and politicians on matters of environmental health and justice. Its approach to political advocacy is to demand that the voices of those community members who are the most harmed by environmental exposure be heard by the government and other decision makers. One of the rhetorical successes of the national environmental justice movement has been the emphasis on low-income and communities of color speaking for themselves (exemplified by the phrase "We Speak for Ourselves").[12] WE ACT's collection of these stories is an attempt to put these principles into action. For example, community resident Sheila Hester, who lives across the street from an MTA diesel bus depot in East Harlem, provided testimony at a New York City Council hearing on the effects of bus and truck idling. A child of a WE ACT volunteer, Elizabeth Soto, age six, spoke on a television segment about the problem of bus idling: "When the buses drive by, the smoke gets in little people's eyes."

Northern Manhattan also suffers from the problem of diesel trucks, especially garbage trucks. WE ACT organized a letter-writing campaign to the city council and the New York City Department of Transportation about the impacts of trucks on local residents at a specific facility on 100th Street in East Harlem. Addie Jones wrote: "Every morning, my family and I are awakened by garbage trucks, diesel fumes, engine gas and yelling from sanitation workers. . . . These trucks are left idling for 20 to 40 minutes . . . and my apartment becomes filled with engine fumes. Our only defense is to turn on a fan and direct it towards the window." Margarita Cruz added: "I live on the fifth floor and have to continuously have screens on the windows because of the flies. You can't see through the screens because the smoke made it black." Katherine

Keyes wrote: "My son was six when we moved here. He developed asthma after we moved here. Every time he had an attack he had to be hospitalized. Eventually he moved to my sister's house in the Bronx and since then, his asthma has not been acting up. Since he moved to the Bronx, he hasn't been to the hospital once. He also has severe nosebleeds whenever he comes to stay here." (These are from stories collected by WE ACT, all dated September 15, 2003.)

WE ACT is also the community partner in a nationally recognized collaboration with Columbia University's School of Public Health through the Columbia Center for Children's Environmental Health (CCEH). WE ACT has transformed its environmental justice activism into a vibrant and significant force in community-based public health research that is generating new knowledge about asthma. The CCEH was founded in 1998 as one of eight Centers for Children's Environmental Health and Disease Prevention established jointly by the National Institute of Environmental Health Sciences and the EPA. The Columbia Research Project on Asthma is charting links between signs of asthma in very young children and exposure to allergens and pollutants in their homes and outdoor environment, the role of nutrition, and the impact of air pollution on birth weights. Preliminary findings of air quality tests in the homes of the first group of mothers suggest virtually universal exposure to two highly toxic pesticides during pregnancy, and biomarkers in maternal and cord blood show high rates of exposure to allergens, air pollutants, and second-hand tobacco smoke (Perera et al. 1999, Miller 1999). The study also found that air pollutants are linked to lower birth weights and skills in African American babies. This research suggests that the problems that low in-come urban children face, and the health effects of pollution exposure, begin before birth. (Chapter 6 discusses WE ACT's health research program in greater detail in the context of a larger discussion of community-based health research in New York City.)

## Conclusion

The environmental justice movement has made an enormous contribution to explicating complex debates about asthma in particular, and the politics of gender, race, and urban environmental health more generally. Asthma rates in New York City are finally starting to fall, at least in part because the sense of community crisis catalyzed an action and research agenda that forced the bureaucracy to act.[13] The politicization of asthma as an environmental justice issue in New York City contributed at least in part to the success in chipping away at the racial disparity of the disease (Flanders 2001). The larger political contribution the environmental justice movement makes is in reenvisioning environmental policy-making, reintegrating the health aspects of environmental policy, and engaging questions of risk assessment, all while prioritizing the voices of those with asthma, in particular, children of color.

Asthma is a complex disease. The high rates of asthma in minority communities are probably due to an intersection of genetics and environment and indoor and outdoor factors. The politics of asthma causation, the answer to the problem of racial disparities in asthma rates, and the gender politics of asthma management are tremendously complex, and much more research needs to be done on the questions and issues raised here. As tremendous federal and scientific resources pour into asthma research leading to increased research on causes and interventions, the next generation of health research on the problem is beginning. It is particularly important for the voices of those who are most affected to be heard, which is why seeing and listening to environmental justice asthma activists matters.

# 4

## The Racial Geography of New York City Garbage: Local and Global Trash Politics

New York City is known for its dedication. . . . The city fights to lead the world in so many areas that to name them would seem an aggressive act of braggadocio. . . . New York excels in crime, punishment, graft, corruption, carbon monoxide levels, prostitution, poverty. . . . Indeed, New York City is recognized in the best of circles as the garbage capital of the world.
—Katie Kelly, *Garbage*

On December 2, 2002, the Monday after Thanksgiving, in a small hearing room in the Bronx Overall Economic Development Corporation, about twenty people, mostly representing the New York City Department of Sanitation (DOS), and elected officials, awaited with little excitement for the opening of the Bronx public meeting on commercial solid waste issues. Harry Szarpanski, DOS assistant commissioner, began the proceedings twenty minutes late, waiting in case any public speaker or community member showed up to comment on the topic of the night, the DOS's preliminary report on New York City's commercial solid waste. Szarpanski asked if anyone was prepared to speak. No one volunteered, and many in the room tittered in nervous embarrassment, looking around at the audience yet avoiding eye contact with him. After an awkward silence, Szarpanski closed the meeting.

After the stenographer had gotten up from the table and put away her machine, a young Latino male walked in. The DOS representative manning the sign-in table outside came in and announced that Omar Freilla from Sustainable South Bronx wanted to speak. The stenographer unpacked her machine, and everyone settled into their chairs. Freilla, a resident of Hunts Point, spoke about the need to shift from a truck-based garbage export system to a system based on rail or barge. He cited the high rates of asthma in the South Bronx as a reason to move away from relying on trucks to transport garbage, since trucks produce particulate air pollution from diesel fuel. He pointed out that 30 percent of the students at one local South Bronx elementary school, P.S. 48, suffered from asthma. After about fifteen minutes (far exceeding the allotted time of three minutes per speaker), Freilla ended his comments. Szarpanski waited a minute and then adjourned the meeting a second time. Was it possible that this would be the fastest of the five borough meetings called on the issue of commercial solid waste? This seemed impossible in the Bronx, where passions about garbage, stemming from the Bronx-Lebanon incinerator campaign, run deep.

Suddenly (or dramatically, as is his wont), Carlos Padilla, president of the South Bronx Clean Air Coalition and a long-time veteran of the incinerator battle walked in. Szarpanski reopened the meeting for the second time, and again everyone settled back to listen. After apologizing for being late, Padilla spoke passionately and angrily about garbage and community health, the problems of corporate consolidation, the need to move from trucks to rail, and the problems of the "revolving door" for corporations, politicians, and regulators. He railed against the former state attorney general, Dennis Vacco, who, after he lost his election, became a garbage lobbyist in Albany. Padilla complained about dust, cockroaches, diesel fuel emissions, traffic backup, pervasive odors, and noise around waste transfer stations, where garbage is carted and then sorted for export. In 2004, there were sixty-six waste transfer stations that handled over 47,000 tons of waste per day. Waste transfer station neighbors commonly complain about home invasions by large and aggressive rats fat from eating endless supplies of garbage and about children and elderly who could not breathe because of the truck and garbage fumes.[1] He also directly refuted the notion that concern about garbage meant selfish disregard for other communities.

In advocating a more responsible approach to garbage, Padilla spoke of the need for all New Yorkers to be responsible for waste and to reject garbage incineration in communities outside the city. Padilla urged DOS representatives to come out for a walk with him to see the idling trucks filled with garbage that travel on streets not designated as truck routes and that come perilously close to hitting children and elderly pedestrians, and the fly-by-night illegal operations that unload and reload garbage at two in the morning.

After Padilla's twenty minutes, Szarpanski attempted to end the meeting for a third time. Yet again, a community member walked in. Padilla's longtime ally, Marian Feinberg testified. Feinberg echoed many of the same concerns as Freilla and Padilla, adding a labor and class analysis to the environmental justice critique of garbage policy. She critiqued the city's lack of regulatory enforcement and concern over the operations and poor working conditions at waste transfer stations. She accused the city of turning a blind eye to the low-wage, nonunionized labor at the facilities who face dangerous working environments. Finally, Szarpanski was able to officially close the meeting.

This public hearing represents the persistence of community concern in the South Bronx over garbage, echoed throughout the city wherever waste facilities, especially waste transfer stations, are clustered. The meeting was not an occasion for mass mobilization but an example of how representatives of community organizations continue to speak publicly on policy issues that are important to their neighborhoods. These community representatives recognized the performative aspects of the hearing and the fundamental lack of power they represent (Padilla said, "You can have hearings until the cows come home"), yet they continued to press for policy change. In part, they came because they believed that agency representatives like public participation on their terms: short meetings without controversy, where no one shows up, and a free pass from the public is implicitly given.[2]

This hearing, but a sliver of the environmental justice activism around garbage that has taken place in the past two decades, nonetheless illustrates the complex power dynamics around garbage activism in terms of public participation and the racial framework of environmental justice activists' engagement with garbage policy. This chapter examines the wide range of contemporary organizing and activism in response to New York City's solid waste policy, which radically changed in 2001 when the city closed its last municipally owned and operated landfill, at Fresh Kills in Staten Island. It explores the attempts by community organizations and local residents to make messy, and democratic, debates over the serious policy question of how to deal with New York City's garbage.

In 2000, New York City residents and businesses generated approximately 43,000 to 45,000 tons of waste per day, of which 40 percent was managed by the city department of sanitation and the rest by the private sector (Independent Budget Office, February 2001). Until 1996, the DOS had operated the entire residential waste stream, with the private sector responsible for the commercial waste. Private contractors have always been an important part of the garbage-handling picture in New York City, and garbage has long been a lightning rod for conflict (Corey 1994, Miller 2000). This chapter looks at contemporary urban and racial politics and the changing economic structure of garbage, specifically trends of privatization of municipal residential solid waste. Additionally, the politics of garbage in New York City are intimately linked to the politics and history of recycling. Recycling, waste reduction, and export are all municipal garbage-handling strategies and directly related, especially in terms of financial and budgetary priorities. Thus, I also discuss the city's recycling politics.

In 1996, Mayor Giuliani, with Governor Pataki, announced the closure of Fresh Kills, the largest landfill in the world. It was universally despised by Staten Island residents and politicians for its rancid odors, air pollution, and leakages of garbage and toxic leachate into the surrounding ground and water.[3] It is perhaps generous to call Fresh Kills a landfill. It is more accurately described as an open dump. In 1945, Robert Moses, the New York City parks commissioner, transformed Fresh Kills from a 500-acre tidal wetland, which he described as "an unsightly and unsanitary wasteland," into parkland. To make the area into parkland, he filled it with garbage. Fresh Kills opened in 1948 as a temporary waste station, and despite its temporary status, it grew to cover 2,200 acres or three and a half times the size of Central Park. Fresh Kills did not have a permit to operate, yet it generated a high amount of landfill methane, a gas that contributes to global warming. Methane is thought to contribute 16 percent of the greenhouse gas effect (Gandy 1994).

The closure of Fresh Kills marked the first time in New York City's history that the metropolis would not be burying or burning trash within its boundaries. Although Fresh Kills still had an estimated twenty-year life span, it was closed by the Republican mayor and governor as political payback to the solidly Republican, overwhelmingly white borough, the only borough in the city with those political and demographic characteristics (Miller 2000). At the height of its operation, it received approximately 13,000 tons of primarily residential trash brought daily by barge from nine city-owned and -operated marine transfer stations (MTS). Marine transfer stations are where collection vehicles tipped their garbage loads onto open barges that then traveled to Fresh Kills. The nine transfer stations are located throughout the city, well distributed geographically, and taking advantage of New York City's particular geography of being surrounded by water.[4] Four of the city's boroughs (Manhattan, Staten Island, Queens, and Brooklyn) are islands, and the fifth, Bronx, is defined by its waterfront. The MTS system minimized the health effects of truck traffic because garbage traveled by boat, not by truck.

The closure of Fresh Kills was met with immediate concern by particular communities. Specifically, neighborhood groups that had a history of problems with local waste transfer stations organized against the new policy. Waste transfer stations, long a part of the New York City industrial landscape, were a relatively small problem until the late 1980s, when the city increased the tipping fees for dumping commercial waste at Fresh Kills from $18 to $40 per ton in an effort to prolong the life span of the landfill. Previously, commercial waste had also traveled by MTS to Fresh Kills. Giuliani's initial proposal for a post–Fresh Kills New York City was to privatize residential waste, replacing a municipally owned and operated MTS infrastructure with a system based on contracts to multinational waste corporations, with garbage processed at waste transfer stations on the industrial waterfront. As a result of organized community protest and a change in mayoral administrations, garbage policy and the public discourse that shaped policy discussions altered in minor and significant ways.

This topic is an urban and racial matter, with political, economic, and geographic implications, because of the land use and demographic patterns in New York City and the debates about the negative effects of multinational waste trade on local communities. The neighborhoods particularly vulnerable to changing garbage policies are poor and working-class neighborhoods: Williamsburg/Greenpoint and Sunset Park/Red Hook in Brooklyn, and the South Bronx. More than half of the fifty-four private waste transfer stations (for putrescible, or smelly, garbage and construction and demolition debris) are located in just two neighborhoods: South Bronx with thirteen and Williamsburg/Greenpoint with seventeen facilities (see figure 4.1). In 2004, according to information from the DOS compiled by New York Lawyers for the Public Interest, these two neighborhoods handled 73 percent of the city's putrescible and construction and debris waste.[5]

Many of the garbage environmental justice activists became involved in the issue since the late 1980s because of the growing waste transfer station problem that emerged when tipping fees at Fresh kills increased for private carters. They had worked for years, and helped to pressure the city council to pass Local Law 40 in 1990, mandating that DOS come up with siting regulations for waste transfer stations where there had

**Figure 4.1**
Waste transfer station map
(Credit: Pratt Center for Community Development)

been none previously. Community groups were also plaintiffs in a series of lawsuits.[6] But the regulations were weak. In 1997, community residents' ire was raised by the 400-foot rule for a buffer zone to protect residents from waste transfer stations.[7] This rule was announced approximately at the same time as Mayor Giuliani's attack on sex shops in his Quality of Life campaign, where sex shops had to be kept 500 feet from schools and other facilities. At one protest at the DOS on the siting regulations, environmental justice activists protested that waste transfer stations were considered less of a problem than sex shops. Some even held signs asking, "What about my quality of life?" to highlight how quality-of-life discourses were applied unevenly by the mayor.

This chapter unravels a local policy question and links it to larger transformations in racial, social, economic, ecological, and political processes in the urban sphere. It looks at how issues of environmental racism and the discourse of the environmental justice movement were used to frame garbage activism. The local health and environmental impacts of garbage-handling infrastructure were major factors in this activism. Community activists, veterans of earlier land use and environmental pollution battles, transformed their local fights to organizing on a citywide level, with a critique of global multinational waste corporations through the vehicle of the Organization of Waterfront Neighborhoods (OWN), a coalition that formed in 1996 when Fresh Kills was closed.

OWN was founded by the New York City Environmental Justice Alliance (NYCEJA), a citywide organization focused on environmental justice issues (NYCEJA itself was founded by activists involved in the four campaigns examined in chapter 2). OWN was co-coordinated by New York Lawyers for the Public Interest (NYLPI) and functions like a network. OWN's twenty-four organizational members were from neighborhoods that were already heavily burdened by waste transfer stations on the waterfront.[8] It thus was a citywide coalition committed to advancing an environmental justice agenda.[9] OWN members objected to city policies that they thought exacerbated the disparate racial impact of pollution from waste transfer stations and truck traffic and their associated health effects, specifically regarding asthma. OWN mobilized over 4,000 people to various hearings, demonstrations, and public events from 1997 to 2000 (Eddie Bautista, personal communication, May 2002). It focused on residential and commercial solid waste, since, as one activist put it, "a transfer station is a transfer station, is a transfer station." The bureaucratic and technical distinction between commercial and residential waste is meaningless at the community level.[10] OWN's platform highlighted several themes that the other organizations and coalitions working on garbage issues ignored in their public materials: fair share of burdensome facilities and "Don't Waste Our Waterfront." Neighborhoods organizing around solid waste, primarily low-income neighborhoods with high populations of people of color, asked important questions about the distribution of benefits and burdens of city services and how the allocation of these burdens and benefits was influenced by race, class, and politics. In their public statements and in practice, OWN supported "equity," *not* not-in-my-backyard (NIMBYism), especially in promoting policies like borough equity and self-sufficiency, which has racial and geographic implications. Borough equity or self-sufficiency is the idea that each borough should handle its own waste. The biggest barrier to this concept is Manhattan, which is the richest borough and generates 40 percent of the city's commercial waste, all of which is handled through Brooklyn, Bronx, and Queens. I examine how racialized discourses of environmental benefits and burdens were successfully mobilized. In documenting OWN's campaign, I investigate the claim by politicians and Staten Islanders that all garbage activism was necessarily NIMBYist politics that sought to perpetuate the injustice of Fresh Kills. I suggest how and why the claims of NIMBYism made against low-income and communities of color are not equivalent to NIMBY politics by elites in the area of environmental racism claims and within the environmental justice movement (Gregory 1998).

The particular formation of the problems of urban solid waste and the discourse of environmental justice that I untangle (along with the environmental, legislative and regulatory context, and debates about public participation) are what make this current organizing distinct from earlier waves of garbage policy, history, and activism. The proposed privatization of residential solid waste; the legacy of two decades of federal, state, and municipal environmental legislation; the codification of public participation into policymaking; and the discourse of environmental justice are all new factors that affect the management of urban solid waste in New York City.

## Local-Global Environmentalism, or The Politics of Place and Urban Garbage

Keil's "world city environmental problematic" brings to light conflicts over democratic decision making and land use planning processes as key areas of study. Land use and economic and development processes are tied to privatization and globalization in a postindustrial New York City, as the focus on municipal solid waste reveals.[11] Waste management options have global impacts: more waste going to landfills creates more greenhouse gases, and increased use of virgin resources such as wood for paper affects forests and global climate change and biodiversity (Grover and Grover 2002). Furthermore, there are significant negative health effects, ranging from asthma attacks to premature death, of New York City's emissions of greenhouse gases (Cifuentes et al. 2001).

Urban geographers have written at length about contemporary patterns of consumption in New York City within the framework of postmodernity. Garbage is a key theme and ideological symbol, as well as a litmus test for policies that gauge attitudes toward the public and private spheres. For example, David Harvey (1989) offers a framework for understanding urban garbage that links the material with the cultural and ideological spheres:

In the realm of commodity production, the primary effect (of the postmodern condition) has been to emphasize the values and virtues of instaneity (instant and fast foods, meals, and other satisfactions) and of disposability (cups, plates, cutlery, packaging, napkins, clothing, etc). . . . It meant more than just throwing away produced goods (creating a monumental waste disposal problem), but also being able to throw away values, lifestyles, stable relationships, and attachments to things, buildings, places, people, and received ways of doing and being. (286)

Harvey uses garbage as a metaphor for the postmodern condition and as a material object (the monumental waste disposal problem) to represent changing forms of capitalism. This form of capitalism, based on instantaneity and represented by packaging, is also a proxy for the increasing alienation of workers from the fruits of their labor and the alienation by users of objects from production and consumption, and ultimately disposal. Social and political relationships between classes of people and between people and things are reduced to the market.

Harvey (1989) notes the fundamental disconnect from the "real," or older, forms of industrial production in relation to New York City's economy. He suggests a trend that is related to a crisis in economic value and structures: "The biggest physical export from New York City is now waste paper. The city's economy in fact rests on the production of fictitious capital to lend to the real estate agents who cut deals for the highly paid professionals who manufacture fictitious capital" (p. 332). Similarly, in *The Assassination of New York* (1993), Robert Fitch describes what he calls the "poverty of post-industrial life in New York." According to Fitch, "the rest of the world sends us cars, bananas, cocoa, electronic goods, all manner of ingeniously made and rare commodities. We ship back waste paper. This is what our economic metabolism with the rest of the world comes down to" (259).[12]

The central paradox of globalization and how changing forms of political economy reshape geography is that the less important spatial barriers become, the greater the sensitivity is of capital to variations of place within space and the greater is the incentive for places to be differentiated in ways attractive to capital. In New York City, these political-economic transformations meant that the city's real estate became "too valuable" for manufacturing uses. This dispersal of manufacturing prioritizes the intellectual capital concentrated in world cities over that of labor capital. In New York City, this transformation meant a shift in the political, economic, and cultural sectors of the city based on production. The material manifestation of this transition from a production to service sector economy, as Harvey and Fitch note ironically, is the overproduction of New York City wastepaper. As urban space is deemed "too valuable" for manufacturing or waste disposal within the boundaries of the city, the hierarchization of uses within the city becomes even more classed and racialized, so that Manhattan garbage cannot be processed in Manhattan (or at least affluent Manhattan below 125th Street), since cheaper land is found in the outer boroughs. The city's financial capital also translates to a more complete command over rural space throughout the region (broadly defined geographically) in communities hosting landfills for New York City garbage. These communities are facing their own difficult transitions from an industrial to service sector economy (an example is steel and textiles in Pennsylvania). It is not a surprise that the rural communities that import urban trash are often the same communities vying for prisons, since prisons and landfills are similar types of nonproductive industries requiring large swaths of land.[13]

These spatial and political implications were suggested in the controversy that developed after the Fresh Kills closure announcement and the city's first plans for a post–Fresh Kills era, dependent entirely on regional export. In response, New Jersey Governor Christine Whitman told Mayor Giuliani to "drop dead." Anti–New York City garbage sentiment reached a new high in the wake of Giuliani's inflammatory statements about why Virginia should take the city's trash as "payment" for New York City's services as a cultural and business capital. He said, "People in Virginia like to utilize New York because it is a culture center and business center. What goes along with being a business center is that we're very crowded, and we don't have room to handle the garbage . . . so this is a reciprocal relationship." The Virginia legislature passed a bill to curb imports of New York City garbage into the state, a decision that was struck down in federal court (Spencer 2000). This trash-for-culture comment is more than a flippant idea. Rather, it reflects an attitude about the command of financial global capital in world cities to extend control, through cost, over cheaper urban and rural space.

This changing role of urban space is exemplified by the transformation of the industrial waterfront in New York City, a shift that is both central to and symbolic of the larger shifts of the political economy of city. Policies that alter the waterfront from active manufacturing or industry to nonproductive, acceptably pollutable space, (characterized by a proliferation of waste transfer stations) signify this historical process of New York City's transformation to a city that increasingly sees its space as too valuable for working-class uses. This transition does not imply a shift from nonpolluting to polluting uses; manufacturing and industrial waterfronts are also polluting, after all. What is different is that employment from these industries provided compensation for this pollution, whereas the proposal to increase the extent of the garbage infrastructure on the waterfront is seen by activists as frustrating the efforts by communities to develop their waterfront for employment and housing, as I describe in chapter 6.

## Privatizing Garbage

The argument over what the role of private companies should be in handling New York City garbage is not new. New York City's eagerness under

Mayor Giuliani to privatize city sanitation services stands in marked contrast to the urban reform era movements in the late nineteenth and early twentieth centuries to municipalize services in order to avert corruption and monopolies. Public services were believed to offer increased accountability. Historian Martin Melosi documents the rise of municipal socialism in U.S. cities, or the belief that government ownership and service delivery is superior to that of private contractors.[14] Whereas a century ago, private contractors were seen as predatory and corrupt, tied into the municipal corruption of the political machine, today it is far more common for private corporations to be seen in certain sectors as cleaner and more "efficient." Part of this change is tied to the ever-shifting perceptions of public versus private, with the contemporary moment characterized by an ever-shrinking responsibility to any idea of the public. In the case of garbage, this shift means the direct transfers of municipal service operations of residential waste to private transnational waste companies.[15]

This urban reform impulse was also true in New York City. The garbage situation in New York was complicated by the disjointed nature of the solid waste system, in which a division between cleaning, collection, and disposal activities developed over time, with responsibility for performing these functions shifting back and forth between the public and private sector (Corey 1994). The split that emerged, with private contractors handling commercial waste while the city managed residential waste, held true until the Fresh Kills closure. Before 1993, the New York City private waste market was dominated by small carters in the commercial waste sector, with heavy mafia influence as popularized in the television show, *The Sopranos*. The largest multinational waste corporations were shut out of the New York City market through a cartel that survived until 1995, when it was broken by Manhattan district attorney Robert Morgenthau. He indicted twenty-three garbage firms, seventeen executives, and four trade associations for conspiring to fix costs, charging that organized crime controlled the commercial waste sector through an industry trade association that enforced anticompetitive arrangements (Lentz 1995). Prices began to drop as a result of the indictments (estimates range widely from 30 to 75 percent) and the creation of the Trade Waste Commission in 1996.[16]

The rhetoric and ideology of privatization must be explained to understand how it actually functions in the case of garbage. One analyst describes privatization as the initiative to introduce market relationships into the bureaucratic production of public services (Sclar 2000). This introduction of market relationships is particularly complicated regarding public services:

> Although collectively, taxpayers stand to gain the most through sustained market competition, they have less individual incentive to politically defend competitive, public contracting than sellers have to undermine it. Thus, even though competitive contracting seemingly promises more choice and better prices, the potential benefit for individual taxpayers is often insufficient for them to justify the investment of time and money to enforce sustained competition. Contractors, on the other hand, stand to reap a great deal individually by ensuring that the public market structures work to their advantage. Therefore, they are willing to invest the necessary resources to shape public markets in anti-competitive ways. (2000, 11)

Additionally, the longer the term of the contract is and the more complex the service provided, the smaller the role played by market competition in terms of the benefits of privatization. The power of competition lies in large part in the threat to jobs of public employees. However, if government has been providing a service for a long time, outsiders rarely have the knowledge or the expertise to take on the job done by the public agency. Thus, contracting can be a cumbersome and expensive instrument for the delivery of public service, especially if there is insufficient regulatory oversight. In part, the push for privatization is "fueled more by an ideological desire to shrink government than a wish to enhance public service" (Sclar 2000, 94). The assumption is that the private sector is more efficient, innovative, entrepreneurial, and flexible than the public sector. Privatization proponents assume a zero-sum relationship between the inefficient government and the market economy, and its advocates often describe the move to private control as a no-cost win-win, leading to lower costs for consumers.

One powerful argument against privatization is that the "best cannot mean cheapest or most efficient, for a reasonable appraisal of alternatives needs to weigh concerns *of justice, security and citizenship*" (emphasis added; Starr 1990, 110). Privatization transfers decisions from one realm of choice—and constraint—to another. These realms have different interests and abilities, typically differentiated as citizens and consumers (Cohen 2003). As one privatization critic explains, "The public realm recognizes equal voting rights, the market unequal purchasing

power. The two realms provide different environments for forming preferences. Democratic politics is an arena for explicitly articulating, criti-
cizing and adapting preferences. Democratic politics pushes participants
to make a case for interests larger than their own. Privatization dimin-
ishes the sphere of public information, public deliberation, and public
accountability. These are the elements of democracy whose values are
not reducible to efficiency" (Starr 1990, 118). Privatization tends to
produce diminished access that limits distributive justice outcomes.

These criticisms of privatization are certainly made by advocates who
focus on the environmental and corporate factors that shape garbage
policy at local, regional, national, and international levels. One long-time
garbage privatization critic writes: "Neither has public knowledge (particularly in the U.S.) been served by the further privatization of waste
policy and practices through the use of the courts as the ultimate arbiters
in disputes between citizens and the waste industry, government and the
industry as well as between waste firms themselves" (Crooks 1993, 261).
Such critiques are echoed by environmental justice garbage activists in
New York City in their critiques of privatization in garbage policy.

### Globalizing Garbage

The unyoking of New York City from its previous spatial limits reflects
the intensification of processes of deterritorialization. Deterritorialization, or what Manuel Castells (1983) call the "delocalization of production and consumption," is the removal of a city from its physical
limits of production and consumption, signifying a transition from previous spatial practices. In New York City, this condition of deterritorialization depends on the commodification of local urban garbage as a
commercial export product to rural or international landfills, in a system
increasingly managed and owned vertically by multinational waste corporations. The changing nature of urban garbage, and the fate of marginalized communities in the cities, is intimately linked to rural
impoverished populations through class and race. The increasing privatization and geographic mobility of garbage exemplify what David
Harvey (1989) identifies as changing experiences of space and time, or
"the time-space compression." This compression does not mean a concentration of capital within national or local borders. In fact, Harvey

argues the opposite position: that "capitalism is becoming more tightly organized *through* dispersal, geographical mobility and flexible responses in labor markets, labor processes and consumer markets, all accompanied by hefty doses of institutional, product and technological innovation" (159).

To illustrate, New York State's garbage (of which a large percentage is New York City's) ends up in Connecticut, Florida, Illinois, Indiana, Kentucky, Maryland, Massachusetts, Michigan, Ohio, Pennsylvania, Virginia, and West Virginia (Goldstein and Madtes 2001, Holusha 1991). The route that any given bag of New York City garbage travels on any given day is subject to the whim of a midlevel manager of a multinational who may choose to send trash to one of a number of available landfills under contract. For example, Brooklyn Heights garbage may end up in Charles City County, Virginia, while garbage from nearby Prospect Heights may come to rest in Scranton, Pennsylvania (Lipton 2001a). At one point, about 1,850 tons a day of Manhattan and Queens garbage was incinerated in Newark, New Jersey, and Hempstead, New York.[17] Increasingly, U.S. garbage may end up in Mexico or other Third World nations, where environmental regulations are laxer and pollution control technology less sophisticated (recalling the voyage of the *Mobro* and the 1986 voyage of the *Khian Sea*, which left with Philadelphia toxic incinerator ash; traveled to the Bahamas, Bermuda, the Dominican Republic, Honduras, Guinea-Bissau, the Netherland Antilles, and Panama; then dumped part of its load on a beach in Haiti).

Geographical dispersal of local garbage is inseparable from the globalization of the waste industry, increasingly concentrated since the 1980s in the hands of a few (and rapidly decreasing number of) multinational corporations, as documented by Harold Crooks in *Giants of Garbage* (1993). This corporate consolidation is not unique to the waste trade; in 1997 alone, a record $1 trillion in mergers took place, up from 1996's record $647 billion level. In 2000, the top four waste industry players accounted for 85 percent of total industry revenues.[18] This industry consolidation was the main reason for the increased export of garbage. In 1989, only thirteen states and the District of Columbia exported trash. In just eleven years, that number jumped to forty-seven states (plus Washington, D.C.) (O'Connell 2002).

These trends have local impacts in particular communities in New York City. The first private contract awarded for the interim export of Bronx residential trash went to Waste Management Inc., a company with an atrocious environmental and community relations record.[19] Browning Ferris, which also entered the market, has a similarly abysmal record.[20] In two years, from having no position in the New York market, one multinational waste corporation (USA Waste/WMI, the product of a merger) came to control approximately 40 percent of the local trash industry and approximately 70 to 90 percent of the volume at waste transfer stations at the time of its merger.[21] The Waste Management–USA Waste merger was the subject of a U.S. Department of Justice antitrust investigation, settled only when the company agreed to sell three large waste transfer stations. Waste Management was also the subject of a U.S. Department of Justice (DOJ) investigation, joined by New York, Pennsylvania, and Florida, because of its acquisition of Eastern Environmental Services. In January 1999, Waste Management reached a settlement with the DOJ after agreeing to give up Eastern's right to bid for the New York City residential waste contract. Yet in 2002, Waste Management still controlled 32 percent of out-of-town transport and 38 percent of disposal capacity within 100 miles of New York City. In 1999, Waste Management–USA Waste was the largest carter in New York City, Eastern and IESI the next largest, and BFI the fourth (Lentz, March 15, 1999). By 2001, Waste Management/USA Waste and Allied/BFI controlled approximately 65 percent of waste transfer station capacity (Lentz 2001).

When Waste Management was awarded the Bronx contract, several policy analysts and proprietors of small waste companies cautioned that the bidding companies were low-balling bids so that a monopoly could be established. Once contracts to the large corporations were awarded, analysts argued, small businesses would be driven out of existence, and prices would likely increase. There are many potential problems in placing residential garbage handling in the hands of multinationals: structural, political, and environmental. Chief among these is the fact that corporations that own both waste transfer stations and landfills (which charge by the ton) see garbage as a valuable product, and thus have no incentive to reduce the amount of garbage handled in order to cut into their profit margins. In making garbage a commodity, it is against their self-interest to reduce the amount of waste handled, as well as the resulting pollution from their commodity. Another key political issue for garbage activists is that there is no guarantee that the out-of-state landfills will not close their doors to New York City's trash. Pennsylvania, Ohio, and Kentucky have proposed limiting the importation of out-of-state garbage, though these proposals violate the Interstate Commerce Act (Gold 1990). In 2001, Pennsylvania Governor Tom Ridge unsuccessfully attempted to introduce a landfill permit moratorium in his state. Additionally, in 2001, congressional representatives introduced, albeit unsuccessfully, provisions for the Solid Waste Compact Act to empower state governments to limit the amount of trash imported into their states. In 2005, Representative Paul Kanjorski of Pennsylvania reintroduced the bill (Govtrack 2005).

## The Meaning and Roots of Environmental Justice Garbage Activism

In 1992, New York City's ten-year solid waste management plan (SWMP) was approved by the city council and the state DEC; it was modified in 1996 to expand the city's recycling program and review the environmental impacts of proposed incinerator projects, primarily the controversial Brooklyn Navy Yard incinerator. There are four phases of the post–Fresh Kills landscape spanning two mayoral administrations: the interim export phase, the 1998 formal draft solid waste management plan, the May 2000 SWMP modification, and the 2002 conceptual plan. I will detail each in turn in order to explain OWN's position and how it was able to intervene in ongoing debates on the city's garbage policy.

Mayor Giuliani and Governor Pataki established a task force to develop a plan for the closure of Fresh Kills (several OWN leaders sat on this task force). In November 1996, the committee released *The Fresh Kills Closure Task Force Report: A Plan to Phase-Out the Fresh Kills Landfill*, which recommended waste reduction and recycling as preferred waste management alternatives. It proposed preserving and reusing the existing marine transfer station system for handling garbage, cautioned against export, and expressed a commitment to fair share and borough self-sufficiency. But to the dismay of the task force and activists, the mayor ignored the central principles of the task force plan. DOS policy emphasized the opposite: under Mayor Giuliani, it rejected the use of the

marine transfer stations, it depended on export, and it rejected the principles of fair share and borough self-sufficiency.

Turning to OWN, the first thing to note is that the name OWN evokes
NIMBYism. However, its structure as a citywide coalition contradicts
this assumption of geographic parochialism. Indeed, its platform and
political analysis defy any definition as a NIMBY group. OWN became
involved at every stage of the planning and political process, because of
the proven intransigence of the DOS and inability to do the right thing,
specifically in promulgating siting regulations (Local Law 40) and in
recycling (Local Law 19). OWN members took every opportunity to
testify formally and, in certain cases, to organize public actions and
demonstrations. It organized numerous public demonstrations against
the city's positions at various hearings at city hall and the DOS (see figure
4.2), as well as at other public meetings. OWN's platform was a new
version of the three R's: reduce, reuse, and recycle. Its platform, "Recycle,
Reduce and Retrofit," was aimed to "recycle, reduce our waste stream,
and retrofit existing marine waste transfer stations." A retrofit is the
physical modification of an existing marine transfer station so that the
waste could be compacted and containerized for direct export by barge,
as it had been when the residential garbage was going to Fresh Kills.
Once compacted and containerized, the waste would be hauled by barge
to railheads or directly to landfills.

The privatization of residential solid waste began under the interim
export plan. Short-term contracts were first issued in 1997 for borough
trash, with varying bid costs and destinations.[22] Export costs drove up
DOS's operating expenditures from $590.5 million in 1997 to over $1
billion in 2002 (New York City Department of Sanitation 2002). To give
a sense of scale, the total New York City budget in 2001 was $41 billion
(thus, garbage comprises approximately one-fortieth of the budget, just
slightly less than the total City University of New York budget in
2000–2001).

In April 1998, the DOS issued its formal draft solid waste management plan, which ignored the recommendations of the 1996 task force
report. That December, Mayor Giuiliani released 2001 and Beyond: A
Proposed Plan for Replacing the Fresh Kills Landfill, which called for
two huge transfer stations in Red Hook and New Jersey. The plan also
called for the export of Manhattan and Queens residential waste, to be

**Figure 4.2**
OWN campaign flier

processed through waste transfer stations in Carteret and Newark, both in New Jersey. These facilities included the siting of permanent enclosed barge unloading facilities (EBUFs) to be built without adapting or reengineering the existing city-owned marine transfer stations. The city's 1998 plan called for new facilities, despite the lack of an engineering study to show why existing facilities could not be retrofitted for expanded capacity. All of this increased export, OWN activists feared, would translate directly to increased truck trips and increased exposure to particulate pollution.[23]

OWN critiqued the 1998 plan on privatizing residential garbage on the basis that the city was creating "mini–Fresh Kills" in their local neighborhoods, as well as in landfill communities outside the city. At the same time, OWN was pressing the DOS to look more closely at commercial solid waste, because the distinction between commercial and residential waste, and between private and city-owned waste transfer stations, are bureaucratic in terms of their health effects and impact on local communities. OWN helped to draw serious attention to the problems of the commercial waste stream by forcing the city to conduct its first study of commercial waste. Previously the city had collected few data on the commercial waste stream, although it constituted a huge portion of the overall waste stream (O'Connell 2001).

OWN's Red Hook and Brooklyn member organizations were particularly incensed by the disregard embedded in DOS's attempt to build one of the two large waste transfer stations in Red Hook. Red Hook's docks and piers were a center of New York City's waterfront activity from the mid-nineteenth to the mid-twentieth century. In the 1940s, Red Hook Houses were built as a model New York City public housing project, and the Red Hook recreational area was built to house one of the city's largest acreage of open spaces, at 40 acres. The decline of the waterfront started in the 1950s when the phasing out of the Bush and Army terminals began as a result of containerization; the shift in the global economy as exports shifted from the Americas to Asia, specifically the Far East; and increasing competition from West Coast and other East Coast ports (Muñiz 1998). Shipping operations shifted to the New Jersey side of the harbor due to Port Authority policy (the New Jersey side also has superior access to the national transportation network). This shift has led to the underutilization and abandonment of the Brooklyn piers. Red Hook has been hammered by a combination of economic trends, government policy, and neglect. For example, the building of the Brooklyn Queens Expressway and the Brooklyn Battery Tunnel during urban renewal effectively cut off the area from other local neighborhoods. As a result of urban renewal and tax policies in the 1970s and 1980s, large numbers of properties were taken by the city and left unsold or undeveloped.

OWN's official platform was shaped greatly by Eddie Bautista, chief organizer in his capacity as community planning director at New York Lawyers for the Public Interest (NYLPI). Bautista grew up in Red Hook in the 1960s, when 8,000 longshoremen still toiled on the docks and Erie Basin was one of the busiest shipping centers in the country (Century 1999). Red Hook has a long and sordid history of municipal neglect and a rich history of political activism against that neglect. The area was devastated by Robert Moses's highway building, the condemnation of housing to clear room for a container port that was never built, waste transfer stations, seven sites that may warrant Superfund designation, three hazardous waste facilities, and a Toxic Release Inventory site (Raver 1999). The community board worked for several years on a neighborhood revitalization plan that was approved by the city planning commission in 1996, the first such plan to be approved in Brooklyn (Williams 1996).

Bautista's youthful route to environmental activism was rooted in the culture and history of Red Hook. His father was a longshoreman in the 1960s, and their backyard abutted the home of "Crazy Joey" Gallo, New York's flashiest gangster, taken out by a mob hit in Little Italy in 1972. Bautista recalled: "I remember never being able to sleep because Gallo had these huge lights on all the time to prevent a secret attack" (Bautista 1998). His consciousness of the role of the city on his life became clear in the 1970s. According to Bautista, "The year 1977 was a turning point, not only for myself, but for our whole community. Hip-hop began to emerge as a street culture, and the Yankees won the World Series. . . . The City began a sewer reconstruction project [in 1976] that stretched along one block, and abandoned it when the fiscal crisis hit. We were exposed to the sewer, which we called 'the trench,' for over a year. Me and my friends would take garbage bags, and build rafts. Like urban Huck Finns, we swam in the trench alongside giant sewer rats."[24] He described another critical moment in Red Hook that same year: "In

August, the building across my street collapsed, killing my neighbor Marisol, who was 9, and her father Paco who had run back into the building to save her." The collapse of the buildings was precipitated by the sewer project. City surveyors had not adequately examined the housing stock before commencing the project. He remembered the community anger at Mayor Abe Beame, who came to the neighborhood after the collapse hit the front page of the *Daily News*: "We chased him out of the neighborhood, but not until I was sent to try to get money for the funeral." The city responded to the collapse by condemning dozens of buildings and promising to build replacement housing for the community, but it ultimately reneged on that promise: "Entire families never recovered from this trauma, and the community was destroyed." For Bautista, based on his experiences in Red Hook, the city was a force of either neglect or active destruction that must be counterbalanced by community activism. This experience shaped his activism and stance toward the city's garbage policy.

One of the campaigns that Bautista worked on was the 1992 fight against the city's proposal to build a sludge plant in Red Hook. The campaign included leadership from Red Hook Houses, the public housing unit that houses 80 percent of Red Hook's residents. Red Hook residents used the history of municipal intervention in the area, such as the building of major highways by Robert Moses that cut off their neighborhood, in their waste transfer station and garbage organizing. This history ensured that local residents understood garbage policy as an attempt by the city to frustrate the renaissance of a neighborhood that the city itself had set into decline through destructive public planning.

Because their communities have largely been victims of NIMBYism (as the victims of projects forced out of other neighborhoods by more successful NIMBYists) and poor urban and economic development policies, OWN activists were sensitive to issues of race and class in the positions they formulated on garbage policy. OWN rejected NIMBYism by paying close attention to where the garbage ultimately ended. As Bautista said, "It's not environmental justice if our garbage ends up in a poor working class or African-American community elsewhere, like in Charles City County."[25] Another example of OWN's rejection of NIMBYism was when its members traveled to Baltimore in 1998 to attend a regional garbage activist meeting organized by the Center for Health, Environment and Justice to network with other garbage activists, mostly from rural working-class communities. Results of this meeting were mixed and revealed the difficulty in forming cross-racial, regional alliances. Garbage activists in Virginia and Pennsylvania used the "spectre" of New York City garbage in their own activism. According to a Pennsylvania environmental activist present at the meeting, this language was used in order to spur up racialized fears of "city" garbage, while underplaying the extent of local activism in the city and not paying sufficient attention to the racial stratification faced by communities of color in New York City (Mike Ewall, personal communication, December 10, 2002). Nevertheless, some limited networking did emerge out of this meeting. For example, New York City activists were able to persuade regional garbage activists to submit letters and make phone calls to the New York City Council on the Draft Solid Waste Management Plan. Pennsylvania activists also called on New York City garbage activists to respond to their action alert to shut down the old and dangerous Harrisburg incinerator, sited in a predominantly poor (near a housing project) and minority (African American and Vietnamese) community. This incinerator is a large source of dioxin.[26] Mayor Giuliani visited Harrisburg for a Republican fundraiser and was met by anti-incinerator activists, who had also sent fifty pounds of trash to his office in New York City (In Pennsylvania, Giuliani Draws Protest on Incinerator, 1999). Harrisburg's mayor, Stephen Reed, specifically sought New York City's trash for his controversial incinerator (Randall 1999).

OWN members worked closely to raise environmental justice perspectives and community concerns with U.S. Representatives José Serrano (who represented the South Bronx) and Nydia Velasquez (who represented parts of Manhattan and Brooklyn). Both filed civil rights complaints with the U.S. EPA that cited discriminatory actions in the permitting of waste transfer facilities. These complaints were filed under Title VI of the Civil Rights Act of 1964.[27] Serrano, along with a coalition of community organizations, filed a letter with the EPA Office of Civil Rights in 1998 seeking an investigation into possible discriminatory practices by the city and state in relation to the siting of waste facilities in the South Bronx. EPA agreed to conduct the investigation. Velasquez filed a similar complaint in July 2000 on waste transfer stations and other hazardous substance—handling facilities in

Greenpoint/Williamsburg and Red Hook, but it was thrown out on procedural grounds.

After two years of public hearings, the draft environmental impact statement of the SWMP modification was released in May 2000.[28] The main feature of the modification approval was that it endorsed a long-term borough-based export plan. It retained use of five marine transfer stations through retrofitting, which the city has previously described as a technical impossibility, although it still focused primarily on private companies and export. The plan called for six waste transfer stations—two city owned and four privately owned—to handle the waste (New York City Department of Sanitation 2000). For the privately owned facilities, the city would enter twenty-year contracts with private vendors. A centerpiece of this plan was for 6,500 tons of garbage to be handled at a proposed rail trash depot in nearby Linden, New Jersey. Browning Ferris won a $6 billion, twenty-year contract to handle residential waste. From Linden, it would be moved to trains to be hauled to landfills in Illinois, South Carolina, and Georgia.[29]

The city reconsidered retrofitting existing marine transfer stations only after intense political pressure by environmental justice activists, among others. As a result of the organizing by local communities, the DOS changed its SWMP modification to reflect a central critique about the first plan, in particular the failure of the city to examine retrofitting. The 2000 plan also endorsed two good ideas previously ignored in the 1998 plan: the principle of borough equity and that garbage move by rail or barge instead of truck.[30] After negotiations with DOS, the city council, and the mayor's office, the council approved the SWMP modification, and Mayor Giuliani signed the bills authorizing the draft modification and a study of the commercial solid waste management system into law. The November modification was submitted to the state for final review, and the DEC approved the SWMP modification in February 2001.

In 2001, New York City elected a new mayor, who made garbage policy one of the cornerstones of his administration. Mayor Michael Bloomberg announced in the summer of 2002 that his "conceptual plan" had two main goals: reducing the truck traffic while retaining municipal control of garbage policy in order to reduce vulnerability to external and corporate forces. Bloomberg, who won election based on his knowledge of the corporate world and private business and vaulted into power in part because of his vast personal wealth, which he used to fund his campaign, favored preserving public control instead of privatization on largely economic grounds.[31] In sharp contrast to Mayor Giuliani on the issue of municipal control and the health effects of garbage, Bloomberg announced, "We are not going to continue to give our kids lung diseases, no matter what the cost is" (Lipton 2003). Bautista heralded this as the "biggest victory for environmental justice in the history of our city" (see figure 4.3).[32] Under the new plan, the system of transfer stations was to be run by the city, a significant victory for municipal workers, who retained their jobs (Johnson 2002).

**Figure 4.3**
OWN victory press conference, Eddie Bautista at the microphone

## Messy Garbage Politics?

It is important to recognize that within the universe of garbage environmental justice activism, there are significant and complicated differences among community-based organizations in the positions they take and the tactics they use. For example, although West Harlem Environmental Action was a founding member of the New York City Environmental Justice Alliance and initially an OWN member, the organization objected to the reopening and expansion of the marine transfer station in West Harlem, a key OWN platform item, and ultimately it left the coalition. WE ACT objected to DOS's decision on the grounds that the community was already overburdened from noxious facilities (Cecil Corbin Mark, personal communication, May 2003). Two other conflicts reveal this complexity, both in the South Bronx: the Harlem River Rail Yard paper de-inking facility and the American Marine Rail proposal.

In 1992, the Natural Resources Defense Council (NRDC) and Banana Kelly, a community-based housing development group that originated from urban homesteading activism in the 1970s, began to collaborate on a paper recycling facility in the South Bronx (Holusha 1994). The recycling operation was to be run as a for-profit company called the Bronx Community Paper Company on a 19-acre site in the old Harlem River Rail Yard. The project was announced with great fanfare and lauded by President Clinton. The goal of the project was to reduce the use of virgin paper for New York City newspapers through a recycling process to create de-inked paper pulp for the newsprint market and to produce jobs. It was seen as an innovative project—a state-of-the-art example of brownfield reclamation of previously polluted land that was to use cutting-edge technology such as reclaimed water use, air pollution control, and energy efficiency (Hershkowitz 2002). The plant was to be sited in Hunts Point, on property leased to Francesco Galesi, who held a ninety-nine-year tax-free lease from the State Department of Transportation to develop the property.[33] The plant was to be designed by world-renowned architect Maya Lin (Holusha 1996).

However, other community groups, such as the South Bronx Clean Air Coalition, objected to the plant based on the premise that increased air pollution emissions would exacerbate the asthma crisis in the South Bronx and that the facility would frustrate the development of the

Harlem River Rail Yard as a rail transit hub (thereby alleviating the community of the health burden of diesel trucks). The coalition sued and won in state court, with its lawyer arguing that the site should be used exclusively as a rail-yard hub. But the decision was overturned on appeal (Van Natta 1995), and the state issued a permit in August 1997. The main facility proponent, Allen Hershkowitz (2002) of NRDC, dismissed the community complaints as "turf wars" and thuggish attempts at extortion. Unsurprisingly, he gave little credence to SBCAC complaints in his account of the project.

This conflict exploded along complex community and racial lines when the *New Yorker* magazine reported that facility opponents had anonymously characterized NRDC's environmental justice representative, a founder of WE ACT, using an antiblack expletive. This expletive implied that the representative had compromised the South Bronx and "the community" because she was employed by NRDC, which was promoting the recycling facility (Harris 1995). The plan was ultimately called off for a variety of political and economic reasons, not least of all the highly polarized debate that ensued.[34] Ackerman and Mirza (2001) discuss the controversy over the NRDC South Bronx paper mill in order to highlight the difficulties of implementing a paper recycling plant as a community economic development tool. These conflicts represent intracommunity struggles for authenticity and leadership related to the internal contradictions of what constitutes sustainable community development (Pellow 2002).

The South Bronx was also the site of another controversial garbage facility that bitterly divided the community. Over 500 community members mobilized to a public hearing in the South Bronx against American Marine Rail (AMR), which applied for a permit to build a new 5,200-ton-per-day marine-to-rail solid waste transfer facility (including 3,500 tons of non-Bronx waste). SBCAC, which had organized against the Bronx-Lebanon medical waste incinerator and had struggled against the NRDC paper de-inking facility, supported this proposal on the grounds that it represented a good example of community economic development. OWN opposed it, as did several community groups in the South Bronx. Waste Management and Republic, two other large waste corporations, operated existing facilities in the same area. The three companies were competing for bids for the barge-to-rail export of garbage from the South Bronx. Different community groups accused each other of taking payoffs and of selling out their community, with charges of hypocrisy and betrayal leveled left and right. On one side was SBCAC, which supported AMR because it was owned by a minority stakeholder (a former linebacker with the New York Giants) and because it proposed to move waste by barge and rail, as opposed to the more polluting trucks (Stewart 2000). On the other side was the Point Community Development Corporation, which argued that the proposed waterfront site could be used for recreation (Waldman 1999). Initially, DEC and DOS decided that the AMR proposal did not require a full environmental impact study (Critchell 2000). Along with a number of community groups, the Point, aided by legal counsel from New York Lawyers for the Public Interest, sued over DEC's "negative declaration" on the AMR permit on the issue of fine particulate pollution (the result of a "neg dec" is that an environmental impact statement is deemed unnecessary because the environmental impacts are considered negligible).[35] After two days of hearings in 1999, where over 500 community residents were mobilized, the neg dec was overturned by an administrative law judge with DEC, which required that an environmental impact statement be done, and the AMR proposal was effectively defeated.

**Recycling**

In its platform, OWN explicitly supported recycling and reduction efforts over export as a garbage-handling strategy. One of its primary objections to the city's overall garbage policy was that municipal services, especially around garbage and waste, were inequitably distributed by race and political power. Recycling services, for example, were poorly run and stratified citywide. Different boroughs and districts received different levels of service (in materials recycled or in frequency of pickup). In 1998, nine districts were restored to weekly recycling, twenty-one more were added in 1999, and the final twenty in 2000. Only since April 2000 have all districts received the same level of service. But in 2002, Mayor Bloomberg suspended certain facets of the recycling program in New York City to save money, although components of the program were later restored.[36]

New York's recycling politics have large political and environmental implications. New York City's housing stock (primarily multifamily housing) and extreme population density are unique nationally. Because of its sheer size, the city is looked at as a symbol of larger trends and is treated by major environmental groups as the great "lost cause" of the recycling movement, hobbled by institutional inertia and lack of creative thinking about recycling.[37] New York State passed the State Solid Waste Management Act in 1988, which required a 50 percent reduction of the waste stream by 1997: 8 to 10 percent through waste prevention at source and 40 to 42 percent achieved through materials recycling. At the city level, Local Law 19, passed in 1989, required that 25 percent of the city's waste be recycled by 1994. In 1992, New York City was successfully sued by NRDC, in part because the city had only one recycling plant (Gandy 1994). The city has repeatedly gone to court to subvert its legal mandate. OWN activists pointed to its inability to follow its own laws and argued that if the city seriously strengthened its recycling program, the waste stream could be reduced. Since 1989, when Local Law 19 was passed, the city has been ordered seven times by state supreme and appellate courts to make sufficient investments to achieve the mandated recycling rate.

Recycling and reuse have long histories in American history. It is, in fact, the throwaway culture that is a relatively new phenomenon. In the early days of the twentieth century, 80 percent of cities with more than 25,000 people required separation of organic garbage or ashes for recycling and reuse (Strasser 1999). Recycling politics reflect their historical and cultural moment and particular definitions of recycling.[38] There is a hierarchy of recycling options, each with associated drawbacks and benefits: waste reduction, preconsumer recycling, product reuse, primary recovery, and secondary recovery. Most of the attention on recycling is primary recovery through three methods: collection and curbside programs, street collection and recycling centers, and centralized sorting facilities (Gandy 1994). Recycling proponents argue its benefits: conservation of domestic and imported natural resources (timber, waste, and mineral ore), pollution prevention (from manufacturing), energy savings, reduction of landfilling and incineration and pollution associated with both. Other associated benefits are the protection and expansion of manufacturing jobs and an increased sense of community and responsibility (NRDC 1997). Recycling opponents argue that recycling costs more resources that it saves, causes pollution, is more expensive than landfilling (also because landfilling space is abundant), and that government mandates subsidizing recycling are cost-ineffective.[39]

In between the extremes of recycling rhetoric (pro versus con) lie the reality and complexity of recycling in its current incarnation. Recycling is a commodity-based, profit-driven competitive industry in which large private firms using public dollars dominate. Recycling is also an increasingly global business with large economic and geopolitical implications (Weinberg, Pellow, Schnaiberg 2000). Pellow (2002) examines the contradictions of recycling politics in urban low-income communities of color. He focuses on Chicago's Resource Center and the discourse and practice of community-based recycling, the goal of which is to create social and environmental change through education and action rather than focusing on the bottom line. The unintended negative consequences of recycling show how social movement groups can support new policies and technologies that create their own injustices (facility siting and pollution). He examines the recycling industry because it is the latest development in solid waste management and emerged as a response to the environmental movement. He states that "the environmental justice and toxics movement now seemed to have reached a consensus that city dumps, landfills and incinerators are bad for the environment and bad for people's health. Thus far, there seems to be no consensus on recycling" (157).

Pellow uses an ethnographic approach that highlights the hard work, low status, and occupational hazards of recycling laborers. His focus on workers and their voices on the front line suggests the source of environmental inequalities in recycling facilities: that there is convergence of interest among community groups, environmentalists, industry, and government support for recycling and that managers have much control of work conditions. Recycling work is rendered invisible because environmentalists are invested only in setting up recycling programs, without focusing on the actual experiences of workers, and because the highly polarized economy versus environment debate is so controversial that critical discussions of recycling are often impossible. Recycling workers are often the most marginal (primarily low income and minority), and thus ignored as befits their out-of-sight, out-of-mind status. He identifies the central contradiction in the deep disparity between the ideology of pro-environmentalism and fact of environmental hazards that support for certain environmental programs create.

This complex view of recycling helps to make some sense of the conflicts that beset New York City garbage and recycling politics.[40] On the one hand, the conflict over the Harlem River Rail Yard in the South Bronx exemplifies the contradictions and limits to paper recycling operations and the difficulty in implementing sustainable community development programs. OWN activists, in their support of recycling, were not sufficiently critical of the complexity of recycling beyond the "feel-good" rhetoric, in part because the city has never allowed recycling to develop beyond a certain level. Thus, the contradictions and the complexity that Pellow describes in Chicago in terms of race, class, and labor have not yet been fully realized and recognized in New York.

To this day, the city lacks the infrastructure to process recyclables, known as materials recovery facilities, owing to poor planning and ideological resistance. The department of sanitation had two main options: build the infrastructure and assume the market risk in selling secondary materials, or pay the cost of letting other parties assume the risks. It chose the latter (New York City Department of Sanitation, 2001a). Since the beginning of its recycling program, the DOS has argued that it is the most successful municipal recycling program in the country.[41] It claims a 34.9 percent recycling rate, including construction and debris material, abandoned cars, and other disputed materials such as asphalt, millings, and dirt reused from lot cleaning operations (and it tried to add the tonnage from 9/11 World Trade Center debris to its numbers). Environmental groups and some city council representatives cried foul in response to this cynical attempt to boost its record by inflating the recyclable amount, which other municipalities do not generally count.[42]

The reality is that New York City is certainly not the worst recycling city in the country, although the percentage of financial resources dedicated to recycling lags far behind that of other major cities (it comprises a smaller percentage of the budget, compared to other major cities and to the $1 billion dedicated to garbage export). New York City's program is also extremely inefficient.[43]

## Conclusion

Over the past two decades, beginning with the rise in tipping fees at Fresh Kills and the marked increase in the number of waste transfer stations, low-income and minority neighborhoods have been concerned about the localized health and environmental effects of garbage and recycling policies. Activists grew tired of the relentless stream of garbage trucks in their communities and perceived that not all neighborhoods in the city shared equally in the burden of handling solid waste. At the same time, DOS and different mayoral administrations proved time and again to be hostile to local needs, from the waste transfer station issue to recycling. With the closure of Fresh Kills and the rise of the discourse of environmental justice, community activists organized themselves into a citywide coalition that focused on the racially disproportionate health effects of garbage policy, especially in terms of trucks and air pollution.

Garbage politics in New York City are by their nature complex, contradictory, and messy. It is hard to make simple pronouncements about what falls under the rubric of garbage environmental justice activism as well as its larger meaning, which exists on multiple levels. On the one hand, this activism was NIMBYism of a sort. But it was also more than self-interest, as OWN's networking within and between low-income and minority communities and with regional activists reveals. Garbage environmental justice activism also reflected the desire of communities of color to protect and defend their neighborhoods from policy and in a historical context of blight and decay initiated and facilitated by the state forces, such as urban renewal and highway building. The changes in the city's garbage policy and the rapid transformation of the industry into an increasingly privatized and global sector also reveal garbage to be an excellent case study to examine the intersection of local-global environmental politics, changing notions of corporations, and the relative merits of the public and private spheres.

OWN was partially successful in its overt political goals. As a result, in part, of OWN's activism, New York City reconsidered retrofitting of the existing marine transfer stations and endorsed two ideas previously ignored in the 1998 plan: the principle of borough equity and that garbage move by rail or barge instead of by diesel trucks. Furthermore, Mayor Bloomberg's 2002 Conceptual Plan supported two parts of OWN's platform: reducing the current truck traffic while retaining municipal control of garbage policy in order to minimize vulnerability to external and corporate forces. But despite these minor successes, New York City's garbage system is still based on export and private companies, and garbage remains a highly contentious flash point for community activism.[44]

OWN's larger success was in terms of the politics of representation, broadly defined. It used its disproportionate pollution exposure, especially to air pollution, as a means for community mobilization. OWN succeeded in reformulating garbage as an environmental health and air pollution issue and in centering race and the lives of children of color into discussions of garbage policy. These are no small feats in a city and within an agency that thinks of garbage as merely as a problem of moving things out of the streets and communities as obstructions to that goal. OWN forced the city and policymakers to think about who garbage hurts (in this case, local neighborhoods, particularly communities of color) and who it benefits (the multinational garbage corporations). In forcing a closer look at the politics of garbage, OWN enabled a much-needed discussion about the environmental impacts of the politics of consumption, the perils of corporate privatization, and the effects of globalization in and on local communities and communities of color.

# 5

## Power to the People? Deregulation and Environmental Justice Energy Activism

On February 26, 2002, the New York State Energy Board held hearings in Manhattan and Brooklyn. At issue was the state energy plan, drafted by the New York State Energy Planning Board which is intended to provide strategic direction and energy policy guidance.[1] The board, through the plan, coordinates New York State government activities and responses to energy issues, including the siting of power plants. Under state law, the plan is supposed to be revised every four years, with a participation process conducted through public hearings. The midday Brooklyn hearing, which took place in the main auditorium of the Brooklyn Museum of Art, was almost empty, with an audience of about 20 in a room with a capacity of over 1,000 people. Elizabeth Yeampierre, executive director of UPROSE, the oldest Latino social service agency in Brooklyn and a community-based organization active on environmental justice issues and community development in Sunset Park, was one of the few people there representing a neighborhood perspective. Yeampierre, a Puerto Rican woman in her forties, got up to the microphone and blasted the state energy board representatives sitting on the stage for organizing public hearings at a time when community members, especially low-income working people, could not attend. She critiqued the board for not addressing the power plant siting issue, which she called an example of environmental racism, and invited them to hold a hearing at night in Sunset Park, where there were three power plants proposed. Yeampierre promised to monitor the plan and the process and, if need be, to file lawsuits and apply community pressure on the power plant siting issue.[2] Members of the audience reacted sharply to Yeampierre's testimony—some for bringing life to a previously dull meeting, others visibly uncomfortable with her tone and statements.

The next day, at the trendy W Hotel in midtown Manhattan, I took an elevator up to the hotel lobby and walked through it to a small conference room packed with businesspeople, lobbyists, and government representatives, all of whom seemed to know each other and who were there to monitor the future direction (and possible profits) of the state's energy policy. The hip hotel scene was at odds with the conservative suits inside, engaged in lobbying rituals in the air-conditioned room. The "suits inside," largely male and predominantly white, greeted each other with an easy familiarity. To an uninitiated outsider, it felt like a lobbyist's convention or the hallway outside the Albany legislature during a late-night budget negotiation. There were no representatives from community-based organizations testifying that day, although there were a few people from citywide and national environmental and public interest groups. There were no Elizabeth Yeampierres to stir the crowd with anything other than business as usual.

In both the Brooklyn and Manhattan hearings, at the museum and at the trendy hotel, the location and the physical space reinforced a message: no outsiders to the process need attend. Although it claimed to be a public hearing where ordinary citizens could weigh in, the culture of the hearings contradicted this claim to an open and democratic process. Both hearings evoked clubby exclusion and insider politics, despite the presumption that these were public hearings to deal with important energy policies with large environmental and public health implications in local communities.

This chapter addresses the claims made by environmental justice activists like Elizabeth Yeampierre that energy policy, and particularly the issue of power plant siting, represents a salient example of environmental racism. It also examines the culture and the politics of energy policy decision making. I look at issues of race and power by closely examining energy policy. At their most basic levels, power and empowerment are metaphors for the ability to do things, either by oneself or by making someone else do something (through force). Power as a political concept has been well explored for centuries by theorists such as Thomas Hobbes and John Locke. More recently, slogans such as "Power to the People" and "Black Power" have been used by proponents of democratic social movements seeking greater inclusion into previously closed political and cultural systems, defined by class or race exclusion.

Contemporary struggles over energy policy have racial dimensions, especially when viewed through the framework of environmental racism and the environmental justice movement, which links local and community-based activism with broad-based energy activism at larger scales—citywide, regional, national, and global. It analyzes how energy is racialized through the politics of energy regulation and deregulation and of distribution (Sze 2005).[3] Environmental justice energy activism also emerges as a result of political discontent with intensifying trends regarding the expansion of capital with a simultaneous decrease in government intervention and regulation. These dimensions can be most sharply seen, and most vehemently debated, in the negative costs of energy systems, manifested through environmental pollution and their disproportionate impact on poor and minority populations. Community-based activism against power plant siting is a direct result of an increased number of proposed plants under conditions of electric utility deregulation. Community responses to these racial dimensions are exemplified by environmental justice campaigns against the siting of power plants in California and New York State. The case study in this chapter is about a citywide community-based coalition, Communities United for Responsible Energy (CURE), which organized in 2001 in response to the siting of power plants in low-income and minority communities in the wake of electricity deregulation in New York City.

I draw from historian David Nye's approach to analyzing energy in *Consuming Power: A Social History of American Energies* (1998), in which he argues that energy constitutes a "social world." Energy systems are results of historical negotiations between people alongside technological change. The social world is a set of social constructions of home, factory, or the city that are "inextricably connected to a dominant energy system. Machines are extensions of human lives—someone makes it, markets it, opposes it, uses it, and all interpret it" (5). Nye focuses on how people shape technology, emphasizing human choice, agency, and cultural difference. The focus here is not on the scientific or technological dimensions of energy systems (the dominant mode in which energy is usually discussed) but how energy system choices are given social and political meaning, contested, and culturally shaped (Tatum 2000).

I begin with a general overview of energy history and development and the emergence of the old and stable regulatory system that governed how utilities operated. This history contextualizes contemporary debates about changes to the system in the form of deregulation. This approach further illuminates the changing nature and power of corporations at the beginning of the twenty-first century, particularly in the debates about public and private power and the role of the state in mediating the influence (and corruption) of corporations through regulation. I also highlight the relationship of racial politics to changing energy systems in the context of deregulation. In doing so, I show how and why energy policy and environmental justice analyses are linked. I look at the effects of deregulation on local communities and communities of color in the California energy crisis and then turn to the New York City case study of activism against power plant siting.

Environmental justice energy activism reflects the specific interpretive responses of people of color to the implementation of energy systems that are particularly destructive toward racial minorities in the U.S. context. The burdens of large-scale energy production have destroyed myriad communities in many nations across the world, whether energy is generated by coal (on the Navajo and in Appalachia), oil (Shell's activities in Nigeria, Texaco's in Ecuador), or hydropower (dam projects displacing hundreds of thousands of people in Quebec, India, Chile, Brazil, and China). At the same time, the international fossil fuel lobby is fighting the Kyoto Protocol and other international attempts at regulation.[4] A changing climate raises sea levels, alters precipitation and other weather conditions, threatens human health, and harms fish and many types of ecosystems, and the adverse impacts fall heaviest on the poor in the United States and the global South.[5]

There is a growing awareness of the interconnectedness of global climate change and environmental justice issues. To press the administration to adopt Kyoto, the Environmental Justice and Climate Change Coalition (EJCC) formed. The EJCC is a coalition of twenty-eight U.S. environmental justice, climate justice, religious, policy, and advocacy groups that formed to pressure the Bush administration and Congress on climate change and the Kyoto Protocol. The group's 2002 fact sheet stated, "People of color are concentrated in urban centers in the South, coastal regions, and areas with substandard air quality. New Orleans, which is 62 percent African-American and 2 feet below sea level, exemplifies the severe and disproportionate impacts of climate change in the

U.S. . . . . Wealthy homeowners are able to move, whereas low-income people (who usually rent) cannot. Also, low-income people typically lack insurance to replace possessions lost in storms and floods. Only 25 percent of renters have renters insurance."[6]

I am not suggesting the burdens of energy production are unique to people of color in the United States. However, I suggest that in the U.S. context, race and racism are useful frames for understanding how pollution harms from the energy sector are socially distributed, as well as the larger political meaning of community and environmental justice activist responses to changes in energy policy. These examples of activism are a significant challenge to energy companies' attempts at unilateral decision making on energy issues to promote a pro-business government ideology, exemplified through deregulation.

## Energy: Economic and Environmental Effects

The United States consumes far more energy than any other nation and leads in per capita consumption. Energy has been a crucial force in the shaping of American capitalist development and history and its political ideologies (Nye 1998, Melosi 1985, Jacobson 2000). Historian Martin Melosi describes general periods of American energy history, characterized by two interlinked beliefs: the inexhaustability of supply and cheapness of fossil fuels.[7]

Historians have shown how the energy industry is an excellent prism through which to understand the changing nature of the corporation and its relationship to the state. From the mid-nineteenth century onward, energy has been a big business and corporate enterprise. During the second half of the century, coal, oil, and electricity came under the control of large corporations, closely related to the growth of big business and the merger wave at the end of the ninetieth century.[8] The degree to which government regulates industry and the nature of the energy market have been contested by producers, consumers, and regulators for well over a century, and the lack of a national energy policy has been a persistent feature of American energy history (Melosi 1985). Energy companies have also been the perpetrators of some of the largest and most spectacular corporate frauds and failures in American history, from the fall of the House of Insull in 1932 to the Enron scandal in 2001.[9]

The electric utility industry grew rapidly in the twentieth century. By 1970, electric utilities were the largest industry in terms of capital assets in the United States. This created a host of new problems since energy systems are also major contributors to environmental degradation.[10] Emissions from electric power plants generate about 33 percent of all carbon dioxide emissions. Worldwide, fossil fuel power plants produce about 60 percent of all greenhouse gas emissions. Most harmful are older coal-fired steam plants, which produce a large volume of air pollution, particularly sulfur oxide and particulate matter (fine particle pollution). Three decades of health and environmental research have led to increasing state and federal legislation, most notably the historic 1970 Clean Air Act, the comprehensive federal law that regulates air emissions from area, stationary, and mobile sources. This law authorized the U.S. Environmental Protection Agency to establish National Ambient Air Quality Standards (NAAQS) to protect public health and the environment. By the 1990s, a large volume of data from public health practitioners and researchers had begun to document the relationship between electricity production and environmental degradation and their human health effects.

## Electricity Overview

Electricity services constitute big business in the United States.[11] Electricity is a unique commodity in several ways because it must be provided on demand, which means that it cannot be stored or saved. There is also complicated jurisdiction over it (local, state, and federal). The electricity service industry provides four separate but related functions: power generation, transmission, local distribution, and, most recently under deregulation, retail services such as meter, billing, and energy efficiency.[12]

Almost immediately after Faraday's creation of an electric motor in 1821, which formed the basis of electromagnetic technology, practical and commercial applications were sought to harness the power of electricity. Thomas Edison's utility business, established in the financial district of New York City in 1882, consisted of steam engines, generators, and a wiring network designed to illuminate electric lights in restaurants and shops.[13] Samuel Insull, Edison's private secretary and later vice president of GE, bought out rival firms, consolidated their equipment, and supplied power to an increasingly large base of users with cost-effective turbine generators (McDonald 1962).

In the wake of rapid consolidation within the electrical industry, the major debate at the end of the nineteenth century was the role of the public sector versus that of the private in delivering power. This debate was not confined to energy, but extended to most municipal systems, such as garbage, transportation, water, and sewage systems.[14] The debate was particularly intense between the 1890s and 1910, as the number of home rule systems (publicly owned power) increased. But the tide soon turned. In 1926 alone, there were more than 1,000 mergers, in many cases involving municipally owned facilities selling out to private companies (Melosi 1985).

In the early twentieth century, electricity systems and use grew rapidly. The number of private residences served increased from 6 million to 20 million. Electricity had a widespread impact on culture through the adoption of electrical appliances, in propagating popular culture through radio and movies, and as objects of consumption (de la Peña 2003, Platt 1991, Nye 1990). By 1929, the United States produced more electricity than the rest of the world combined. Other entrepreneurs vertically integrated the electrical industry, which grew from a small number of telegraph supply firms in 1870 into a $200 million industry by 1900. Utility holding companies revolutionized the industry, not by producing or distributing commodities or service but by acquiring many smaller operating companies through control of their stock (Melosi 1985).

Regulation emerged historically as a reaction to unbridled corporate power, particularly the large-scale growth of utility holding companies and their corporate machinations. Abuse in the industry was great, whether through blatant profiteering, stock manipulation, or pyramiding, as exemplified by the 1932 fall of the House of Insull. The main political debate was whether to municipalize energy or to regulate.[15] In 1907, states began to regulate the rates charged to retail customers, and by 1935, the federal government began to regulate wholesale electricity rates through the Public Utility Company Holding Act (Brennan et al. 1996). The hybrid that developed by the 1930s, private companies and public regulation, is what energy historian Richard Hirsh (1999) calls the "utility consensus." Regulators assumed central importance as mediators of conflicting interests.[16] Government regulation won, with the support of the utility companies.[17]

Regulation firmly established the notion that utility companies constituted natural monopolies. Natural monopolies made sense in principle because the transmission and distribution costs of service were high and inflexible. Thus, competition was seen as duplicative and inefficient.[18] The consensus also legitimated the utilities because government oversight meant that they were seen as permanent, stable, and safe investments (Hirsh 1999).

## Race and Energy

Given the history and the large scope of energy and electricity development, along with its associated benefits, how does any social group make particular its claim to energy policy? What does energy (or electricity) have to do, if anything, with race? Generally energy is widely seen as a technological issue, not like housing or education, both of which are commonly thought of as social issues. Thus, energy is thought to transcend social categories in its universal benefits. But what about its harms? Many environmental justice scholars have argued that whenever there are environmental benefits to be enjoyed and pollution burdens to be avoided, these benefits and burdens tend to be stratified unequally by race or class. That is the case with energy.

A good example of how race neutrality is belied by government energy policy and state retrenchment from energy policy and decreasing regulation can be found in Eric Klinenberg's (2002) account of how race and class intersected with natural disaster in Chicago's 1995 heat wave. This heat wave killed 700 Chicagoans, many of them poor and African American (energy intersects with heat waves in multiple and complex ways, in that air conditioners could help reduce deaths, and in energy efficiency policy). He rejects the rhetoric of natural disaster adopted by politicians as a simplified mode of explanation for who, why, and how so many died.[19] Like Klinenberg, environmental justice activists reject race and class neutrality by forcing a closer look at who benefits and who bears the burdens of power plant siting and, by extension, energy policy. They do so by using standard public policy criteria, such as reports that analyze the racial burdens of energy policy. They also draw attention to the history of harm from corporate entities and exclusion from protection from public agencies, whether at the local, state, or federal level. This combination of standard public policy approaches and attention to histories of racial exploitation and exclusion makes environmental justice energy activism unique within larger environmental and public interest campaigns on energy issues.

The politics of energy regulation and deregulation and distribution generate racialized consequences, especially in the context of the high-energy society and postindustrialism, specifically manifested through rising levels of computerization and other personal electronic, entertainment, and communication devices like cell phones (which require energy to run). Nye (1998) documents what he calls the "high-energy regime" in the United States in the mid-twentieth century that was dependent on a historical anomaly: multiple sources of energy were in oversupply. In particular, the overabundance of oil and petroleum enabled the ascendancy of the automobile and the suburb over the city. He writes, "There was no technological inevitability about the mechanization of agriculture, the exodus from the farm, the preference for motor cars, the decline of central cities, or high unemployment among African Americans. These four American choices were based on energy abundance and they raised new social issues" (209).

The social effects of the rise of the automobile have been well documented. Primary among these is the ascendancy of suburbs, directly relating to the decline of the central cities (Kay 1998). The movement of homes and jobs from the cities to the suburbs has well-known racial and social impacts, concentrating poor and minority populations in the declining inner city. The decline of manufacturing work in the cities, with jobs migrating overseas, has had a particularly destructive impact on African Americans (Wilson 1987). Suburbanization and urban decline were facilitated through racially discriminatory public policies. These ranged from blockbusting and other real estate practices, and redlining by banks, to the subsidization of white flight by the federal government through housing and transportation and highway programs (Jackson 1985, Gregory 1998, Lipsitz 1998).

The growth of the postwar suburb in the United States and the rise of energy consumption through technology led to increasing energy demands that the United States could no longer meet. In the mid-twentieth century, the United States gradually made the transition from an oil-exporting to an oil-importing nation, vastly altering global geopolitics in the process. Other oil-producing nations, such as Venezuela, Saudi Arabia, and Iran, increased production throughout the latter half of the twentieth century. The Arab oil embargo from October 1973 to May 1974 highlighted the crisis that the lack of national energy policy and development in the United States had created. The 1970s signaled the end in the confidence in the high-energy regime based on electricity, oil, and natural gas, shaken as a result of the oil crisis when price hikes and boycotts by the Organization of Petroleum Exporting Countries (OPEC) stalled the U.S. economy, leading to long lines at gas pumps and a sense of an impending national crisis.[20]

One of the proposed solutions to the energy crisis was nuclear power.[21] Nye (1998) suggests that Ronald Reagan's election as president was related to energy politics because it signified a public declaration of faith in the old order in which high energy consumption went hand-in-hand with the ideology of personal and individual success and the resurgence of the American dream (237). At the same time, a shift in global capitalism resulted in radical shifts in production and consumption. This shift was enabled through changing technologies and communications, documented by David Harvey (1989) among others. Computers were a key component in the electronic energy regime: they put white-collar knowledge workers at the center of the economy, relegating the majority of U.S. workers from blue-collar to service sector employment. Postindustrialism and increasing computerization are also intimately connected. Large-scale adoption of computerization has produced racial impacts through increased production of computers and rising pressure and demands on electricity grids.

Computers, seen in the public eye as a clean technology, are in fact highly toxic to produce (Szasz and Meuser 2000). This distribution of pollution, especially in the production process, is racially stratified. The computer industry is the most chemically intense in the world, using up to 1,000 different chemicals, including arsenic, cadmium, lead, and mercury. The computer production line workers in Silicon Valley, California, who face these occupational health hazards are overwhelmingly nonunionized, low-income Asian and Latina immigrant women workers (Pellow and

Park 2003). The health and environmental effects of computer production line labor are numerous and are particularly destructive to reproductive and nervous systems, triggering miscarriages, for example.[22]

There are also toxic implications for computer disposal, which contributes greatly to toxic dumping and toxic leachate in landfills, in the United States and globally. Finally, steadily increasing electricity demand as a direct result of increased computer use is a primary factor driving the flurry of electric power plant siting proposals. Thus, a complex set of technological innovations and demands for energy and global economic restructuring in the manufacturing sector intersects with existing racial, gender, and economic inequalities.

### Energy Deregulation: Heartbreak Hotel

The original idea of energy deregulation in New York sounds like something that Austin Powers might have thought up. Consumers . . . would be divorced from their old ball-and-chain utility companies, and the electricity marketplace would become a kind of giant dating game, full of come-ons and casual liasons: no long-term commitments, no guilt. (Johnson 2003)

The increase in the numbers of proposed power plants (and thus campaigns over power plant siting in California and New York State) is linked at least in part to energy deregulation. For that reason, it is important to understand its ideological and legislative roots. Deregulation is a retrenchment from older forms of state regulation, but its proponents use the language of liberation to advance their ideological agenda. The actual record of deregulation is much more ambivalent and complex, signifying broken dreams alongside opportunity. Hirsh (1999) identifies three stresses on the old system of regulation and the utility consensus, which had ensured stability in the system: technological stasis, the energy crisis, and ecological critiques. Technological stasis meant that limits of efficiency had been met, the 1970s energy crisis disrupted old systems, and the environmental movement grew hostile to nuclear power as popular social movements increasingly challenged utility companies. These three stresses diminished the authority of utility executives and the power of utility companies in two important ways: by questioning the ideology of growth and through growing environmental legislation that decreased utility companies' unilateral decision-making power.

The largest threats to the utility consensus emerged in the post-1970s energy crisis period. Chief among these was new federal legislation, specifically the Public Utility Regulatory Policies Act of 1978 (PURPA). In 1977, President Jimmy Carter had urged the nation to respond to the energy crisis with the "moral equivalent of war" and sought to advance federal policies that addressed the weaknesses in the energy system laid bare by the oil crisis. PURPA opened the door to elements of deregulation in the system. It sought to increase energy efficiency by reforming the way customers paid for electricity and to remove barriers to entry in the generation sector. The law allowed unregulated electricity producers to contest the monopolistic position of power companies.[23] PURPA created new classes of participants in the electric utility community.[24] It also spurred innovation and small-scale technologies outside the realm of the traditional utility system and large-scale utility production facilities.[25]

In short, PURPA invalidated the philosophical and practical justification for the natural monopoly system by introducing free market principles such as the creation of a competitive market and pay-for-performance. It altered the demographics of power within the utility system by decreasing power held by the utilities and increasing that of regulators and other stakeholders.[26] The Federal Energy Policy Act of 1992 further encouraged competition among wholesale power producers and gave states the prerogative to introduce retail competition. The act allowed regulated utilities to spin off their generation facilities to become exempt wholesale generators. Deregulation depended on open access to transmission networks and tended to fracture the modified consensus based on demand-side management and integrated resource planning.[27] The overall impact was that power companies lost control over the system as the utility consensus vanished.

In 1996 the Federal Energy Regulatory Commission (FERC) issued Order 888, which forced utilities to open their transmission lines to other utilities and electricity wholesalers. It also forced the functions of generation, transmission, and distribution to be separated from one another and to be priced separately. This background is the legislative and historical context for large-scale state-level deregulation, most disastrously enacted in California when rolling blackouts swept the state (McNamara 2002, Sweeney 2002). In 1996, California proposed the most sweeping statewide electricity industry restructuring in the nation. Environmental and low-income advocates in California vigorously fought the dissolution of environmental and public interest requirements in the face of deregulation. The story of California's disastrous experiment has been well documented, but the impact of California's experience on other states, such as New York, is less well understood. In fact, California's energy crisis shaped the political discourse of power plant siting and environmental justice activism against power plants in New York City in 2001 and 2002.

### Race and Air Pollution: Environmental Justice Power Plant Activism

The rush of power plant proposals in the wake of industrywide deregulation brought to the forefront the relationship among race, pollution, and power plant siting. That is because, in general, proposed power plants were to be sited in communities of color.[28] Power plant pollution is a major contributor to global warming and air pollution, the impacts of which are racially disparate. According to a national report published in 2002 by a broad coalition of civil rights, public health, environmental advocacy, and environmental justice organizations, *Air of Injustice: African Americans and Power Plant Pollution*, 78 percent of African Americans live within thirty miles of a power plant, as opposed to 56 percent of the white population (Black Leadership Forum et al. 2002). In addition, African Americans account for 17 percent of people living within five miles of a power plant site, statistically higher than the percentage of the population that they make up nationally.[29]

New power plant siting in California and New York, largely a result of deregulation, also has racially concentrated effects. A Latino Issues Forum report, *Power Against the People* (2001), analyzed eighteen proposed power plants in California in the wake of the California energy crisis and showed that for 80 percent of the plants, the proportion of Latinos in the surrounding population exceeded state averages. In terms of income, for 83 percent of the plants, the family income for nearby residents was less than $25,000 per year, far below the state mean household income. The report also criticized the expedited review process for the siting of power plants, instituted by Governor Gray Davis. This fast-track legislation for siting and approval was extremely controversial because it essentially skirted environmental review, specifically the

California Environmental Quality Act. The legislation, supported largely by power companies eager to build, was passed despite rising political controversy from consumer advocates and environmental and environmental justice organizations.

Power plant siting is a major community organizing issue in California. In South Gate, a largely Latino and immigrant neighborhood in Los Angeles, a community coalition organized by Communities for a Better Environment (CBE) won an informal neighborhood vote against a proposed power plant, which the builder respected (Soller 2001). In the Bay Area, community-based organizations such as CBE and Bayview Hunters Point have been involved in multiyear campaigns to shut the Hunters Point Power Plant and stop the expansion of Potrero Plant in African American communities in San Francisco. According to the California Air Resources Board, the Potrero and Hunters Point plants are the biggest and second-biggest industrial air polluters in San Francisco. Community anger at the expansion of these power plants forced agencies to reject the operations and plans for expansion.[30]

In the political controversies over the concentration of power plants and their impact on the health of people of color, the social construction of the issue links these diverse campaigns. That is, the generalized dissatisfaction with living near an existing or proposed power plant is made racially specific. Rather than being a general environmental, public health, or community issue, the power plant issue becomes a racially charged example of a larger problem as crystallized under the rubric and umbrella of environmental racism. Energy and power plants become yet another example of how people of color are harmed by a large-scale technological system and a political process unresponsive to their communities and needs. This system is increasingly guided by free market principles and the profit margin in an era of deregulation. For communities of color living near power plants, deregulation is a concrete policy that hits their neighborhoods hard, with little protection or regard for their health or environment.

## New York State Power Politics

What were the statewide politics that provided the context for the siting of power plants in low-income neighborhoods and communities of color in New York City? In 1997, in response to Order 888, power providers in New York State filed a proposal with FERC to create a competitive wholesale market through the formation of the New York Independent System Operation, known as the NYISO (Lentz 1999b). The ISO is a non-profit Albany company that regulates energy supply for New York State.[31]

In the early 1990s, electricity demand in the state had increased approximately 10 percent at the same time that state spending on energy efficiency and conservation dropped dramatically.[32] The state's increased demand was driven by population growth and increased use of computers and was exacerbated by Governor George Pataki's 1995 targeted, controversial, and roundly criticized cutbacks in energy efficiency and energy policy planning in anticipation of deregulation.[33]

In 1997, New York State's peak demand for energy was 28,700 megawatts. Governor Pataki sought to avoid passing state legislation on the issue (as in California), going instead through the Public Service Commission (PSC), the state body that regulates utilities (including electricity, gas, telecommunications, steam, water, and cable) and whose members he appoints. In 1996, the PSC ordered competition in the wholesale market to start the next year and mandated the introduction of retail access in 1998. The PSC's ideology is clearly stated in its mission statement. According to the PSC's Web site, one of its central goals is to *"promote competitive markets and streamline regulation. . . . We believe customers are best served by competitive markets. Therefore, we will promote their development and will increasingly use output oriented, performance based approaches to regulated areas that are not competitive. Once markets become sufficiently competitive, we will eliminate regulatory involvement to the extent permitted by law"* (emphasis added). As Gerald Norlander of the Public Utility Law Project (PULP), which advocates for low-income and rural utility consumers, noted, the PSC left issues of affordability off the table. The PSC implied that broadened taxpayer-funded programs or "energy stamps," be implemented to address the needs of low-income consumers, although it did not address the political viability of such a solution. The PSC's view that competition would bring greater efficiency and lower prices dominated the public discourse, despite critiques from consumer advocates.

Deregulation proponents argued, both practically and philosophically, that the market would be a perfect self-regulating system that would ultimately require that the PSC phase itself out its own existence. The political and ideological belief that deregulation would "magically" lead to lower prices was not unique to New York. It was also the driving force behind California's experience. The rhetoric of inevitable price reduction saturates the language of deregulation advocates, who believe that freedom from regulation necessarily cuts costs. At the beginning of his deregulation experiment, Pataki promised "more competition and lower prices." Despite this promise based on the "let-the-markets-rule" ideology, New York State's energy costs were 70 percent higher than the national average in 2002—higher than when Governor Pataki took office in 1994 and before deregulation, when the costs averaged 50 percent higher than the national average (Barrett 2002).

The PSC forced the state's utilities to sell their generating plants and instead buy electricity from independent generators in new wholesale markets, a provision lauded by deregulation advocates. "Selling the plants is enormously important. . . . This was the true "success story coming out of New York," according to Howard Fromer, director of government affairs in New York State for soon-to-be-disgraced but at the time still-high-flying Enron (Lentz 1999c). At the same time, the PSC plan was criticized as not going far enough. The *Daily News* bemoaned the retail plan as its implementation began, its editorial page declaring (preenergy crisis in California) that "energy deregulation in New York is a bust." New Yorkers, who wanted "real electric competition and real savings won't find it here. They'll have to move to California." The editorial page quoted Fromer's criticism that New York had only an "illusion of competition" because the New York plan was to deregulate the generation of electricity only, which constitutes just 25 percent of the total bill, since the other parts of the bill are in distribution, transmission, and delivery costs (Rate Reform lacks energy, 1998).

The media spectacle of the California energy crisis intervened as different actors used the blackouts to promote their respective agendas. The public relations battle over energy deregulation in New York State and the battle over power plants in 2001 in New York City were clearly shaped by the California energy crisis. Community advocates charged that New York State was "using a climate of fear" (of the California crisis) to speed through the political and regulatory processes. Proponents of deregulation and new power plant construction in New York

City warned ominously, "Every day's delay will push New York City one day closer to California" (Johnson 2001). New York State's deregulation proponents (agencies and companies) fear-mongered that communities unhappy with an expedited environmental and siting review process were selfishly and dangerously placing New York City in harm's way, closer to blackouts. In New York City, the charge of NIMBY politics was marshaled by power companies that claimed a larger public good in their actions, separate from their own economic profits and interests. CURE addressed this claim of NIMBYism in its literature: "While both the press and NYPA would like to paint the opposition as a 'not in my backyard' situation, it is important to note that the areas where the plants have been proposed all have at least one thing in common: all the neighborhoods are low-income communities of color! All these neighborhoods are already disparately impacted by poor air-quality and an overabundance of pollution sources," and NYPA did not show that the need was real in the time frame laid out.

As California had found, so did New York State discover that deregulation did not guarantee or magically lead to lower prices.[34] For example, Con Edison was at the mercy of the deregulated wholesale market as it was forced to buy electricity from plants it had been mandated to sell. That, combined with the scarcity of supply and the rising costs of natural gas and oil, led to increasing prices. Electricity bills jumped 43 percent in the first summer after deregulation, while delivery costs, which were still regulated, remained stable (Lentz 2000c). Deregulation also led to cutbacks on other noneconomic criteria. Under deregulation, utilities such as Con Edison had a major incentive to increase sales rather than promote energy efficiency or clean generation. For example, Con Edison's energy efficiency investments declined greatly, from $124.7 million in 1993 to $37 million in 1997. Postmortem analyses of the energy crisis found that it was the flawed structure of deregulation and the machinations of power companies that led to blackouts, not lack of supply.

## New York City: Race and Power Politics

The New York City energy market, one of the nation's largest, is worth about $7 billion. The city produces 7,700 megawatts of electricity and imports 5,000 megawatts, for a total of 12,700 megawatts. Demand surges in summer, largely due to air-conditioning (New York Power Trip Up Threatens Growth, 1999). The city's energy market is severely constrained by geography because there are only three transmission hubs through which power can flow into the city. Thus, there is a limit to how much power can flow through the system, much like a traffic bottleneck. New transmission lines are difficult to site because of the population density surrounding the city, high property values, and the extended time to receive permit approval. For those reasons, the independent system operator has a rule that requires that 80 percent of New York City's peak load be located in New York City.

In 2002, there were eight private power plants proposed for New York City, in addition to ten quasi–public power plants proposed by the New York Power Authority (NYPA), one of the largest state-owned public power enterprises, with a significant impact on state and city energy politics.[35] In 2000, it announced a plan to install ten 44 megawatt natural gas power turbines throughout New York City, at a cost of approximately $510 million.[36] These sites—four in the South Bronx (on two sites), two in Astoria (on one site), one in Williamburg, two in Sunset Park (on one site), and one on Staten Island—are in industrial waterfront communities (see figure 5.1). These plants were supposed to be temporary, although residents of these communities were innately suspicious of this temporary status, on the logic that it is harder to get rid of a facility that has already been built. Their suspicion was justified when NYPA announced that the turbines were not temporary (as promised) and that they would possibly be sold to private companies (Pérez-Peña 2001a).

The shape that deregulation took in New York City was racialized by activists who focused on the siting of power plants, which was concentrated in low-income areas and communities of color. The NYPA plants were sited in communities with a strong history of environmental justice activism and where residents shared a political and historical framework that interpreted city, state, and corporate initiatives to site noxious facilities as examples of environmental racism. Opposition to the NYPA plan was strong and immediate, mainly based on the impact of air pollution and exacerbation of asthma rates from these facilities on local communities of color. As in the garbage case study, there are many community

**Figure 5.1**
Existing and proposed power plants in New York City (as of February 2001)
(Credit: NYPIRG)

and environmental groups with different agendas working on the power plant issue.[37]

Communities United for Responsible Energy (CURE) was the citywide environmental justice and energy coalition that emerged with member organizations from throughout the city.[38] Its platform was comparable to that of other clean air and energy advocates, but it differed in that it emphasized a racial discourse and foregrounded the language of environmental justice.

There were also important structural and ideological connections between CURE and the Organization of Waterfront Neighborhoods (OWN) coalition. This overlap was evident in terms of organization, membership, and structure. For example, Eddie Bautista was the primary community organizer for both OWN and CURE. There was also a

**Figure 5.2**
Garbage or generators? A long-time garbage group (Neighbors Against Garbage)
changed its name to reflect its new battle: Generators
(Credit: Photo by author)

natural link between the garbage and the energy issues, because these
facilities were targeted for the same geographic areas, particularly the
South Bronx, Williamsburg, and Sunset Park (see figure 5.2). According
to Bautista, "We [the OWN coalition] were blindsided by the NYPA plan
and the power plant issue, which seemed to come out of nowhere" (personal communication, May 16, 2002). There were also some important
differences, particular to the energy case study. For example, although
the CURE coalition worked, like OWN, primarily within the discourse
of environmental racism and environmental justice generally, CURE
worked primarily in Latino communities. There were no power plants
proposed for West Harlem, a historic stronghold for environmental
justice activism. Also, the Chinese community in Sunset Park was
not involved in the power plant activism, which they saw as being more
physically distant from their neighborhood stronghold away from the
waterfront.

Many of the ideas being promoted by CURE and its allies are basic to
energy reform and environmental perspectives, and not necessarily
unique to communities of color: increasing conservation and efficiency
programs and completing an overall energy needs assessment and

comprehensive planning process. Some of CURE's platform was standard in terms of representing the consumer, public interest, and environmental perspectives: calls for rate regulation protections (which is the actual cost of producing the power with a certain prescribed profit factor to set the rate for each generator), energy demand reduction, transition to clean alternatives (renewables such as solar, wind, and fuel cell technologies), and the demand that no new plants be built until older plants were fully repowered (CURE platform). Repowering refers to an upgrade of an existing power plant's infrastructure, where turbines, boilers, and other plant components are replaced with more efficient and less polluting technology, allowing some portion of an existing facility to continue operation as part of a new or reconfigured system. Repowering usually involves gas, oil, and coal-fired boilers.

Some of CURE's demands were more radical in terms of their environmental, health, and democratic implications. These proposals included imposing a temporary moratorium on permits for new power plants. CURE also called for a community-based planning process that included access for underrepresented constituencies, the protection of the waterfront, and the need to promote open space for recreation (this issue is a key one for waterfront communities, which have fewer areas of recreation and open space than other neighborhoods). Finally, CURE called for "cumulative review," which would look at the total number of environmental facilities in a particular area, rather than at single sites, as a way of measuring total, cumulative environmental and health impacts on local communities.

CURE members were incensed by the siting proposal itself, as well as NYPA's top-down approach and arrogance toward local neighborhoods. According to NYPA's fact sheet, "Power NOW!" the schedule for implementation was set and predetermined, impervious to community demands: "To be prepared for the summer demand season, these new plants *must be ready* to begin operation June 1 2001" (italics added). NYPA's self-imposed deadline of June 1, ignored any time or process for state-mandated review, normally through an environmental impact statement (EIS) under the State Environmental Quality Review Act (SEQRA). Also, in three sites there were two proposed turbines at 44 megawatts each (for a total of 88 megawatts). NYPA promised to produce only 79.9 megawatts for minimal environmental review in order to go under the

80 megawatt threshold detailed under Article X. Article X of the New York State Public Service Law is the unified and expedited review process for applications to construct and operate electric generating facilities with capacities of 80 megawatts or more.[39]

NYPA requested that the siting board shorten the public comment period from twenty-one to ten days, a request that incensed communities who felt shortchanged by the process.[40] The board approved both the exemption from Article X and the shortened public comment period. On November 20, 2000, a mere four days after the siting board's Article X waiver, NYPA issued a negative declaration, which means a project has been deemed to have no significant environmental impact. Two days later, the day before Thanksgiving—another move that outraged communities who saw the scheduling as an obvious and cynical attempt to reduce public participation—the New York Department of Environmental Conservation (DEC) issued draft air permits. The DEC scheduled public hearings for December 13, 2000, with a notice for public comments by December 22, 2000, three days before Christmas. The three public hearings in Bronx, Brooklyn, and Queens were all scheduled for the same time, making it impossible for activists to attend multiple meetings and support their allies, in what CURE saw as a divide-and-conquer strategy. All in all, within a two-week span the DEC and the siting board waived Article X and EIS requirements and issued the required regulatory permits. This expedited review ensured that NYPA was not forced to examine alternative processes or sites or to mitigate the impacts of its operations (Bautista 2001).

Not surprisingly, community groups in the affected neighborhoods were outraged by the fast-track process and lack of public participation at every stage of the process. Community organizations and especially CURE members attempted to mobilize speakers and a large turnout for these public hearings. But because they had little time to organize, the groups met with limited success. Given the failure of the regulatory process, community groups then sought legal redress. In 2001, a coalition of community groups, represented by New York Lawyers for the Public Interest, sued NYPA over its ten turbines and the expedited review process. The groups included organizations in neighborhoods long associated with environmental justice activism in New York City like UPROSE (Sunset Park), El Puente, and We Stay/Nos Quedamos in the

South Bronx. In the NYLPI case, Judge Lawrence Knipel ruled in favor of NYPA that there had been no violation of the law (Riccardi 2001). The community groups, through their lead counsel, responded to this decision that it sent "the message that the process can be manipulated and maneuvered to ram projects through, particularly in low-income and communities of color."[41]

The power politics of electricity was also a major political issue at the city and the state levels during crucial elections that were shaped to a certain degree by race and class considerations. Energy deregulation was most closely associated with Governor Pataki, who pushed NYPA to install the turbines and expedite the building of new power plants throughout the state. His 2002 gubernatorial opponent was New York State comptroller Carl McCall, who was attempting to become the first African American governor in New York. It was not altogether surprising that McCall released a critical report attacking the state's deregulation plans. In it, he raised concerns about NYPA's management and spending and criticized it for not providing information in a timely manner for the audit. He also questioned the need for so many generators, although he did not focus on the racial dimensions of the siting (Barrett 2003).

Mayor Giuliani joined the fray and declared his enthusiastic support for the NYPA facilities: "This has ramifications beyond just the economy. It goes to whether people are going to live or die. Whether people are going to be safe." In response to community skepticism at this claim, Giuliani sneered back, "I am good at teaching people reality" (Lipton 2001b). In sharp opposition, Bronx Borough president Fernando Ferrer cited the asthma epidemic and air pollution concerns in the South Bronx as a reason to reject the South Bronx facilities (Lentz 2000b). Ferrer, a long-time Giuliani foe, was locked in a battle with Mark Green in the Democratic mayoral primary. He objected to Judge Knipel's decision, saying that "when it comes to building a multi-screen cineplex or Disney, they roll out the red carpet. . . . but when the Power Authority need to construct new generators that could foul the air with dangerous toxins, the state immediately looks to Black and Hispanic neighborhoods in the outer boroughs" (McKinley and Cardwell 2001). This theme fit well with Ferrer's campaign theme, "The Other New York," in his bid to become the first Latino mayor of the New York (he lost the primary). This slogan captured the idea that working-class New Yorkers and communities of color were being shut out of the city's economic boom. It addressed a host of issues where people of color and low-income communities felt marginalized by police brutality and criminal justice policy, education, economic development, and environmental concerns.

Ferrer also spoke at a rally held in front of one of the NYPA sites in Sunset Park on Mother's Day in 2001, which attracted about seventy participants, including representatives from CURE groups from other neighborhoods who came to give their support, as well as local and city-wide politicians who came to show solidarity with the neighborhood on the power plant issue. Ferrer blasted Governor Pataki for what he called hypocrisy on race and the environment, evident, said Ferrer, in Pataki's support for ending the navy's occupation of Vieques, a major environmental and civil rights issue for Puerto Ricans (in both New York and Puerto Rico), seen as an attempt to win Latino votes, at the same time as he was forcing Latino communities in New York City to live with more power plants and air pollution. The rally attendees marched in a circle, chanting and holding signs that accused the Department of Environmental Conservation (DEC) of neglect. "DEC = Department of Environmental Crime," one sign read. Others called for "Power Planning, Not Profit." Still others focused squarely on the asthma and air pollution problem, calling for "Less Wheezing, More Breathing" and "Less Asthma and More Justice."

Less than a month later, on June 1, 2001, the day the NYPA turbines were being turned on, CURE organized a protest of about 250 people in front of Governor Pataki's office in midtown Manhattan. The outreach flier for this rally read: "While Manhattan gets one skyline, the rest of NYC gets another. Are Power Plants Pataki's idea of how to fight asthma?" The visuals are of the World Trade Center (this event took place three months before the World Trade Center was destroyed by terrorists), contrasted with two power plant stacks spewing smoke. The two faces are a smiling Pataki and a black youth with an asthma pump in his mouth gasping for air during an asthma attack. This visual contrast of the state's most powerful politician with a child of color with asthma is a literal representation of CURE's essential politics and belief systems, which seek to place the lives and health of children of color at the center, not the periphery, of public view (see figure 5.3).

## <u>Friday, June 1st at 5pm</u>

Join people from across New York City to
Protest Pataki's Plan to poison our air.

While Manhattan gets
one skyline, the rest of
NYC gets another. Are
Power Plants Pataki's
idea of how to fight
asthma?

## Demonstrate against the NYPA Turbines at Pataki's NYC Office 663 Third Ave. ( btw E 42/ E 43 St.)

For more information contact Eddie with Communities United
for Responsible Energy (CURE) at 212.244.4664 or contact:
with                                        at 718.      .
& find out how you can help your community locally.

Figure 5.3
CURE flier

At that rally, a racially diverse mix of community residents from a number of affected communities, accompanied by politicians, marched and spoke out against the governor's energy policies. CURE drove a car to the rally with three artistically rendered power plant stacks on the roof of the vehicle. People wore gas masks and carried signs that read: "South Bronx Is Choking." These signs reminded viewers and passing pedestrians that air pollution may kill, even if does so "Slower Than Guns." The rally forced the midtown business crowd, mostly white-collar workers and executives, to see the community anger over an issue that is literally, politically, and figuratively rendered invisible and marginalized to the periphery of the city's poorest and most vulnerable neighborhoods of working class and people of color. The rally made the noonday crowd stop and look at poor people, sick people, and children and think about where the city's energy comes from and who is possibly harmed in the process of its creation and usage (see figure 5.4).

It is impossible to gauge the direct impact of these demonstrations on politicians and the regulatory process. Environmental justice energy

**Figure 5.4**
CURE Protest, June 1, 2002
(Credit: Photo by author)

activism has made its clearest impact in the legal arena, which is para-doxically insulated from this type of community pressure. The legal history of this campaign exemplifies the limits and successes of using the courts as a means to achieve environmental justice, since lawsuits can be dragged out and appeals can overturn both good and bad decisions.[42] What is significant about the public displays of community anger is that they are crucial parts of a multipronged organizing strategy on the energy issue that mobilized local residents to participate in what is traditionally a closed process and made political a normally technocratic issue left in the hands of experts. At the same time that there were public demon-strations, CURE also wrote an extensive and detailed letter to the state energy planning board outlining its objections on three issues: cumula-tive impacts, PM 2.5 (small particle pollution), and Article X reform (on the siting of power plants), and the need for energy efficiency and clean, renewable energy. Activists thus transformed what is normally treated as a complex technological and scientific issue into a legitimate political subject open to vigorous public protest and debate.

## Race and Siting: Contrasting Causality

So why exactly were the NYPA facilities sited where they were? The answer to this question is crucial, and thus the source of much political controversy. NYPA claimed that the sites were chosen by nonracial and noneconomic criteria: these areas had the right zoning and electricity and gas hook-ups, and could be in use by the summer of 2001. At the same time, NYPA conducted its own internal environmental justice assess-ment, which looked at poverty and race demographics around its ten sites. But it refused to release this assessment publicly, despite several Freedom of Information Act requests. It thus was hidden from public view until the NYLPI lawsuit uncovered it through the discovery process.

NYPA's own 2001 In-City Project Environmental Justice Assessment showed that areas around NYPA sites had higher poverty rates and higher proportions of minorities within a half-mile radius than the city-wide average. The citywide averages are 19 percent below poverty, 29 percent black, and 24 percent Hispanic. (These numbers are based on the 1990 census data. Racial populations do not total 100 percent because "Hispanic" can include members of all different racial categories.)

At five of the seven sites, the poverty level exceeded the city average. The most extreme cases were in the South Bronx: at the Harlem River Rail Yard site, the rates were 51 percent in poverty, and at Point Morris, 44.1 percent poverty. The racial overrepresentation was most dramatic at Harlem River, where the population was 36.9 percent black and 64.7 percent Hispanic, and at Point Morris, where the percentages were 48.5 percent black and 52.3 percent Hispanic. In Williamsburg, the poverty rate was 28.7 percent, and the population was 7.5 percent black and 57.9 percent Hispanic. In Sunset Park, the poverty rate was 27 percent, and the population was 8.5 percent black and 52.3 percent Hispanic.

Local communities and their allies looked at these numbers and drew their own conclusions that social, racial, economic, and political factors, not race-neutral ones, were the primary reason that these sites were chosen.[43] Local communities interpreted these data to mean that their neighborhoods had been deliberately targeted for their racial and social demographics. Community groups determined that their neighborhoods were seen as easier targets than wealthier and whiter neighborhoods, and had less political and social capital. Communities of color drew this conclusion in part because of NYPA's secretive and top-down approach, an attitude the agency would not use in more affluent neighborhoods. In its talking points for a NYPA hearing in December 2001, a CURE flier critiqued the lack of community participation, the lack of health assessment of the affected neighborhoods, and the harm to air quality, which NYPA ignored in its draft EIS. CURE outlined these objections in more detail in a December 27 letter to NYPA, again moving between public and bureaucratic critiques for different audiences.

Even the *New York Times,* which historically supported controversial environmental projects despised by local communities (such as the Brooklyn Navy Yard incinerator), blasted NYPA in an editorial (The Turbine Mess, 2001). The *Times* charged that New York State "ignored governmental processes, cut regulatory corners and exploited a loophole in state laws to dodge full environmental review." The environmental review did not study the effects on noise, air quality, water quality, land use, or community character even though the proposed sites were within 400 feet of houses, schools, and parks. The editorial cited numbers generated by the Natural Resources Defense Council that New York City had access to greater megawatts than its anticipated generated load and that NYPA was depending on "secrecy, speed and dubious tactics."

With NYLPI's assistance, community and environmental justice groups appealed Judge Knipel's ruling even as the turbines were turned on in June 2001 as originally planned by NYPA (see figure 5.5). In July 2001, the Brooklyn appellate court overturned the decision, ruling that New York State had violated the State Environmental Quality Review Act. The ruling did not block operation of the turbines, but the appellate division did order an environmental impact study and directed NYPA to study the plant's output of soot particles as small as 2.5 microns

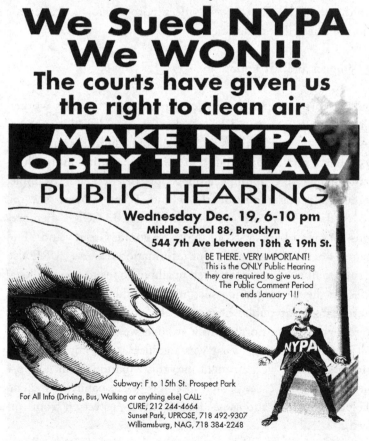

**Figure 5.5**
CURE-NYPA flier

as opposed to the larger 10 microns.[44] This ruling was a legal break-through, the first of its kind in a New York court. The court sided with environmentalists who demanded that the plants meet a much stronger standard for particulate pollution than one traditionally enforced by the state. This appellate court ruling was later upheld by the state's highest court, which affirmed that the Pataki administration had acted illegally in installing the plants without conducting environmental reviews. Because the court of appeals was upholding a lower court's decision, it was not a statewide ruling. It applied only to the Appellate Division Second Department, but that included a large region of the state and encompassed most of the proposed power plants (Pérez-Peña 2001c). As a result of the combined legal and political pressure, NYPA developed pollution reduction, also known as "offset" programs, to reduce air pollution in the affected communities.

### Cumulative Impact and Air Pollution

Throughout the tortuous and lengthy legal process as the cases worked their way through the system, CURE worked on its political campaign. It organized public demonstrations and conducted education and public outreach on energy and its contribution to the air pollution and asthma problem and highlighting its impact on people of color. For example, CURE organized protests outside the Hunts Point subway station, where two of the NYPA turbines were to be sited. CURE members carried signs that read "Public Need, Not Corporate Greed" and "End Environmental Racism," and passed out informational fliers. CURE also organized town hall meetings in affected neighborhoods to educate local communities on the power plant issue, and individual CURE members spoke out repeatedly at public hearings. The opposition between the public interest and the corporate profit motive was made explicit and was not altogether surprising. What was significant was how problems of environmental racism were brought into this equation. That is, those most vulnerable—in this case, people of color—were painted as exem-plifying the public interest and as needing the most protection from cor-porate greed.

The problem CURE identified was not just with the NYPA facilities. With the exception of Staten Island, every neighborhood with NYPA turbines—Sunset Park, Williamsburg, the South Bronx and Long Island City—had additional proposals for power plants by private developers. In addition to the ten NYPA turbines, there were seven proposed facilities as of June 2001. This concentration of power plants raised the issue of the cumulative impact of multiple air pollution sources on communities of color, a concern long focused on by community members and environmental justice advocates. In that sense, the cumulative impact issue echoes the garbage activists' rejection of the distinction between private and city-owned residential and commercial waste as functionally irrelevant. The division of public and private energy facilities, like that of commercial and residential waste, is a bureaucratic and technical distinction, while communities focus on the lived realities of what those multiple facilities mean in their entirety.

Nydia Velasquez's Twelfth Congressional District, comprising the Lower East Side and the Brooklyn waterfront, was particularly hard hit by multiple industrial facilities, both proposed and existing. As she stated at a Mother's Day rally in front of the NYPA site in Sunset Park, "It's getting hard to keep up with these power plant sitings. I find myself running up and down my district tracking these proposed sites." Her district alone was slated to host the two 44 megawatt NYPA turbines in Sunset Park, a 520 megawatt plant on a barge owned by Sunset Energy Fleet, a proposed reopening of the Hudson Avenue Plant to generate 60 megawatts, a generating barge in Williamsburg, the two 44 megawatt NYPA turbines in Williamsburg, and the Con Edison East River expansion.[45]

At a nighttime Community Board Six hearing on the Sunset Energy Fleet proposal held at an elementary school, UPROSE's youth group, the Environmental Enforcers, comprising twenty-five teenagers (mostly Latino and some Middle Eastern), came out in full force, some wearing gas masks and others with asthma pumps in hand. Several of the Enforcers testified at the community board, talking about their asthma and the clean air problem in the community and their effects on youth of color in Sunset Park. Several of the youth complained about the lack of trees in their community, the problems with the Gowanus Expressway, and the fact that they already had problems breathing. One teenage youth asked the community board, "Why do you want to put *something else* bad here? Don't we have enough?" (personal communication, June 11, 2002).

UPROSE's youth contingent constituted a crucial part of its empowerment and community organizing strategy. Energy issues were the means to illustrate other larger problems of community and democracy and through which to achieve larger social, political and educational goals. According to Yeampierre, UPROSE's executive director, "I moved the organization from social service to empowerment model. I want to focus on young people and make people realize through workshops in relationship to what they learned and what they see in their communities. Trees are political. Urban planning is political. Air is political. Energy is political. This kind of knowledge is political. We learn what we need to know to be knowledgeable for environmental justice: science, social science and geography. Environmental justice issues get the youth excited about education. Thus, participation in the public process is part of their political education" (personal communication, April 8, 1999).

## Conclusion

Despite attempts by the city, state, and NYPA to minimize debate, environmental justice groups, alongside their environmental and consumer protection allies, have inserted themselves into the public process and made public a serious debate on energy. As of 2005, this process continues to be long, contentious, and complicated. But CURE remains seriously engaged in the process and was appointed in 2003 to Mayor Bloomberg's Energy Task Force to develop recommendations to prevent future blackouts and ensure adequate energy supply in New York City after massive blackouts that swept the Northeast and Midwest (Barrett 2003). This task force produced an extensive report in 2004 that, according to CURE, was the first "public recognition that there is no hysterical energy crisis."[46] Rather, the report provided information and a "fair and strategic plan," which included energy conservation and efficiency, green building design, and a commitment to repowering. CURE was a key factor in inserting these principles and language into the Energy Task Force Report.

The pace of power plant construction slowed in New York City. By far, the biggest factor was the slowing enthusiasm for energy projects, in part a result of a post-Enron and post-California energy crisis disenchantment with deregulation as well as changing economic circumstances as power companies failed to obtain financing for their projects. Community protests against power plants in New York City contributed to the sense of instability clouding new power plant construction. But in general, environmental, environmental justice, and public interest constituencies in New York City had little concrete to show for their effort. According to the state energy plan's 2003 annual update of the state's progress on reaching its performance goals on energy, the state admitted its many failures on two key policy goals: achieving a clean and healthy environment and fair and equitable consumer protections. Repeatedly under these two categories, such as mitigating environmental impact, the state admitted "no significant progress." The same holds true for reducing greenhouse gas emissions and increasing renewable energy sources. And the same failures hold true for implementing principles from the Department of Environmental Conservation's Environmental Justice Advisory Group.

Nonetheless, community groups, particularly CURE member organizations representing communities of color and environmental justice perspectives, understood that in an ideological climate that favors deregulation over regulation and the private sector over the public good, concerns of low-income areas and communities of color were guaranteed to be ignored unless they forced their way into this complex and technocratic policy debate to get their issues on the table. The only chance at improving the health and environmental consequences at their neighborhood level depended on inserting themselves into ongoing debates on energy issues.

# 6

# The Promise and the Peril or, Can Community-Based Environmental Justice Initiatives Reintegrate Planning and Public Health in the Urban Environment?

One of the principles of the national environmental justice movement is that low-income and communities of color can speak for themselves and act on their own behalf to improve health and environmental conditions. New York City environmental justice activists have used this principle in fighting particular noxious facilities, as well as forming coalitions on garbage and energy policy. They are also building an agenda of community-centered action, a potentially transformative act when it is introduced into populations and neighborhoods that historically have been lacking social and cultural capital, political power, or economic clout.

Community-based initiatives come in many forms. In this chapter I examine two related but distinct forms of community-based action: environmental health research and planning in New York City. As discussed in chapter 1, public health and urban planning reforms were historically linked in the late nineteenth and early twentieth centuries, although the two diverged in the Progressive era. It is in the arena of environmental racism and through the environmental justice movement that the two fields are being reintegrated because of its growing recognition of the complexity of the relationship between race, class, health, and the urban environment. Moreover, community-based attempts to remediate conditions of environmental racism and promote environmental justice contain both seeds of promise and peril in environmental health research and planning that have larger implications for community groups nationwide.

Community-based planning and environmental health research are not unique to New York City or environmental justice issues. For example, the basic features of community-based environmental justice research are central to trends in community-based research, community science, or popular epidemiology more generally. The community turn to research is also significant in terms of its engagement with the larger politics of mainstream scientific knowledge and research. Citizen participation in science potentially rejects the dichotomization of citizens and experts, technical facts and cultural values, and can create a more democratic scientific practice through different forms of knowledge (Fischer 2000, Wynne 1996).

Community-based environmental justice research (CBEJR) is important to examine in that it may help remediate particular environmental and pollution threats in communities of color and generate new knowledge about the relationship of race, poverty, health, and the urban environment (Corburn 2005). I begin by explaining how community-based research differs from traditional research, and thus how communities of color in New York City have engaged in the politics of scientific knowledge and research. The results of this research are commonly used by community organizations in political campaigns to reduce health and environmental risks in disempowered communities. CBEJR emphasizes the multidimensional components in terms of analysis and methodologies. Such holistic approaches exemplify the environmental justice movement itself, a multifaceted analytical worldview joining social justice and environmental perspectives.

Community concern over asthma rates has been a key catalyst for environmental justice activism in New York City. One way in which local communities responded to air pollution was through community-based environmental health research. Community-based asthma research helped to produce new knowledge and information about the disease and its relationship to race, class, and urban life in general. This chapter looks at community-based research initiatives on environmental health conducted by WE ACT. It builds on Corburn's (2005) description of El Puente's asthma research in Willamsburg as a form of what he calls "street science." He defines street science as a framework that joins local insights with professional scientific techniques, with concurrent goals to improve scientific inquiry and environmental health policy and decision making. He argues that street science at its best identifies hazards and highlights research questions that professionals may ignore, provides hard-to-gather exposure data, involves difficult-to-reach populations, and expands possibilities for interventions, resulting in what he calls "improved science and democracy." Community-based organizations like WE ACT use a variety of tools to measure air pollution and the health effects of this pollution (Brown et al. 2005). These include health surveys, air monitoring, and traffic counts. As I discussed in chapter 3, WE ACT works in collaboration with the Columbia School of Public Health Research Project on Asthma at the cutting edge of environmental health and asthma research.

In the area of community-based planning in New York City, local neighborhoods attempted to reshape and improve their local spaces, long neglected by other political or municipal forces. This chapter focuses on community plans and planning initiatives emerging from West Harlem and Sunset Park (there are also community plans from the South Bronx, Williamsburg, and Red Hook), where fierce and well-publicized campaigns against particular noxious facilities left a political legacy of organizing and advocacy around issues of land use, health, and racially disproportionate pollution exposure and generated a natural constituency for community planning. I base my analysis on information provided by the Campaign for Community-Based Planning, the umbrella campaign for the numerous individual community plans throughout the city.

This analysis of the success and failures of community-based initiatives for environmental justice in planning and public health examines the dual impact in terms of outcomes and process, also understood as the distinction between procedural and distributive justice (Young 1990, Lake 1996). I contend that the success or failure of community-based planning or environmental health research as a strategy to remedy environmental racism revolves around issues of procedural justice and community empowerment. That is, do particular initiatives advance the resources of the local community broadly defined? For example, is community leadership developed, and if so, what are the effects of this development? These questions follow from Fischer's (2000) view of citizen participation as ideology and practice and of its potential contribution to increased democracy in environmental decision making.

## Community-Based Environmental Justice Research

In *Community-Based Research in the United States* (1998), the Loka Institute, a think tank that works on science and democracy issues, defined community-based research (CBR) as "research that is conducted by, with, or for communities (e.g. with civic, grassroots, or worker groups throughout civil society)."[1] It thus stands in contrast to the bulk of research and development (amounting to $170 billion per year) in the United States performed on behalf of business, the military, the federal government, or academic/scientific research. *Community-based research* is an umbrella term that includes all research by, with, or for communities. These distinctions (by, with, or for) are important to understanding the different terms of how research is designed and implemented with respect to power relations.[2]

Environmental justice issues constitute an important and rapidly growing focus of community-based environmental health research. Its community practitioners identify politically and strategically with the environmental justice movement, and are located or housed in community-based settings and nonprofit organizations. Its academic practitioners are housed primarily in university settings that are not explicitly linked to the environmental justice movement.[3]

The environmental justice movement's engagement with community-based science and research is part of the tradition of community science and popular epidemiology that challenges conventional practices of health research and environmental risk assessment (Tesh 2000, Brown and Mikkelson 1990, Wing 1998). Community-based research is situated in the context of local circumstances and "local knowledge" (Fischer 2000). Community-based environmental justice and environmental health research endorse a "make science better" position through their critique of traditional risk assessment.[4] As Corburn (2005) shows in his study of Williamsburg, street science is not a form of populism where the "community" replaces "experts," but something that works to create better knowledge through an improved understanding of how knowledge coproduced among local and professional constituencies leads to better health, science, and politics.

Certain sectors of the environmental justice movement have chosen community-based research in an attempt to quantify and use methodologically sound techniques in making policy claims. In part, this push is a rejection of the idea that communities and grassroots actors are unempirical in making risk claims and seeks to counter the perception that their political action is based on emotional, irrational, or countermodern perspectives. Community-based research seeks to improve the science and politics of conventional risk assessment and epidemiology, not to discount it. Political scientist Sylvia Tesh provides an overview of the history of risk assessment, its methodology, and main critiques.[5] The traditional scientific method that underlies environmental risk assessment is based on an idealized model of risk systems best practiced under laboratory conditions (Wing 2000). This structure of risk assessment tends to produce knowledge that does not address where risk exposures are from and ignores questions such as who is producing the risk, who benefits from this production of risk, and why certain groups and not others are exposed (addressing questions of social power and corporate corruption). Finally, feminist philosophers of science critique discourses of objectivity that privilege a separation of researchers and object of research (Keller 1985, Harding 1993).

Brown (1993) defines popular epidemiology as the process through which laypersons gather statistics, create knowledge, and marshal the resources of experts in order to understand the epidemiology of disease. Popular epidemiology diverges from traditional epidemiology in terms of research methods, especially with regard to causation, estimation of data, methodology, accepted levels of measurement, statistical significance, and relations between scientific method and public policy.[6] Some of these alternative research methods include such projects as "bucket brigades" and health surveys. "Bucket brigades" are specially fitted buckets that do a "grab sample" of air pollution levels. The bucket, affordably fitted with a $5 tube, a $10 air vacuum, and an $80 valve, sucks in an air sample, which is sent to a lab for a variety of tests. The value of this method is that it quantifies a "bad smell" to empirical air sampling data, which can then be used to leverage action from the particular corporation or to urge environmental or health agencies to take stronger regulatory action. The method of the bucket brigade is the same basic technology that businesses and governments use to sample air data. Bucket brigades have been successful in documenting air toxins releases around oil refinery communities in Cancer Alley in Louisiana and in Richmond, California (Lerner 2005). "Cancer Alley" refers to the roughly 125 oil and chemical plants in the chemical corridor between New Orleans and Baton Rouge in Louisiana, where a series of low-income, predominantly African American rural communities are located.

The state reports over 8 tons of toxic waste per year per citizen, and cancer and respiratory illness rates in the region are among the highest in the United States. This research is community based in that local residents take an active role in collecting the data, from "sniffers" who detect a possible problem or pollution release to "samplers" who take the sample. Health surveys can be constructed in a myriad of ways and levels of detail, either primarily qualitative or quantitative.

Lay participation and popular epidemiology can help to identify many cases of bad science (poor studies, secret investigations, and failure to inform local officials). It can show that normal science has limits.[7] Examples of such limits are not being interested in environmental health effects, lack of willingness to investigate disease clusters, demanding standards of proof that may be unobtainable or inappropriate, and being slow to accept new ideas about toxic causality. Lay participation and popular epidemiology can also encourage citizens to seek alternate sources of information and analysis and can yield valuable data from new sources.

One of the main areas of conflict between "experts" and "laypeople" that Brown (1993) identifies is the level of statistical significance required for intervention. Often a cancer cluster has too few cases to achieve the scientific threshold of statistical significance. Another major difference between traditional and popular epidemiology is that while scientists often err on the side of rejecting environmental causation and seek to avoid a false positive, community residents who take up popular epidemiological strategies tend to err on the side of causation. That is, epidemiologists prefer to claim no association or causation even when there is one rather than to have claimed an association when there is none. The structure of epidemiological studies, and of scientific evidence, is constructed to act as a bias against causation and commonsense notions of causality because scientific standards are held to a higher standard of proof than nonscientific interpretation. To local communities experiencing environmental pollution, that often means the burden of scientific proof is such that it is meaningless outside laboratory conditions.

The environmental justice position on environmental risk and community-based research transforms the discourse of objectivity and abstraction that Tesh (2000) asserts is shaped by its "preenvironmentalist" limits. Preenvironmentalist research does not adequately explain how environmental change occurs and does not look at long-term effects of pollution. Environmental justice positions are consciously governed by a discourse of interestedness, aligned with specific racial and political identities, and which take seriously the history of specific places, peoples, and racial oppression. CBEJR is also counterposed against the most egregious examples of exploitative research, beginning with the notorious Tuskegee experiments and most recently exemplified by the Kennedy Krieger lead level debacle in the mid-1990s.

Between 1932 and 1972, the U.S. Public Health Service (PHS) conducted an experiment on 399 black men in the late stages of syphilis. The men were never told that they had the disease and were not treated for it. It is often cited as an example of abusive and coercive research and of a research, racial, and cultural climate that led to an absence of medical and professional ethics where informed consent was not received.

In the second example, the Kennedy Krieger Institute, affiliated with Johns Hopkins University, received $1 million in federal grant money for a childhood lead poisoning study. The study paid landlords up to $7,000 to recruit families with healthy children to live in houses where lead was only partially removed. The purpose of the study was to determine the minimum amount of lead clean-up that could be undertaken and still protect the health of children. Lead exposure leads to developmental delays that can affect learning. In fact, lead levels in healthy children rose, yet families were uninformed that they were taking part in a study. First Appellate Circuit Court Judge Dale Cathell has compared this study to the Tuskeegee syphilis study (Pinder 2002, Roig-Franzia 2001).

Finally, CBEJR is distinct from traditional research in terms of research process, for example, in encouraging cultural sensitivity and community specificity in research design. Rather than use a neutral language of scientific research with no particular community in mind, this research is designed with particular cultural audiences—racial, religious, or cultural in nature.[8] Research studies, historically a source of disempowerment in minority communities, are often structured to facilitate empowerment.[9]

The major critique of community-based environmental justice research is that there are few scientific evaluations published of the research and empirical analyses of whether this research is "good" or "bad" science (for an extended discussion of these critiques, see Corburn 2005). Thus, critics suggest, data can be manipulated to serve a particular political campaign or agenda. A related possible critique is that since the community members often own the data (as a response to past research that is taken out of the community), these data cannot be independently verified, and independent verification is a central method of scientific review. This paucity of formal critiques of community-based research can be explained in part because the body of this research is already marginalized within the traditional scientific community. It cannot enter into the process of normal science through procedures such as peer review, although this is slowly changing in certain subfields of scientific and medical research.[10]

Another critique hinges on defining what constitutes good or bad science on the contested terms that Brown (1993) identifies: the level of statistical significance, the size of the sample, and the replicability of the research. Mainstream research methods require a high threshold of statistical significance, agreed upon within a scientific community; a large data set; and an understanding that experiments be replicated. Community-based research, because of its small nature and scale, fails the measure of "good science" based on these criteria. The question of what counts and evaluation of the research is necessarily a political one. Empowerment is a key goal in community-based research, and one that makes this research "good" from the environmental justice or community perspective. But the question of whether empowerment is a valid goal in scientific research is a controversial one, both as aim and in terms of how to quantify or measure this goal.[11] Traditional science would disagree with this goal as marginal to the research, in addition to the difficulty of empirically measuring empowerment (Wallerstein 1999).

### Community-Based Environmental Health Research

In New York City, innovative community-based research has been conducted in West Harlem and Williamsburg around asthma and environmental health issues.[12] Local community-based organizations like El Puente and WE ACT have transformed their activism around environmental justice and clean air issues into research programs that emphasize community empowerment in study design and data collection. This research is not unique to New York City. Community-based asthma education is increasingly recognized as an effective tool to deal with the growing problem of asthma in low-income and minority populations (Ford et al. 1996, Wilson et al. 1998).

WE ACT is the community partner with the Columbia School of Public Health, and its Center for Children's Environmental Health (CCEH) has been engaged in community-based environmental justice research on air pollution and its impact on child health, in data collection as well as in providing a community voice in study design. For WE ACT, the political and practical implication of its collaboration with research partners such as Columbia University is that it provides documentation of the problem and strengthens the organizational goal of an overall reduction in pollution exposures that negatively affect the community, specifically children's environmental health in northern Manhattan. WE ACT's youth programs grew alongside its programs in community-based participatory research and environmental health. However, rather than participating in the "drive-by research" that has characterized many academic studies in communities of color, WE ACT developed the position that communities of color are not objects of study but rather must be active collaborators with researchers and institutions to assess and eliminate the causes of poor health (Shepard et al. 2002, O'Fallon and Dearry 2002).

According to WE ACT's executive director, Peggy Shepard, preparing the next generation to understand and confront environmental racism is one key factor in sustaining hard-won environmental justice victories while WE ACT also prioritizes how youth programs can enhance the individual development of its participants. Thus, youth leadership is a key component of WE ACT's overall organizational goal. Its major youth programs have taken two forms (and with names and acronyms chosen by the youth themselves): the Earth Crew Youth Leadership Program (Earth Crew), which ran from 1993 through 2000, and the more recently developed Young Women of Color Organizing Project (whose participants took the name Diverse Individuals Fighting for Environmental and Reproductive Rights Now 'Til Tomorrow—DIFFERENTT).

Earth Crew developed the leadership potential of youth of color (primarily African American and Latino) by using the urban environment, specifically in northern Manhattan, as a classroom laboratory. The Earth Crew program taught over 200 young people skills such as public speaking, environmental audits, pollution monitoring, and community leadership. Earth Crew was both a summer program, funded by the City of New York Summer Youth Employment Program, and an after-school program. Any young person from Upper Manhattan or the Bronx could be involved. Recruitment was conducted through churches, schools, and community meetings. The participants were overwhelmingly of low to middle-low income socioeconomic status, and there was a deliberate effort to balance the group in terms of gender and between African American and Latino (with a small number of white and Asian participants). The numbers of participants ranged from fifteen up to thirty-five depending on whether it was a summer or after-school session. The smaller groups were considered more effective.

In the summer of 1996, WE ACT's Earth Crew teamed up with researchers from the Columbia School of Public Health to measure air pollution at four intersections in Harlem. The study measured two kinds of pollutants: fine particulate matter and black carbon (or soot), which is used as an indicator of diesel exhaust. The study also made traffic counts. The goal of the study was to see whether there was an association between the volume of traffic, especially diesel exhaust, and the pollution measured at each intersection. The intersections were chosen by community residents as being representative of a range of traffic density, from relatively quiet intersections to extremely busy, dirty ones. The members of the Earth Crew were trained as field technicians for this study. They learned how to operate the air monitoring equipment, which they wore in backpacks as a way of indicating personal exposures, and conducted the traffic counting every day for a week. This study also showed how community residents, especially youth, could learn new skills in the process of collecting data on pollution exposure. By helping select the intersections where data were collected and by wearing air-monitoring backpacks, the Earth Crew participants helped develop a snapshot of what kinds and levels of pollution people were exposed to daily. This issue is important, since air monitors tend to be placed on top of buildings, where the air is not necessarily representative of the air people on the ground are actually breathing.

The study found that the level of black carbon that was measured varied a great deal from site to site and was in fact associated with diesel traffic density at all sites, with one important exception. The highest levels of black carbon were measured at a site near the Manhattanville bus depot, although relatively few buses were seen during the time the youth were counting traffic. This finding suggested that the diesel bus depots may act as a stationary source of diesel pollution even when buses were not actively driving to and from the facility. The research led to a five-year epidemiology study to assess diesel exposure in four high schools in northern Manhattan and testing for an association between diesel exposure and asthma symptoms. The work of the Earth Crew in conducting this study has also been a critical tool in WE ACT's ongoing struggles with the MTA to convert its fleet to clean fuels and reduce the disproportionate numbers of diesel buses garaged uptown. Notably, the MTA agreed to convert the entire fleet of buses at the Manhattanville depot to hybrid electric models, which produce considerably fewer emissions than traditional diesel buses, and it agreed in 2000 that all new bus depots would be designed to house compressed natural gas buses rather than diesel buses.

The Earth Crew's history is rich with examples of youth projects that develop and demonstrate leadership skills and concrete accomplishment, no small task for Earth Crew's primarily minority and low-income youth. In one project, the Earth Crew identified abandoned city lots they wished to reclaim for community use. To do so, they researched city land transfer regulations, made a formal public presentation to the community board that gained the board's support, and filed a formal request with the city for the lots. In another project, the Earth Crew designed and built a green oasis in front of the Adam Clayton Powell Jr. State Office Building on 125th Street and programmed it with activities for rappers, spoken word artists, and senior citizens. Earth Crew participants have traveled to Boston to participate in a youth summit; handed out fliers and educated community residents about the toxins in fish found in waters off Harlem's shores; and designed, distributed, collected, and analyzed peer surveys on smoking, teen pregnancy, domestic violence, and rap music.

In the summer of 2001, WE ACT's youth group (then named Planet Rock Youth) was composed almost entirely of young women. Although this composition was not by design, the staff noticed a significant shift in the dynamics of the group from the previous summer. With only two young men present, the remaining ten young women appeared much more comfortable with voicing their opinions and taking leadership within the group. This observation coincided with a growing interest by other WE ACT programs in better understanding and addressing the specific impacts of environmental exposures and pollution on the health of women and of children. WE ACT's involvement since 1998 as a community partner with Columbia University in a large mothers and newborns study helped the organization begin to make connections between pollution exposure and birth outcomes as part of a growing body of evidence that suggests the long-term impact on reproductive and developmental health is linked to certain chemical and pollution exposures.

The gendered turn that WE ACT's work took is tied to Allen's (2003) analysis of feminist science workers combating health and environmental injustices in Louisiana. As she argues, methodologies used by feminist science workers exemplify philosopher Sandra Harding's strong objectivity paradigm that centers local knowledge, specifically, gendered and racialized perspectives (1991). The gendered focus also represents a further broadening of the term *environment*, which was a key ideological contribution of the environmental justice movement. WE ACT expanded "environment" to include the internal and bodily environment, a central focus of feminist analysis and activism and itself a focal point of women's health movement activism.

In 2002, WE ACT launched a new youth group, this one focused on cultivating new voices and advocates for issues that affect the environmental health, reproductive health, and environmental knowledge of the participants, while at the same time mentoring and enriching the knowledge base of twenty young women of color aged fifteen to eighteen (this group was 30 percent Latina, 20 percent native Carribbean, and 50 percent African American). The Young Women of Color Project (whose participants chose the name DIFFERENTT) fostered the desire among these girls to challenge the status quo, look critically at and analyze their communities, recognize the importance of being active participants in shaping the norms within their immediate environments, and organizing around issues that are important to themselves and their families. The program prioritized experiential learning and an interactive teaching approach, using group discussions, shared personal experiences, outings, and guest speakers, to facilitate the young person's active involvement in the learning process.

DIFFERENTT focused on the relationship between environmental hazards and the health of young women of color using the logic that the reproductive health agenda encompasses the unmistakable connection between environmental exposures and reproductive disorders. Women of color often live in communities that are disproportionately exposed to lead, mercury, industrial solvents, and dioxin, which are widely thought to contribute to miscarriage, infertility, and menstrual abnormalities. An understanding of the reproductive system and how it works, clear information about the issues involved in reproductive health, and education about the impact of the environment on reproductive health was seen as essential to helping young women of color become advocates within their communities and throughout the United States and to transforming the reproductive health rights agenda to reflect the full range of concerns of women of color. DIFFERENTT was designed to give the young women a working understanding of how their bodies function to ensure that they recognize and learn to expose the environmental factors that contribute to poor overall and reproductive health, help them identify the links between their health and exposure to environmental hazards, and enrich their interest in political and community organizing to reduce exposure. Overall, the main objectives were to provide health education and advocacy skills training that incorporated messages and issues that gave voice to the perspectives, ideas, and realities of young women of color in sexual, reproductive, and environmental health.

Each of the experiential learning activities was developed by WE ACT staff to provide a balance between individual and group activities, foster curiosity, and make the experience fun. For example, DIFFERENTT members engaged a group of their peers in a community treasure hunt activity. The activity began with the young people sharing information with their peers about things and places in the community that they liked or treasured and why. The information was mapped onto a full-size map drawn by the young people themselves, and then the youth visited these sites. The "treasure" tour was integrated with a "toxic" tour to highlight sites that might be harmful to individual and community health. In conducting both of these tours, DIFFERENTT reinforced a belief that there are both treasures and potentially harmful facilities and land uses in their neighborhood. The activities succeeded in getting participants to look deeply at their surroundings. One seventeen year old wrote in an evaluation, "Why is all this stuff up in our hood, I have a lot of questions I didn't have before the treasure hunt and toxic tour—now I want to do something and not just ask questions!"

In addition to the lessons, take-home assignments were given by the youth coordinators based on current events relevant to the topic at hand. This helped to broaden the perspective of the young women and stimulated their thinking about the issues covered during the session. The young women were also encouraged to keep journals and record their feelings. Finally, the young women made group presentations on asthma, diesel depots, the principles of environmental justice, and childhood lead poisoning. This practice reinforced their presentation, public speaking, and communication skills. The group was also given a qualitative and quantitative survey and evaluation. The quantitative survey focused on how much information the young women were able to retain, and the qualitative survey provided an opportunity for the young women to evaluate the instructor and educational materials and share their thoughts on areas that could be improved. All of the participants were able to identify local environmental pollutants and their effect on health; explore their local environments and identify strategies to make their environments safer and cleaner; connect local and community health issues with global struggles; identify skills needed to run an environmental justice campaign; and develop their organizing and advocacy skills through a public presentation. Exit interviews revealed that the program succeeded as well in expanding previously narrow definitions of environment and health. For example, according to one seventeen-year-old participant, "I never really thought the environment was everything around me and that I had the right, no I mean the responsibility of making sure everything was all right in it." One fifteen-year-old participant said after completing the program about the relationship between knowledge and action, "I believe all women have the rights to make their own choices—but that means being aware and involved."

WE ACT's various initiatives revealed important facts and raised new questions about environmental health, asthma prevalence, treatment, and causation in northern Manhattan—information and data that potentially have larger relevance in similar communities throughout New York City and nationally. Another interesting bridge between their environmental health research and land use planning interests can be seen in their development and sophisticated use of geographic information systems (GIS) to map their organizational concerns. WE ACT has an in-house community member trained in GIS, Carlos Jusino, who has produced maps such as the "Asthma Diesel Connection," and "MTA Diesel Bus Depots in Communities of Color" that illustrate the relationship between race, land use, and health concerns using census tract and other official data from a wide array of sources.[13] As Corburn (2005) argues, mapping in general and GIS in particular function as crucial tools that can be effective communicators of information, identity, and community. At the same time, like other kinds of maps, community maps can distort or be selective in terms of the information and perspective provided. Nonetheless, WE ACT uses them as both an environmental health and community planning research tool.

## Community-Based Planning for Environmental Justice

This section identifies how community organizations used the concept of environmental justice to create community plans to promote their neighborhoods. I examine whether the increasing importance of the language of community input in land use planning has empowered low-income and racialized minority communities to remediate the conditions of disproportionate pollution exposure. Again, the emphasis on planning as a tool to remediate environmental racism and promote environmental justice is not unique to New York City. Harwood (2003) argues that advocacy planning is an important tool to contest environmental racism. Advocacy planning, she explains, like community-based research, rejects value neutrality in planning. Rather, advocacy planners advocate for "those values on the margin, those often of low-income groups" (26). What has been underanalyzed is whether and how community-based planning for environmental justice (using the principle of "speaking for ourselves") or advocacy planning has been successful in New York City, where there has been a great deal of focus on community plans.

First, the instruments of participatory models for community planning in New York City must be explained. The New York City Charter of 1963 divided the city into sixty-two community planning boards, established as advisory bodies. Each board was given responsibility for advising the city planning commission on "any matter relating to the development or welfare of its district." In 1968, Section 84 of the charter that established community planning boards was repealed and reenacted under Local Law 39.[14] There are three main mechanisms that affect community planning: the Uniform Land Use Review Procedure enacted in the 1970s, "Fair Share," and the 197A provisions of the 1989 New York City Charter Revision.

Section 197-c of the city charter, adopted by voters on November 4, 1975, stated that "applications by any person or agency respecting the use, development, or improvement of real property subject to city regulation shall be reviewed pursuant to a uniform review procedure." On June 1, 1976, the Uniform Land Use Review Procedure (ULURP) was adopted, mandating that a community board review and vote on all land use applications, such as zoning actions, special permits, acquisition and disposition of city property, and urban renewal plans. But ULURP is only an advisory process, so the city can ignore board's votes. Fair Share regulations call for "equitable balancing considerations" in the siting of city facilities, although private facilities are exempted. Section 203 of the 1989 City Charter required the city planning commission to adopt criteria "to further the fair distribution of the burdens and benefits associated with city facilities." The charter provisions were a reaction against poorly planned and often secretive siting decisions driven by political expediency. In December 1990, the city planning commission unanimously adopted Criteria for the Location of City Facilities, commonly known as the Fair Share Criteria, which became effective in July 1991 (New York City Department of City Planning 1995). The generic name given to community plans is 197A, and most are drafted and sponsored by the local community board. According to the charter, 197A plans are "plans for the development, growth, and improvement of the city and its community districts [that] may be proposed by . . . a community board with respect to land located within its community district." However, no formal process for reviewing 197A plans was mandated. This problem was clarified by the 1989 revision of the city charter, which laid out the review procedure: by borough presidents, the city planning commission, and the city council.

After the 197A plan has been submitted to the department of city planning, a plan can be ignored, accepted, or modified. Some planners and analysts argue that a more inclusive decision-making process, a "collaborative consensus," would necessarily improve conditions for dis-empowered populations (Motley 1993, 220). Others familiar with the reality of the New York City experience have suggested that ULURP and Fair Share are limited because they lack legal power and do not repre-sent a change in zoning practice. While the city charter's original intent was that 197A plans were to be folded into the city's planning decisions, in reality these plans are often ignored. The department of city planning's institutional attitude is an important factor in whether or how commu-nity plans are taken into account. According to one critical assessment of 197A plans, "Rather than seeing community-based plans as building blocks in developing public policy, City agencies regard community plan-ning and policy planning as separate, even conflicting interests" (Munic-ipal Art Society Planning Center 1998). The major features of, and problems associated with, the 197A planning process are a lack of knowledge about and resources for planning at the community board level and the lack of DCP resources in assisting communities in the 197A planning process, reflecting a level of hostility from the department. Many people with experience of the 197A process express frustration that there is a serious disjunct between the rhetoric and the reality of community-based planning. Nevertheless, some would argue that despite the limitations of 197A plans, they still represent the best urban plan-ning being done in New York City. According to Jocelyne Chait, the author of a 1998 study of 197A planning, "My cynical side says 197A plans are a palliative. You make people think they are accomplishing something, but all we're doing is making them feel good while business goes on as usual. . . . My not so cynical side says that people will get so fired up that they will start demanding more and it will lead to changes" (Bressi 2000, 12).

As of January 2002, there were fifty-one community-based plans in New York City, as documented by the Municipal Arts Society, which coordinates a citywide task force and the Campaign for Community-Based Planning. Members of the task force were organizations that had demonstrated an interest in community planning, chose to join the cam-paign, and endorsed its platform. It has strong support and leadership from environmental justice organizations, although the campaign is not exclusively concerned with environmental justice issues. Of the thirty-seven member organizations, fifteen were groups that had worked on environmental justice issues. Significantly, many were also OWN and CURE member organizations. These plans, spearheaded largely by the local community board or community organizations, vary in structure, organization, and official status.[15]

As one flier explaining the platform says, "Community-based plans represent among the best planning done in New York City. In many poor communities, they are the ONLY planning." The Platform for Community-Based Planning in New York City is based on the following principles:

1. Planning in New York City should be community based rather than top down.
2. The city must view communities as partners, not as adversaries.
3. Community-based planning activities must be inclusive.
4. The city should commit to the implementation of completed and adopted plans.
5. Reflecting the common goals of existing community-based plans, the city should adopt the following: plans must meet citywide needs, both burdens and benefits must be equitably distributed, new developments should reflect the existing community context, traffic impacts on local communities must be minimized, a commitment must be made to improve quality of life in communities, the status of public health and a community must be incorporated into planning and environmental assessment, the city must make it possible for communities to have both jobs and a clean environment, and in meeting its infrastructure needs, the city must be guided by principles of sustainability.

It is through this last principle, expressed through the language of equitable distribution, that the environmental justice implications of community-based planning in New York City become clear. The campaign is pushing for a further implementation of the principle of Fair Share. This approach seeks to build on, but surpass, existing city policy on Fair Share provisions regarding city-owned facilities, to encompass private facilities. In a sense, this demand echoes the call for cumulative impact I described in chapter 5, and a rejection of the distinction between private and city-owned facilities and residential and commercial waste as I explained in chapter 4. The distinction between private and public facilities is seen as functionally meaningless for local communities in terms of their health effects and lived meanings.

The 197A plans from Hunts Point in the Bronx, Williamsburg, Red Hook and Sunset Park in Brooklyn, and the Harlem on the River Plan in West Harlem are all community-based plans that respond to their local needs.[16] These neighborhoods share environmental justice and health concerns and a history of activism that catalyzed interest in developing these plans. This next section focuses primarily on Sunset Park and secondarily on West Harlem.

### Sunset Park

The long stretch of waterfront in Sunset Park contains some of New York City harbor's most active and also some of its most derelict pier areas. It is in southwest Brooklyn that competing visions over local and global development are most sharply manifested, because of the potential conflict between dreams of returning the Brooklyn port to its former preeminence in global shipping and local community needs.[17] In the South Brooklyn area, there are currently plans for a container port, a cross-harbor freight tunnel connecting Brooklyn to Staten Island or New Jersey, a waterfront park, and reconstruction of the Gowanus Expressway. All of these redevelopment initiatives have the potential to vastly transform the physical, social, and economic geography of Sunset Park.

The Sunset Park waterfront extends from the mouth of the Gowanus Bay at Twenty-Ninth Street south to the Belt Parkway at Sixty-Sixth Street and east to the Gowanus Expressway/Third Avenue. There is almost no public access to the waterfront (the one exception is a single pier on Fifty-Eighth Street). The waterfront is mostly city owned, while properties between the waterfront and Third Avenue are mostly privately owned. There are also many abandoned sites, chiefly the Bush Terminal—110 acres of mostly city-owned property dotted with unused industrial buildings. This area has the second highest industrial density in Brooklyn, comprising the South Brooklyn Marine Terminal, Bush Terminal, the Sunset Industrial Park, the Brooklyn Army Terminal, and the New York Cross Harbor Railroad providing limited access to continental rail (the Cross Harbor Railroad floats 3,200 rail cars from Brooklyn to New Jersey through 1.5 miles of track at 5 mph). The site as a whole, however, contains underutilized land and facilities, vacant structures, and decayed piers. Despite this history, Sunset Park is still an active employment area.[18] There is complicated jurisdiction over the area between private and public entities, and with different city and state agencies competing for resources and influence. There is also a history of institutional hostility and competition among these agencies.[19] For example, the New York City Economic Development Corporation owns the Brooklyn Army Terminal, the Cross Harbor Rail Road, Bush Terminal, and the Sixty-Fifth Street Float Terminal, and it manages South West Brooklyn Marine Terminal. The Port Authority of New York and New Jersey owns the South Brooklyn Marine Terminal, and the Sunset Industrial Park is privately managed.

It is in Sunset Park that the tensions and trade-offs between local communities and global finance are most sharply defined and debated. Ports and international trade are historically linked, and the importance of keeping New York area ports competitive is a crucial economic issue with regional and national implications. The Port of New York and New Jersey is the nation's third largest port and growing. Estimates are that trade will roughly double in the next decade and quadruple by 2040. Seaports need to grow because virtually all international trade to and from the United States is carried on ships. Currently, the global shipping industry is undergoing a technological transformation, as the size of ships grows ever larger with the new generation of deep-draft container ships—vessels with drafts exceeding 40 to 45 feet. Container ports require sufficient depth and navigating area to be able to deliver their cargo. To accommodate these larger ships, the U.S. Army Corps of Engineers and the Port Authority proposed that the harbor's main channels be dredged on the New Jersey side to a depth of 50 feet or more. To get the port channels to the global modern standard of 50 feet, an Army Corps of Engineers Harbor Navigation Study indicated that dredging would cost nearly $1.8 billion. In 2000, the Port Authority Board of Commissioners authorized a $4 million study of harbor dredging in the Port of New York and New Jersey to identify, develop, and explore innovative and cost-effective ways to remove and dispose of sediment from the port's channels and berths. The use of old and inefficient dredging technology is also controversial because it can pull up long-buried toxic sediment in the silt, sand, and mud. One of the advantages of the Brooklyn waterfront, its advocates argue, is that there are naturally deeper depths on the New York side of the waterfront at 60 feet, thereby avoiding a costly and environmentally questionable process of channel deepening.[20]

Both the New York City Economic Development Corporation (EDC) and the Port Authority have developed plans for a container port on the

Sunset Park waterfront. The EDC is the city's official vehicle for promoting economic growth in each of the five boroughs. In 1999, it published the *Strategic Plan for the Redevelopment of the Port of New York*. In 2000, it filed proposal requests for the 95-acre marine terminal between Twenty-Ninth and Thirty-Eighth streets, looking for tenants with water cargo business. It also selected a consultant to prepare designs for transforming the old Bush Terminal Piers into a public recreational and open space area from Forty-Fourth to Fiftieth Street. This acreage would be the first public access to the waterfront in over one hundred years. This plan has the support of the Community Board 197A committee.

Sunset Park is also being challenged by the Gowanus Expressway reconstruction. This highway has deteriorated as a result of structural decay and lack of maintenance. The American Automobile Association ranks it as one of the country's ten worst traffic bottlenecks. In 1994, the NYSDOT recommended rehabilitation of the expressway with operational and safety improvements at a cost of $598 million and expected to take six and one-half years. This announcement was greeted with disappointment by community groups that sought to address the expressway reconstruction as an opportunity to address wider concerns such as economic and neighborhood development. In 1997, the Regional Plan Association (RPA) released a report, paid by the New York City Council, indicating that a tunnel to replace the elevated Gowanus Expressway was not only technically feasible but also aesthetically desirable to surrounding communities. The estimated cost of the reconstruction project is $600 million to $700 million. The potential problems of reconstruction are numerous for users and local residents. There may be serious consequences for the local neighborhood, especially if 50,000 vehicles per day have to navigate local streets during the renovation. In the worst-case scenario, there may be widespread neighborhood disruption costing $200 million, according to some estimates.

A coalition of community groups, known as the Gowanus Community Coalition and including UPROSE, sued the New York State Department of Transportation and the Federal Highway Administration, alleging that the agencies had violated the Intermodal Surface Transportation Act of 1991, which requires a major investment study before significant transportation expenditures. The groups announced a legal settlement in 2001 that gave them a formal voice in the planning process, provided for $375,000 in state money to fund a community technical adviser, and recognized their status as an official stakeholder committee. The community groups favored a tunnel alternative and were most concerned with the air pollution impacts of the reconstruction (Lueck 2001). In 2001, the NYSDOT began to study thirteen tunnel alternatives for the Gowanus Expressway.

Community challenges to the Gowanus Expressway in Brooklyn were also structurally, practically, and symbolically linked to Bronx opposition to the expansion of the Sheridan Expressway in the Bronx from the Point Community Development Corporation and We Stay/Nos Quedamos, which received technical assistance from the New York City Environmental Justice Alliance (Freilla 2004). As Elizabeth Yeampierre remarked about the various initiatives to reshape Sunset Park, "The issue is what the impact of more trucks would mean in regards to neighborhood displacement, both economic and residential. We need to protect the air, and the jobs in our community. We already have too much asthma and too few trees. Our kids and adults need and want open space *here*, not down in Bay Ridge. Also, all decisions about the rail-freight plan must consult the local community, and we always reserve the right to sue" (personal communication, April 8, 1999). She criticized the process whereby the needs of the residents who would be most affected were not directly consulted.[21]

In recognition of the community's needs, the Sunset Park 197A Plan attempted to address the decline and complex planning issues that the neighborhood faces. UPROSE, committed to an accessible and open planning process, scheduled information meetings in local churches and ensured that all materials would be translated into Spanish.[22] The 197A plan sought to preserve industrial redevelopment in an environmentally sustainable manner. The recommendations were to support the long-term use of the South Brooklyn Marine Terminal, develop a waterfront park, support the development of a state-of-the-art "green port" based on sound environmental design, reconstruct the Gowanus Expressway or replace it with a tunnel, oppose the siting of new waste transfer stations, have a moratorium of new energy plants without adequate consideration of energy conservation or alternative energy sources, promote development of ferry services to Manhattan, and examine the rezoning of manufacturing to mixed use zoning (see figure 6.1).

# Planning a "Green" Port in Sunset Park

The Port Authority of NY/NJ and the NYC Economic Development Corporation are both planning to expand Port activity in Sunset Park, Brooklyn. What will this mean for the people of Sunset Park? Will there be more jobs, or just more trucks?; more access to water, or just polluted air? The answers to these questions will affect residents for decades to come.

The United Puerto Rican Organization of Sunset Park, New York City Environmental Justice Alliance, and the Pratt Institute Center for Community and Environmental Development are holding community meetings, studying local traffic, and researching alternatives to promote a "Green" Port for Sunset Park.

## Creating a Vision

### Clean Air

Diesel emissions from trucks using the Port has made breathing difficult in the community. Residents near the Port, along the Gowanus Expressway, are hospitalized for asthma more than residents further away. Requiring that trucks servicing the Port use alternative fuels would greatly improve local air quality while benefiting the region as well.

### Green Open Space

Not much grass grows in Sunset Park, and in this waterfront neighborhood most people have never stood at the water's edge. Including a large, easily accessible, waterfront park into the layout of the Port is essential to improving waterfront access and increasing parkland in the community. This along with planting trees on adjacent streets and rooftop gardens would create green spaces and improve air quality as well.

### Job Development

In order to ensure that local residents benefit from the expected increase in jobs resulting from an expanded Port, job training programs must be put in place that target local residents. Without such training programs promised jobs are often filled by workers and managers recruited from outside the community. In addition to job training, inclusion of businesses owned and operated by people of color during both construction and operation of the Port, as well as a guarantee that existing businesses will not be displaced, are crucial to promoting economic development that actually benefits the local community.

## Creating a Vision

### Truck Reduction

Reducing dependence on trucks is a vital part of "greening" the local Port. Bringing goods into the Port via a Cross Harbor Rail Tunnel would remove tens of thousands of trucks from city streets. Beyond this, a network of shuttle trains connecting distribution centers to the Port can be developed to further reduce the need for trucks to service the Port. Both of these efforts combined would spare Sunset Park from becoming a magnet for trucks.

### Traffic Calming

Measures can be taken to ensure that trucks stay off residential streets and away from sensitive areas such as schools and hospitals. This can be done using speed humps, wider corners, and other devices that deter heavy trucks while permitting emergency vehicles to pass.

**For more information contact the United Puerto Rican Organization of Sunset Park (UPROSE)**
**Tel: (718) 492-9307 – Fax: (718) 492-9030 – E-mail: UPRISE99@aol.com**

**Figure 6.1**
UPROSE green port flier

But these visions are difficult to enact. Consider funding cuts and changing electoral representation, which complicated plans for the waterfront park. Most of the elected officials who supported the park when it was announced in 2000 no longer represented the area due to mandated electoral term limits. According to the Port Authority, in denying a request for $50 million from the waterfront development fund due to a post-9/11 reevaluation, there was a belief that the authority has "no longer had a role in South Brooklyn" (Farrell 2003).

Despite these setbacks, UPROSE is engaged in community-based planning through other avenues. For example, it has been a key community supporter of the Brooklyn Greenway project, with ultimate plans to connect the bridges over the East River and throughout the city to downtown Brooklyn. This project, supported by funding secured by Congresswoman Nydia Velázquez, is to create a continuous waterfront and recreational space in areas with minimal access. These funds are for the study, design, and construction of a greenway/bikeway and pedestrian access project, including the development of esplanades and bikeways, boat and ferry landing connections, open space, interpretive signage, and safety improvements. UPROSE has sponsored community planning meetings (see figure 6.2) where diverse members of the community envision what the space should look like, with areas for tai chi, and small food vendors (Yeampierre, personal communication, November 15, 2005).

## West Harlem

In West Harlem, as in Sunset Park, conflicts over the direction of waterfront development have flared up in recent years. The city-owned property on the West Harlem waterfront used to be a vibrant area, home to ferry services to New Jersey, Brooklyn, and upstate, with an expansive view of the Hudson River and New Jersey. The area used to be a center for commerce and recreation. Just inland from the waterfront was a thriving manufacturing area, filled with meatpackers and doll manufacturers. The area fell into disrepair over the past half-century, into a litter-strewn stretch of asphalt, largely devoid of people and populated by storage facilities, auto repair shops, gas stations, and parking lots. Its current use is largely restricted to a few people fishing and as a parking lot for the popular Fairway supermarket under the West Side Highway.

**Figure 6.2**
UPROSE community greenway meeting

There are two competing plans to develop the area: the Harlem West Plan and the Harlem on the River Plan. According to government estimates, about $20.2 million in public funds would be needed to redevelop this stretch of the waterfront, with another $4.7 million in public investment (Pristin 2002). The Harlem West Plan was organized by the New York City Economic Development Corporation and is advised by the West Harlem Working Committee, a broad base of local constituents, agencies, and elected officials. The Harlem on the River Plan was a comprehensive community plan, established through a community-driven planning process, initiated by WE ACT, in conjunction with Community Board 9 and other community actors. In January 2000, the DEC announced its commitment to use the Harlem on the River Plan as the benchmark for the Harlem Piers Master Plan Study rather than private developer proposals. The plan received $800,000 from the New York Clean Water Clean Air Bond Act and Environmental Protection Fund.

WE ACT became involved with waterfront planning because of its activism around the North River sewage treatment plant located on the Hudson River and its concern over the historical and continued inequity in open space and parks development and funding (Cecil Corbin Mark, personal communication, December 12, 2001). Its specific recommendations were in the areas of economic development, parks and open space, transportation, arts/culture/entertainment, urban design, environmental restoration, and history. The Harlem on the River Plan featured a landscaped park area along the riverfront, a walkway, a bikeway, and a pier for water-dependent uses (recreational and fishing), including an aquatic learning center. The plan also included connections to Riverside Park and restored piers for ferry service. It featured wholesale and retail marketplace development with entertainment, art, and cultural uses and emphasized improved safety and traffic design to reduce vehicular accidents.

Charles Rangel, the powerful Harlem congressman, sponsored a competing waterfront proposal for the same area that sought to turn the piers into a tourist-driven entertainment center, including a riverboat proposal that could accommodate 2,000 people. WE ACT objected to this plan because of its emphasis on corporate development. As Peggy Shepard said, "The issue becomes, who is the waterfront being developed for? Is it a community benefit, for a community that has been disproportionately affected by pollution on the waterfront, or is it for someone else? Historically, this community has been opposed to the notion that the waterfront is for someone else" (Pristin 2003). Neither the Harlem on the River Plan nor the Rangel-sponsored plan has seen action. The Department of City Planning sent back the Harlem on the River Plan with further recommendation (Municipal Arts Society 2004).

## Contributions and Limits of Community-Based Planning Initiatives

To different degrees, 197A and community plans emerging from communities with a history of environmental justice activism addressed the need for waterfront revitalization and for open space and recreation, housing, and a holistic approach to community development. These plans shared certain features, particularly an inclusive planning process that involved multiple stakeholders and a major leadership role for environmental justice community-based organizations. The careful attention to participatory process was a direct result of the politics of the environmental justice movement, especially the concerns for procedural justice, and formed as a response to the systematic exclusion that these communities have experienced from larger planning, development, and political processes. The form of that inclusive process generally meant, at a minimum, public planning meetings or design processes and Spanish translation.

The plans addressed waterfront development in communities that are all on the waterfront and zoned for manufacturing or mixed use. Many members of community-based organizations involved in these 197A plans were also members of OWN and CURE—West Harlem Environmental Action, UPROSE, the Point, and El Puente, to name a few. The prominence of waste facilities in community plans (the Red Hook plan called for a moratorium on waste transfer stations, for example) was not surprising. Policy changes on solid waste and energy, in addition to the 1992 release by the department of city planning of the Comprehensive Waterfront Plan covering the more than 500 miles of city waterfront, were the two main reasons that waterfront issues became dominant (Bressi 2000). Additionally, as struggles against environmental racism gained prominence in the 1980s and 1990s, a greater level of awareness shaped how communities of color on the waterfront envisioned their access to the waterfront and open space as focal points for environmental justice activism.

It is difficult to make generalizations about the success of environmental justice–driven community plans relative to one another and to the broader universe of 197A plans. The Red Hook and the Williamsburg plans are two of the select few that have been approved by the city council. Others (West Harlem, Sunset Park, and Hunts Point) have not yet had any action taken on them due to a variety of funding and political matters. The experience of those engaged in the 197A process suggests that plans go through an intensive political vetting process that transforms "feel-good" vision documents into plans that have a chance of passing agency and city council review. For example, the Red Hook moratorium on waste transfer stations and truck routes was eliminated as unrealistic and contrary to the larger citywide needs as defined by the DCP (Bressi 2000).

What accounts for these differences between various plans' implementation and successes has to do with degrees of political power and mobilization of technical and professional resources, linked at least in

part to race and class considerations (Gregory 1998). That is why critics
of the city's approach to 197A plans have focused on their larger political impacts. Thus, the generally obstructionist way in which the city has
in the past treated, and continues today to treat, these plans adds to the
distrust and frustration felt by many low-income and minority residents
and can contribute to disengagement from the governing, development,
and planning processes more broadly. Other analysts have suggested that
the goal of community-based planning is not to do planning for planning's sake through a 197A process, but to work on implementation of
a vision through a normal zoning process or a community revitalization
plan.

## Conclusion

Despite the difficulty in making broad generalizations about the success
of community planning and of community-based environmental health
asthma research in New York City, the similarity of their visions and
programs must be recognized. Community plans stand as a testament to
the historical roots of the problems that particular communities face and
provide a guide (if not a consensus) on what must happen for remediation of environmental injustices in New York City. Community planning
cannot be divorced from other planning and community development
processes. Urban failure, decades in the making, makes it exceedingly
difficult for recent proposals to provide a quick fix. However, the process
of developing community capacity and vision represented at least a
partial success. Despite the nonaction on the Hunts Point Plan, for
example, the executive director of a community-based organization, Sustainable South Bronx, maintains that "the plan itself is not as important
as the *planning process* that gets the community active in envisioning its
own future, instead of always fighting something coming in" (Majora
Carter, personal communication, March 1, 2002). For communities long
disempowered from the political process, some argue that the act of
coming together and envisioning their future is an important and a profoundly political and proactive act.

The same can be said about community-based environmental health
and asthma research. WE ACT contributed to the greater awareness of
the asthma problem in New York City. Asthma rates in New York City

finally started to fall in the late 1990s, because of increased awareness and innovative programs (Santora 2005). Their health politics made larger ideological contributions to the broader debates on air pollution, disease causation, and collective illness experiences in the United States (Brown et al. 2003).

# Conclusion: What We Can Learn from New York City Environmental Justice Activism

On November 20, 2004, residents of the tony Upper East Side protested in the cold rain against Mayor Bloomberg's announcement that the Ninety-First Street marine transfer station would be reopened (a key OWN victory as described in chapter 4). As outraged residents chanted, " 'Stop the garbage! It stinks!' " five garbage trucks rented especially for the occasion blasted horns. One resident said, "The noise and smell will be absolutely terrible. . . . I'm angry that they would even think of putting it here." Another added, "It's going to be Cancer Alley here" (Ma 2004).

There are a few important things to note about this protest. First, the facility was already there. The proposal was not to "put it there" but to reopen an existing site, with the explicit aim of lowering truck traffic and air pollution from waste transfer stations in Brooklyn, the South Bronx, and Queens. Second, the reference to Cancer Alley was ironic given the term's centrality in the national environmental justice movement. Cancer Alley has a particular racial and regional meaning that was erased in this protest. That garbage trucks were rented for the occasion also speaks to the class privilege of the protesters and of the neighborhood in general. But perhaps what is most significant is that OWN members were there to protest the protest and to ask East Siders in particular, and Manhattan in general, to look at who would be affected by their actions and to handle their fair share of the city's garbage. As Eddie Bautista said, "This [East Side protest] is a massive display of NIMBY and privilege and it's one what Brooklyn, Queens, and the Bronx will fight back against" (Colangelo 2004).

Environmental justice activism in New York City does not, on the face of it, answer or solve the crucial issues that face the city in terms of garbage, sewage, sludge, and energy. That is too high an expectation for local communities and activists to bear, especially given the long history of poor planning on these issues on larger scales (city, state, and federal). But this activism enables better questions to be asked than those that predominate where there is no environmental justice activism. Who benefits from particular policies? Who is hurt? How does history shape the distrust that particular neighborhoods feel toward the city and why? What if policy priorities shifted (toward principles such as fair share for garbage, increasing recycling or increasing energy efficiency) rather than moving to wholesale privatization of solid waste and energy deregulation where these questions cannot be asked (much less answered)? Why are asthma rates in Harlem and the South Bronx so high? What does it mean for so many black and Latino youth to live with asthma? What do race, class, gender, and geography have to do with all of these?

Ultimately this study of environmental justice activism suggests what happens when you center the lives of those usually disenfranchised from the policy process: the young and the old, the working class and people of color. The answer, as the New York City experience shows, is better policy and environmental conditions for everyone. Without environmental justice activism, the North River sewage treatment plant would still stink daily (instead of being repaired and closely monitored), the Navy Yard incinerator and the Sunset Park treatment plants would have been built to line the coffers of corporate investors, and the corrupt Bronx-Lebanon facility would have been still running with its daily violations of toxic releases. Garbage would be moved exclusively by diesel truck instead of by barge (and perhaps someday by rail) and energy plants built wherever profits could be squeezed. All the while, asthma rates, deaths, and hospitalizations would continue to spiral for youth of color in particular neighborhoods in the city.

Environmental justice activists intervened in all of these complex policy disputes, centering their communities and what these facilities and policies meant in terms of their health and environmental impacts. The perspectives of environmental justice activism dovetail with more general demands for greater public accountability and environmental democracy. Environmental justice activists in New York City also made their case using a racially specific analysis that prioritized their local experiences and perspectives, including those of children and families. They made more democratic crucial debates that were not really debates before they entered. They absorbed the technocratic language of how these issues were dealt with without letting this perspective dominate their world-view. They simultaneously became advocates, community planners, and health workers. And their frameworks are indebted to sanitarians and health activists from the past.

Environmental justice activism is not simple and without conflict. Environmental justice groups diverged on specific policies, from the con-flicts in the South Bronx (over the paper recycling facility and American Marine Rail) to WE ACT's objection to the reopening of a marine trans-fer station in West Harlem, which put it at odds with OWN. Nonethe-less, these groups still shared community and racial histories and histories of activism acting for environmental justice. They also shared a racial perspective that framed their adoption of the precautionary prin-ciple, cumulative risk, and endorsement of community-based research on health and land use planning. Like many movements before, individual groups and personalities split and fissures were created. That itself is a sign of democracy. The larger question, which demands further atten-tion, is what individual groups and the movement writ large learn from these conflicts.

I end with a few examples that illustrate the continuing complexity and relevance of the issues discussed in the book. First is the new-found resurgence of recycling in New York City. In 1997, Visy Paper, a local subsidiary of an Australian recycling corporation, opened a plant on Staten Island when the city gave it rights for a large paper processing facility. Since then, the company has paid $7 a ton for the right to turn city paper into corrugated boxes. This successful contract paved the way for Hugo Neu to sign a twenty-year agreement for a material recovery facility in Sunset Park. Unlike the contentious paper recycling plant in the South Bronx, local groups supported the agreement. UPROSE sup-ported the plant in part because the company agreed to build an envi-ronmental education center on the waterfront and in part because it consulted with sectors of the community. At the same time, UPROSE also negotiated with the New York Power Authority (NYPA), which it had previously sued over its turbines, for the purchase of four hybrid electric shuttle buses that were given to UPROSE, the Chinese-American Planning Council, the Sunset Park Senior Center, and Al Noor School.

Thus, this shows that in Sunset Park, UPROSE does not fight all facilities and all agencies for the sake of fighting. In other words, the perspective is not NIMBY or BANANA (Build Absolutely Nothing Anywhere Near Anything). Rather, their perspective, like the environmental justice perspective generally, is based on community building in a broadly expansive sense. This is perhaps exemplified by their annual Baby Justice Day (see figure C.1), organized by their teen group for young children and the community at large to learn about the environment, peace, and justice through arts and crafts, book readings, and games. Their experience shows it is not only possible but desirable to work with communities, especially those that have long histories of being neglected (by the likes of Robert Moses). But to do so, corporations and agencies have to work with communities. That sounds trite, but in reality, that perspective is often ignored. Working with people is not necessarily obstructionist and counterproductive. It may seem easier to stick with tons per waste and megawatts produced, but in the long run, under-

**Figure C.1**
UPROSE Baby Justice Day, 2004

standing the histories of particular neighborhoods and the perspectives of environmental justice activists leads to a greater ability to work through, not blow past, these conflicts. In other words, increase procedural justice and accountability, and we are more likely, as a society and a city, to increase distributive equity of pollution.

President Clinton's 1994 executive order signified the strength of the environmental justice movement in the policy realm in recognizing how race and class affect environmental policy and the life and well-being of disenfranchised communities. In the decade that followed, the movement saw many gains and losses, especially at the state level (Targ 2005). The recent political marginalization of the perspectives of the movement is exemplified by the Bush administration and the EPA's recent (albeit failed) attempt to minimize a particular meaning of environmental justice. In June 2005, EPA announced that it was removing race and class from special consideration in its definition of environmental justice and set a controversial and abbreviated public comment period. Although it backed down from this position, the concept of environmental justice is still quite vulnerable.[1]

The moment of danger that environmental justice activists face, in New York City and nationally, is a political climate in which the forces that produce the health, environmental, and community assaults they experience are gaining strength and with fewer restraints. Thus, the irony is that the moment when discussions of environmental racism are potentially disappearing from the public sphere and reaching a nadir is precisely the moment when the importance of the principles of the environmental justice movement, protecting the interests of racialized communities and that of the public interest and democracy, is increasing in intensity.

# Notes

## Introduction

1. Garcia was a community leader who fought the city's urban renewal plan, which would have displaced thousands of residents in the Melrose Commons section of the Bronx. Garcia died from a heart attack while this book was written.

2. Asthma is a national problem. Asthma prevalence increased by 52 percent for those ages five to thirty-four between 1982 and 1996 (Wilson et al. 1998).

3. The United Church of Christ wrote the important 1987 report, *Toxic Waste and Race*, which suggested that race was the most significant among the variables tested in association with the location of commercial hazardous waste facilities. Three out of five African Americans and Hispanic Americans and approximately half of all Asians, Pacific Islanders, and Native Americans lived in communities with uncontrolled toxic waste sites (Lee 1993).

4. The National Law Journal Investigation on Race and Protection from Environmental Hazards (September 21, 1992) is discussed in Lavelle and Coyle (1993). For example, there are lower penalties for environmental violations in minority communities. According to the report, which looked at penalties for environmental pollution, "the disparity under the toxic waste laws occurs by race alone, not income. Penalties at sites having the greatest white population were 500 percent higher than penalties with the greatest minority population."

5. A key event in the environmental justice movement is the letter written by Richard Moore of the Southwest Organizing Project and cosigned by 100 community-based activists to the heads of eight prominent national environmental organizations. It highlighted the lack of diversity of staff and of programs, as well as their reliance on corporate funding (Tokar 1997).

6. In 1997, President Clinton also issued an executive order, "Protection of Children from Environmental Health Risks and Safety Risks" (see Gibbs 2002). This order is applicable to the discussion on environmental justice, especially with regard to pesticides and chemicals. See also Garg and Landrigan (2002).

7. Bullard's report, *Environment and Morality: Confronting Environmental Racism in the United States* (2004), provides a good overview of what kinds of issues fall under the rubric of environmental racism.

8. For a comprehensive overview of environmental justice research, see Bowen (2001). For a discussion of first- and second-generation environmental justice research, see Williams (1999). Bowen (2002) argues there is not enough information available to make conclusions about racial environmental disproportionality. The race-versus-class debate pivots around whether a particular population preceded a neighborhood's locally undesirable land uses (LULU), or simply put, which came first: the people or the pollution. For example, one school argues that disadvantaged groups migrate to where land values are cheap and zoning allows industrial use (Been and Gupta 1997). A countervailing view argues that the LULUs are sited where populations are low income or racial minorities (Pastor, Sadd, and Hipp 2001). This tends to be especially stark in the South, where racial zoning was a key tool in segregation (Silver 1997).

9. Morello-Frosch, Pastor, and Sadd's (2002) study of ambient air toxics exposure and health risks among school children in Los Angeles found that African American and Latino youth bear the largest share of the burden of air pollution risks and that these respiratory hazards associated with air toxins appear to have a negative effect on school performance.

## Chapter 1

1. This chapter is not the first attempt to use environmental history as a way to understand environmental justice activism in New York City. Dolores Greenberg (2000) discusses how the conditions of urban life and environmental ills were political issues in the Progressive era in New York City.

2. This also included limited or contingent contagionism—or the belief that infectious diseases are a result of contagion, either specific or nonspecific. Contagion believers held that the diseases could not act except in conjunction with other elements, such as the state of the atmosphere, condition of the soil, or social factors (Rosen 1993).

3. Hygeia outlined the elements of climate, site selection, water supply, storage, street layout, park system, and housing design that together would reduce mortality and transform cities into an ideal environment (Schultz and McShane 1978).

4. Peterson (1979) suggests that sanitary reform proceeded from an environmental premise about the causation of disease rather than from a true interest in the urban setting. That is, sanitary reformers were health planners by design and urban planners by historical necessity due to the fact that nineteenth-century urban populations suffered disproportionately from epidemics related to filth conditions.

5. Specifically, he cites the fragmented quality of twentieth-century urban planning in practice between specialists who worked in ignorance of one another—architects, engineers, traffic consultants, landscape designers, and housing experts, among others.

6. Schultz and McShane (1978) offer a specific look at different professional identities in the sanitary reform movement, suggesting that engineers held a special role through their possession of technical expertise. They outline the professional constituencies concerned with sewers and city planning. Engineers, public health sanitarians, and landscape architects all called for physical solutions to environmental problems, but engineers, seen as incorruptible experts, were the most influential.

7. The role of engineers in the emerging profession of city planning was large. Of the fifty-two charter members of the American Institute of Planning in 1917, thirteen were engineers. Only the landscape architecture profession provided more members, and several of them had some engineering training (Schultz and McShane 1978). Kirschner (1978) documents the adoption of fixed qualifications and formal training in social work, public health, and city planning.

8. The one major exception may be found in the case of a major environmental infrastructure development, water systems. Economic historian Werner Troesken, in *Water, Race and Disease* (2004), argues that African Americans were not discriminated against relative to white residents in terms of the benefits of water supply and waste removal and their impact on overall mortality, typhoid mortality, and waterborne disease. That African Americans benefited from sewage systems is a result of factors such as the relatively high rates of racially mixed communities and the high costs of developing different sewage systems for racial populations.

9. Washington declared at the National Negro Health Week inaugural activities in Baltimore: "I am glad of this movement that it emphasizes the matter of health, the matter of cleanliness, the matter of better sanitary conditions. When food is being prepared, the Negro woman touches the white man's life; when food is being served, the Negro woman touches the white man's life; when children are being nursed, the Negro woman touches the white man's life; when clothes are being laundered, the Negro woman touches the white man's life" (*New York Age*, April 1, 1916).

10. In contrast, zoning in the South was explicitly racialized. See Silver (1997).

11. Another factor was the influence of modernist architecture. Several commentators on the vision underlying the 1961 resolution critique its "antiurban" bias (codified through new zoning requirements) on the part of architects— specifically the vision of the "tower" in the park model of design, a vision that encouraged high "superblocks" for open space, but which paradoxically discouraged street life. This model for housing and office space contrasts to small-scale design elements (Strickland 1993).

## Chapter 2

1. Community boards are local representative bodies in New York City. There are fifty-nine throughout the city. Each consists of up to fifty unsalaried members appointed by the borough president, with half nominated by the city council

members who represent the community district. Board members are selected by the borough presidents. The antecedent to community boards are community planning councils, which began in 1951. The 1989 charter revision clarified the role of community boards in environmental review, but they lack much power in influencing planning and land use decisions (I discuss this problem in chapter 6).

2. Nationally, from 1998 to 2001, the amount of municipal solid waste grew by 66.6 millions tons, or 20 percent, to a total of 409 million tons per year. Of that total, about 60 percent is landfilled, 7 percent is incinerated, and 33 percent is recycled and composted. The number of landfills is declining every year due to reaching of capacity or being shut down for pollution (Goldstein and Madtes 2001).

3. In rejecting the garbage-as-symbol/garbage-as-crisis approach, Miller (2000) echoes garbage historians who focus on the development of garbage policy and management from a technocratic approach, notably Melosi, along with garbage archaeologists like William Rathje.

4. This statement does not mean that cities or consumption preexisted capitalism and industrialism. Rather, these processes took unique shape under modernity under industrial society. Social historian Susan Strasser focuses directly on garbage for what it reveals about the changing nature of production and consumption in the United States. In documenting the history of trash making and reuse in *Waste and Want: A Social History of Trash* (1999), she argues that reuse was central to American culture and economy from the colonial period until the late nineteenth century. This system was replaced by the "throwaway culture" because industrialization and economic growth in the twentieth century were fueled by trash. She also argues that rubbish took on new meanings and forms in an emerging consumer culture.

5. Kitchen waste as feed for pigs and poultry remained an essential part of the waste handling picture until the early 1950s, with 650 tons per swill collected, equivalent to approximately 16 percent of the total incineration capacity (Gandy 1994).

6. Not all garbage was dumped at sea: waste streams in different boroughs faced separate fates. For example, Manhattan and Bronx garbage was dumped at sea, and the ashes and garbage dumped at Rikers Island. Brooklyn garbage was dumped at sea, its ashes were dumped in Queens by a private contract, and its rubbish was incinerated by a private firm. Queens garbage, ash, and rubbish were incinerated and used for roads, like that of Staten Island (Corey 1994).

7. Packaging is thought to contribute about 35 percent of the weight and 50 percent of the volume of household waste in developed countries (Gandy 1994).

8. Unlike incineration facilities in Britain and Europe, few incinerators in the United States ever generated useful energy, in part because of the economic structure of incinerator construction. In Europe, incineration facilities were designed and built under the sponsorship of municipal entities, which focused on the longterm horizon, while U.S. plants were built by private interests concerned with maximizing their short-term profits. The American facilities, reflecting the short-

cuts taken in the design and construction, burned inefficiently, were often out of service, and proved expensive to operate (Miller 2000).

9. In 1952, 4,000 Londoners died from smoke and fog, and many dropped dead in the streets. A year later, a similar blanket of fog killed 200 New Yorkers (Crenson 1971). In New York City, a new agency, the Bureau of Smoke Abatement, campaigned to make apartment incinerators illegal (Miller 2000).

10. These annually emitted 50,000 more tons of greenhouse gases, methane and carbon dioxide combined; thousands of additional tons of nonmethane polyaromatic hydrocarbons such as benzene, styrene, and toluene; and hundreds of additional tons of chlorinated organics such as vinyl chloride and trichloroethane (Miller 2000).

11. Incineration opponents identified at least three major problems with incineration. First, energy production from solid waste acts as an incentive against waste reduction, since there is a need for a constant supply of garbage to feed the incinerators. Second, it is costly. Third, it produces toxic ash, which must then be landfilled.

12. The Clean Water Act is the primary federal law that protects U.S. waters, including lakes, rivers, aquifers, and coastal areas. The act had two fundamental national goals: to eliminate the discharge of pollutants into the nation's waters and achieve water quality levels sale for fishing and swimming.

13. Sludge can be disposed of in five ways, each with different benefits and costs (both economic and environmental): incineration, landfill dumping, ocean dumping, gasification (using sludge to generate methanol or energy), and using sludge as plant fertilizer.

14. The basic provisions of the act have remained virtually unchanged since 1972, when it was enacted to establish a comprehensive waste management system to regulate disposal or dumping of all materials into marine waters that are within U.S. jurisdiction.

15. New York City has also been sued by environmentalists in federal court by the State of Connecticut and New York State for discharging excessive amount of nitrogen-rich waste water into Long Island Sound. Nitrogen pollution creates algae bloom, which can pollute water, foul beaches, and threaten the marine food chain (Saving the Sound, 1998).

16. For a good description and history of this controversy, see Stauber and Rampton (1995). Additionally, in 2000, at a hearing before the Committee of Science of the U.S. House of Representatives, testimony was given regarding EPA's strong-arm tactics against its own agency scientists who cautioned over the lack of credible science on the changing sludge rules (Hearing Before the Committee on Science House of Representatives. One Hundred Sixth Congress, Second Session. March 22, 2000. "EPA's Sludge Rule: Closed Minds or Open Debate," 2000).

17. Dioxin is the name for family of chlorinated organic compounds that are never produced intentionally but are synthesized when benzene rings (compounds that form the basic building blocks of materials such as wood paper and

petrochemical products) combine with chlorine (found in nature in some plants, water, and soil and in manufactured products such as bleach paper, pesticides, and chlorinated plastics). Dioxin was first identified as a by-product of the manufacture of pesticides and herbicides such as DDT and Agent Orange. Disease transmission from spreading sewage sludge on land comes from the microbial pathogens in sludge, such as Taenia and other parasitic flatworms, Ascaris and parasitic roundworms, Protozoan parasites, bacterial pathogens (such as salmonella), and viruses like viral gastroenteritis and viral hepatitis (Lewis-Jones and Winkler 1991).

18. According to the Centers for Disease Control, Class B poses a potential health risk from *E. coli*, salmonella, hepatitis B, and other diseases (Hawthorne 2001). Class B, while more toxic, is more valuable than Class A as a fertilizer because of the strength and number of organisms in it, primarily its nitrogen value (Clapp and Orlando 2002).

19. In 2000, the National Institute for Occupational Safety and Health (NIOSH) released a hazard warning for workers who handle or inhale Class B sludge fertilizer, advising that exposure could pose the risk of either the onset of disease (e.g., gastroenteritis) or in a carrier state of a disease (such as typhoid). In its warning, NIOSH said that because data are sparse on what constitutes an infective dose, workers' contact with soil or dusts containing Class B biosolids should be minimized during the restricted periods.

20. These were proposed for Red Hook and Sunset Park in Brooklyn, two on Wards Island in the East River, Mariners Harbor in Staten Island, two in Maspeth in Queens near the highly polluted Newtown Creek, and in Hunts Point in the South Bronx.

21. According to the NYCDEP, approximately 37 percent is used for land application, 42 percent for thermal drying, 13 percent for composting, and 8 percent for alkaline stabilization.

22. Not surprisingly, the contract process was heavily criticized for its high costs. (Contracts to two companies in 1991 cost the city $580 million. One company charged the city $237 per ton, higher than average.) The contract process was also accused of political patronage and corruption. The Manhattan district attorney subpoenaed documents from the New York Department of Environmental Protection concerning the contracts to investigate the complex relationships between Dinkins administration officials and supporters. The first deputy mayor, Norman Steisel, Democratic National chairman Ronald Brown, campaign counsel Harold Ickes, and Armand D'Amato, brother to New York's senator Alfonse D'Amato, all had financial stakes in the companies that sought contracts or represented their interests before the city (Flynn 1992). The city was forced to dump one of its contracts for $210 million with Chemfix, a company under fire for its poor operating record with ties to Ronald Brown. Brown served on Chemfix's board, and his law firm represented the company in negotiations with the city (Flynn and Calderone 1991b).

23. Riverdale, a predominantly white, upper-income community, was the early focal point of activism. Alyssa Eilenberg, of the Riverdale Committee for Clean

Air, which had formed to help phase out apartment incinerators, was the first to find out about the incinerator, and it was her husband who was legal counsel for the first lawsuit (Sturim, personal communication, July 7, 1999).

24. Medical waste is divided into two general categories: general and special waste. Special waste requires special handling, treatment, and disposal. There are three categories of special waste: chemical, infectious, and radioactive. Infectious waste is known as biomedical, biohazardous, contaminated, and red bag waste. In the United States, over 400,000 medical facilities produce close to half a million tons of infectious waste per year.

25. The coalition shrewdly made national contacts, specifically with the Health Care Without Harm Campaign, a project of the Center for Health, Environment and Justice (formerly known as Citizens' Clearinghouse on Hazardous Waste, the organization Lois Gibbs founded after Love Canal). Love Canal is considered a milestone in contemporary environmental and antitoxics activism. In August 1978, President Jimmy Carter declared a federal emergency at the Love Canal, a former chemical landfill that became a 15-acre neighborhood of the City of Niagara Falls, New York.

26. Waste-to-energy (WTE) facilities handled almost none of the waste stream in 1960. The 1980s saw a rapid increase of WTE construction.

27. In 1936, 8,000 people worked at the facility; by the end of the war, 75,000 worked at the Navy Yard. While not unique to the Brooklyn Navy Yard, defense work was highly segregated by race and gender (by 1941, only 3 percent of 120,000 New Yorkers in defense work were black). Rampant racism at the Navy Yard by private contractors receiving public funds was investigated by the War Manpower Commission and the Fair Employment Practices Commission (Wilder 2000).

28. Miller's account (2000) details the conflicts between and among environmentalist groups, based on different strategies. He focuses on Barry Commoner, the father of the modern environmental movement, and Commoner's analysis of the hard and soft paths of environmental politics in explaining conflicts between Commoner, two national environmental organizations (Natural Resources Defense Council and Environmental Defense Fund), and the New York Public Interest Research Group. Commoner writes, "There is in fact a hard path and a soft path in environmental politics. . . . The soft path is easy one; it accepts the private corporate governance of production decisions and seeks only to regulate the resultant environmental impact. . . . The hard path is a difficult one; it would confront the real source of environmental degradation—the technology choice—and debate who should govern it and what purpose. The hard path is the only workable route to the soft environmental path" (quoted in Miller 2000, 247).

29. Toxics Release Inventory (TRI) facilities are those that must report their releases to the U.S. Environmental Protection Agency. TRI is a publicly available database of information on the release and transfer of nearly 650 chemicals by private companies and government. TRI is mandated by the Emergency Planning and Community Right-to-Know Act (EPCRA) of 1986. According to E.P.A., the law is based on the premise that citizens have a right to know about potentially

harmful chemicals in their communities in order to provide planning for response to chemical accidents, and to provide the public and the government with information about possible chemical hazards.

30. Curlee et al. (1994) document the regulatory changes that led to increased WTE construction, primarily from the post–oil crisis legislation that sought to increase alternative energy sources. This study also documents the consolidation of this industry into few megacorporations, as well as the changing tax policy and regulatory uncertainty of the 1990s that contributed to the abandonment of a number of WTE projects.

31. Rohatyn was a prominent and controversial New York City political and financial leader. The bonds for the incinerator were offered by Rohatyn's investment firm, Lazard Freres. He served on the board of the New York Stock Exchange from 1968 to 1972. From 1975 to 1993, he was chairman of the Municipal Assistance Corporation (MAC) of the City of New York. The MAC was founded to guide New York City out of its fiscal crisis. It did so, critics charged, by clamping down on unions and wages (Fitch 1993).

32. More critically, Miller (2000), who witnessed the campaign in his capacity as director of policy planning for the DOS, suggests the effect of the campaign as primarily a destructive one: "[it] made common currency the magical belief that landfilled ash is more dangerous than raw garbage and made politically correct the notion that exporting ash outside the city was not an acceptable alternative. Accepting these premises left no logical alternative but to recycle everything the City's 7.4 million citizens threw away" (261).

33. Miller (1994, 718).

34. The capacity of the plant was an ongoing concern because the moment the plant opened, it reached its operating capacity. In 1995, the Coalition for a Livable West Side filed an intention to sue under the Clean Water Act because the plant suddenly "lost" 24 million gallons of sewage, thereby paving the way for approval of Donald Trump's massive Riverside South housing development to be added to the city's sewage system (Bunch 1995).

35. According to the New York City Department of Environmental Protection (D.E.P.), construction of the treatment plant went forward in two phases. Work on the advanced preliminary treatment facilities began in 1983; the secondary treatment facilities were started in 1985. In March 1986, advanced preliminary treatment went into operation, eliminating the daily discharge of raw sewage into the Hudson River for the first time in the city's history while secondary treatment began in April 1991. When advanced preliminary treatment began in 1986, it was immediately beset by odors, the source of which D.E.P could not determine for years.

These odors intensified when the plant began its secondary treatment to remove an additional 15 percent of the pollutants up to 85 percent (up from 60 percent). Foul air is collected in a two-step filtering process: the air passes through a chlorine-based scrubbing system and then enters a carbon filter before it is discharged through its stacks. Engineers suggested that perhaps the roof's poor design collected smelly air until gusts from the river blew it through the arches into the community; that the odor came from bacterial action creating hydrogen sulfide stemming from either a broken line of the system handling too much waste; or that staff at the plant were too poorly trained to know what to do.

36. Citywide allies also included Latino leaders and environmental groups, like the New York City Environmental Justice Alliance and New York Lawyers for the Public Interest.

37. This initiative was staffed by Michelle de la Uz, who was U.S. Representative Nydia Velasquez's community liaison at the time. Velasquez, the first Puerto Rican elected representative to Congress, is a major supporter of environmental justice campaigns. Information on Sunset United comes from interviews with de la Uz conducted in 1999.

## Chapter 3

1. President Clinton issued Executive Order 13045, Protection of Children from Environmental Health Risks and Safety Risks, on April 23, 1997, in recognition "of the growing body of scientific information demonstrating that America's children suffer disproportionately from environmental health and safety risks." The order directed each federal agency to identify, assess, and address those risks. The order also created the Task Force on Environmental Health Risks and Safety Risks to Children, cochaired by the secretary of health and human services and the administrator of the Environmental Protection Agency. The task force identified four priority areas: childhood asthma, unintentional injuries, developmental disorders, and childhood cancer (President's Task Force on Environmental Health Risks and Safety Risks to Children, 1999). The task force's 1999 report, *Asthma and the Environment: A Strategy to Protect Children*, identifies joint federal efforts by several departments to reduce asthma onset and attacks as well as asthma health disparities.

2. Many studies on gender and environmental justice focus on similar dynamics, in terms of how identity (defined by class, gender, or race) shapes the way in which debates on health impacts are received. See Di Chiro (1998), Krauss's (1992) work on blue-collar women working on antitoxics campaigns, and Epstein (1997). Allen (2003) offers a different take on science, women, and expertise in a study that focuses on feminist health and science workers.

3. This rise in asthma is not unique to the United States, leading some to speculate that asthma is actually a complex disease of civilization that reflects worldwide changes in how people live, especially in relation to livestock and animals (Shell 2000).

4. A number of studies have found that mainland Puerto Ricans have a higher rate of asthma compared with other Hispanic groups. The occurrence of childhood asthma is three times as high in Puerto Rican children compared with non-Hispanic white children. A study of more than 3,000 Hispanics in New York found that overall, Puerto Ricans reported a 13.2 percent asthma prevalence rate, compared with 5.3 percent among Dominicans and other Latinos (Ledogar et al.

2000). In addition to having higher asthma prevalence rates, Puerto Ricans also have higher asthma death rates compared with other Hispanic groups, as well as with whites and non-Hispanic blacks. According to Beckett et al. (1996), Puerto Ricans had an age-adjusted annual asthma death rate of 40.9 per million, followed by Cuban Americans (15.8) and Mexican Americans (9.2). The rate of non-Hispanic whites was 14.7 per million, and non-Hispanic blacks, 38.1 per million.

5. At least one theorist of asthma describes quality of life with asthma with similarly complex dimensions—what he calls the "existential and the aesthetic" (Drummond 2000).

6. The primary sources nationally are older coal-fired power plants, industrial boilers, and gas- and diesel-powered vehicles.

7. Particulate exposure might also increase susceptibility to bacterial or viral respiratory infections, leading to an increased incidence of pneumonia in vulnerable populations. Particulate air pollution might also aggravate the severity of underlying chronic lung disease, causing more frequent or severe exacerbation of airways disease or more rapid loss of lung function. More than two dozen community health studies since 1987 have linked particulate pollution to reductions in lung function, increased hospital and emergency room admissions, and premature deaths.

8. Whether racial minorities are genetically predisposed to asthma is increasingly a subject of health research, to the general dismay of environmental justice activists for the reasons described in this chapter. For examples of research on genetic roots, see Colp et al. (1993) and Miller (1999).

9. Another important question to consider, and a key area for further research, is how the "correction" of the household environment is done, without implying that poor women or women of color have bad housekeeping practices and blaming mothers for their children's asthma, as historical studies of Progressive health interventions have shown how class and racial biases can permeate seemingly neutral and benign public health programs.

10. The spirit of these promises appeared to be broken in September 2003 when a new twelve-story diesel bus depot was opened in a residential community of East Harlem. Because this facility was replacing the former two-story depot on the same site, the MTA asserted that it was not a "new" facility subject to its agreement to build only new compressed natural gas (CNG) depots. A February 22, 2004, *New York Times* article reported the possibility that the MTA would back out of its commitment to converting the Manhattanville depot to CNG (Luo 2004).

11. Title VI of the Civil Rights Act of 1964 prohibits discrimination on the basis of race, color, and national origin in programs and activities receiving federal financial assistance.

12. For a description of this phrase and its centrality to the environmental justice movement, see the Preface to Cole and Foster 2001.

13. At the city level, the New York City Department of Health (DOH) began the Community Asthma Program and the New York City Childhood Asthma

Initiative that sponsored asthma education campaigns on the New York City train and bus system. The DOH also coordinates the New York City Asthma Partnership, a coalition of individuals and organizations who share an interest in reversing the asthma epidemic in New York City.

## Chapter 4

1. Waste transfer stations are organizing issues not just in New York City but also in Washington, D.C. (Citizens Against Trash Transfer Stations); Roxbury in Boston; and Chester, Pennsylvania; among others. Waste transfer stations have also been addressed by the National Environmental Justice Advisory Council of the Environmental Protection Agency.

2. That same day, Mayor Bloomberg signed a bill authorizing an 18.5 percent property tax hike, in an accelerated process that perfected the art of the strategy of the 7:30 A.M. hearing the Monday after Thanksgiving.

3. DOS operates two gas collection systems at Fresh Kills. The gas is then sold to Keyspan to power about 15,000 homes. According to the U.S. Environmental Protection Agency's Landfill Methane Outreach Program, there are over 325 operational programs in the country and 200 under construction or consideration. Retrievable at <www.epa.gov/lmop/about.htm>.

4. In Brooklyn (Greenpoint, Red Hook, Southwest Brooklyn), Bronx (Hunts Point), Manhattan (West 135th, East 91st, West 59th, Gansevoort), and Queens (North Shore).

5. Williamsburg/Greenpoint is home to seventeen waste transfer stations and the South Bronx to fifteen. (DOS Bureau of Planning and Budget Report Second Quarter 2001), retrievable at <http://www.nylpi.org/pub/solidwaste.pdf>.

6. In 1992, DOS drafted preliminary siting regulations but did not put them into effect. In 1996, several OWN members and elected officials from affected neighborhoods brought a lawsuit against New York City, with New York Lawyers for the Public Interest as counsel, charging that the city violated Local Law 40. The city lost that lawsuit in March 1997, as well as its appeal to the lower court decision at the state appellate court in December 1997. As a result, the DOS drew up weak regulations that were subject to OWN protest in 1998 at the department of sanitation. The weak regulations failed to limit concentration of facilities, grandfathered facilities without a permit, have self-certification standards, and failed to require action by the community board, council member, or borough president. In February 1999, the plaintiffs filed another lawsuit in state supreme court, calling the regulations "deficient, arbitrary, capricious, and an abuse of discretion." As a result of court-ordered mediation, the city agreed to promulgate new siting regulations to address some of the key concerns of communities, especially with regard to overall clustering and increasing the buffer zone. In part, Judge Phyllis Gangel-Jacob accepted the city's contention that there was a solid waste crisis "because of the recent destruction of the twin towers of the World Trade Center," in denying the respondents injunctive relief on December 3, 2001. In 2003, DOS released flawed draft regulations that limited sites in

Community Board 1 in Brooklyn and Community Board 2 in the South Bronx. Several OWN members testified at the public hearings, which were held on April 23, 2003.

7. DOS continued to attempt to promulgate weak siting regulations that environmental justice activists and legal advocates critiqued because they ignored the issues of clustering, proximity to residences, and insufficient standards to address public health and the environment. See Janette Wipper, NYLPI lawyer, letter to Robert Orlin, Deputy Commissioner for Legal Affairs, DOS, July 19, 2004, retrievable at <http://www.nylpi.org/pub/orlinwaterfront.pdf>. See also testimony to the New York City Council on October 12, 2004, retrievable at <http://www.nylpi.org/pub/jantest.pdf>.

8. To be considered an OWN member, a group must agree with the platform, support the Principles of Environmental Justice, support community unity and solidarity, and attend monthly meetings and other activities (like public hearings and protests). As of 2006, OWN community organizational members are: Neighbors Against Garbage, Red Hook Civic Organization, Nos Quedamos, UPROSE, Neighbors United/Columbia St. District, West Harlem/Morningside Heights Sanitation Coalition, El Puente, East New York United Front, South Bronx Clean Air Coalition, Hunts Point Awareness Committee, Lower Washington Heights Neighborhood Coalition, Hispanos Unidos de Greenpoint, Southern Queens Park Association, SI Citizens for Clean Air, MADCAP, OUTRAGE, the Point, Planners Network, Mothers on the Move, and Sustainable South Bronx.

9. There were a number of individual anti–New York City DOS policy groups as well as coalitions with such colorful acronyms as NAG (Neighbors against Garbage), GAG (Groups Against Garbage), BARGE (Boroughs Allied for Garbage Equity), and BRAG (Bay Ridge Against Garbage).

10. This distinction is similar to that explored by Allen (2003) in her study of environmental and health activism in the Deep South. As she notes, in the heavily industrialized region she studies, there is no consensus on the impact of chemicals and their health effects. The same geographic space is also referred to in different terms. What black community and environmental activists call "Cancer Alley," the government proudly calls "The Industrial Corridor." Cajuns call it the Acadian Coast, while other whites call it "Great River Road" to invoke its plantation history and current status as tourist attraction.

11. These discussions have tended to focus on hazardous waste. The Basel Ban on the Control of Transboundary Movements of Hazardous Wastes and Their Disposal was adopted in Basel, Switzerland, on March 22, 1989. The convention was initiated in response to numerous international scandals regarding hazardous waste trafficking that began to occur in the late 1980s. The convention entered into force on May 5, 1992, although the United States has not signed onto the convention.

12. By some estimates, wastepaper constitutes 35 percent of the waste stream— approximately 12,600 tons per day. According to one expert, "The City is nothing less than the Saudi Arabia of wastepaper. Its annual production of

cellulose (the raw material used to manufacture paper) . . . equals anywhere between one half to the total amount of virgin cellulose in the entire Brazilian rainforest (and by other studies, more cellulose per acre than the Brazilian rainforest)" (Hershkowitz 2002, 25).

13. That is not to say that the residents of these rural communities necessarily want these facilities or that they are always opposed to them. Landfills, like prisons, are similar types of facilities where poor rural communities gain revenue and services they would be unable to otherwise afford. It is also important to distinguish between bureaucrats and politicians who seek out this kind of development and local residents since their views may not necessarily coincide (Lake 1996).

14. On garbage services in particular, Melosi (1981) writes, "a municipally operated street-cleaning program was generally regarded as the best means of ensuring effective service," promoted in part as a "cure" for the city's social and physical ills. In 1880, only 24 percent of cities had municipally operated solid waste programs, whereas by 1924, 63 percent of cities ran their own programs (Melosi 2001, 115).

15. Privatization as a movement has three distinct but related aspects: (1) public asset divestiture to private firms by all levels of government, (2) private development of infrastructure facilities, and (3) private provision of services to units of government (Kemp 1986).

16. The Trade Waste Commission regulates the trade waste carters. Members are appointed by the mayor, and the commission is staffed with New York City police detectives, inspectors, and auditors. The commission was created with a mandate to rid the waste sector in New York City of mob control.

17. Most recently, Royte (2005) offers a journalistic account of garbage—its travels and travails.

18. In 1998, USA Waste acquired Waste Management (formerly known as WMX) to form the largest waste company in the world, worth approximately $13.5 billion. Allied Waste then acquired Browning Ferris to become second largest, and Republic is the third (Republic left the New York City market in 1999 in an asset swap with Allied, which was being forced to divest $1.7 billion in assets to get government approval to purchase BFI).

19. Waste Management has faced over 600 government pollution citations. The company paid $28 million in fines and settlements for bid rigging, price fixing, and price gouging between 1980 and 1992. The record of arrests and prosecutions is long and varied, spanning criminal violations, antitrust civil cases, environmental civil cases, and administrative cases (Crooks 1993).

20. In a corporate compilation of a ten-year history of Browning Ferris between 1981 and 1991, the company admitted to 270 civil penalties, administrative orders, permit or license suspensions and revocations, as well as bond forfeiture actions, ten misdemeanor or felony convictions and pleas, twenty-four court decrees and settlement orders, and one pending court case, and it disclosed over $75.5 million in fines and settlement from 1972 to 1994 (Crooks 1993).

21. As a condition of its consent agreement for the merger, the company capped its waste transfer stations for three years. This merger had negative local effects, particularly in the South Bronx. In 1997, Waste Management received a permit to build a $25 million waste transfer station, with the caveat that it would contribute $1 million to build a controversial local community center dedicated to reducing asthma and that it would close other waste transfer stations in the Bronx. With the merger and the sale of some of its holdings, the new company claimed that it no longer had enough waste transfer stations handling putrescible waste (Waldman 1999).

22. The schedule was as follows. In July 1997, the plan called for the interim export for 1895 tons per day (tpd) of Bronx waste at a cost of $54.82 a ton to Virginia or South Carolina; December 1998 was for 2,334 tpd of Brooklyn waste to Pennsylvania for $60.03; December 1999 called for 2,798 tpd from Manhattan and Staten Island to Essex County, N.J., and to waste transfer stations in Elizabeth for $63.75 a ton; September 2000 called for 1,073 tpd for Brooklyn trash for $69.16 a ton (Independent Budget Office 2001). The interim export plan costs an average of $63.23 a ton (versus approximately $43 per ton at Fresh Kills).

23. In January 2000, State Attorney General Elliot Spitzer filed a lawsuit against New York City for not properly accounting for the environmental impact of its trash export plan. The suit was based on complaints that the plan degrades the environment by relying on extra garbage trucks that pollute the atmosphere with foul odors, diesel exhaust, and impermissible noise levels. (Jacobsen 2000). In *Spitzer* v. *Farrell*, the appellate court, in a unanimous decision, reversed the original ruling. The appellate court ordered the DOS to perform an environmental impact statement studying the impacts and effects of PM 2.5 (very small particle pollutants), from their diesel truck garbage plan. But in another later ruling, the state appeals court ruled that there was no technologically feasible method to evaluate the smaller particulate emissions (Hu 2003).

24. Bautista is not alone in identifying 1977 as a pivotal year in New York City's recent history. Jonathan Mahler's *Ladies and Gentlemen, The Bronx is Burning: 1977, Baseball, Politics and the Battle for the Soul of a City* (2005) focuses on the racial, cultural, and political turmoil in that year. He opens with labor strife and police and sanitation worker strikes that created what strikers called "Fear" and "Stink" City.

25. Eddie Bautista, personal communication, May 15, 2002. Charles City County in Virginia has 7,000 residents, 55 percent of them African American, and 12.3 percent of the county's residents live below the poverty line. The local economy is based on forestry and farming of soybeans, wheat, and corn. The families of some of the black farmers have worked this land since Reconstruction. Waste Management made a deal with the county to dispose of its trash for free for forty years, accept the commercial waste at a 20 percent discount, build three new collection stations, and receive tipping fees. At its peak in the early 1990s, the county received $5 million per year, which it used to build a community center, school, animal shelter, and an auditorium; reduce its property tax; build a water and sewage system; and expand an industrial park (Friedman 2001).

26. Scientists say they have pinpointed many of the industrial polluters responsible for the dioxin that ends up in the Arctic. Researchers at Queens College estimate that U.S. sources account for 70 to 80 percent of dioxin in the Canadian territory of Nunavut, populated by Inuits. Researchers modified a computer program designed to track fallout in the event of a nuclear accident. These same researchers in another study further pinpointed that just 35 municipal waste incinerators, cement kilns, and steel plants in the eastern and central United States account for one-third of the dioxin reaching Nunavut (Commoner et al. 2003).

27. While litigants under Title VI must prove that a defendant intentionally discriminated, the regulations implementing the statute state that discriminatory effect, or disparate impact, alone is enough to show unlawful discrimination. Title VI has had limited utility because of the inability or unwillingness of federal agencies to mount serious investigations. (Cole and Foster 2001).

28. Public hearings on the plan modification and the DEIS were held before the city council environmental protection committee in May and June 2000. In June, at the DEIS hearing, over 100 members of the public testified. The final EIS was issued in October 2000, with responses to comments made at the hearing. In October and November 2000, the environmental committee held three additional public hearings.

29. The Linden plan was controversial because of perception of corruption. Mayor John Gregorio of Linden is the father-in-law of the owner of the Linden site. The Linden mayor was fined by the local finance board of the state department of community affairs for using his influence improperly to advance the WTS in which his son-in-law had a financial interest. BFI then offered to buy the land directly to get rid of perceptions of corruption (Smothers 2002).

30. The intense public criticism by OWN directed at DOS was one factor that influenced other agency responses. The public pressure that OWN organized has had several concrete effects and also less indirect impacts. OWN's pressure forced the state DEC to beef up enforcement at waste transfer stations through increased inspections: from 2,929 in 1998 to 5,397 in 2002 (Bryce 1999). The DEC also ruled that the city must upgrade one waste disposal center in each borough to absorb Fresh Kills garbage. The agency noted that the city had not shown credible evidence on the retrofitting issue.

31. The Independent Budget Office found that a city-owned waste transfer station infrastructure would cost the city more in the short term but would ultimately save the city money. Political observers and Bloomberg's supporters suggest that his decisions on garbage policy are tied to his broader management style, which are managerial and technocratic, giving aides a great deal of influence, and less politically abrasive than Giuliani (Rutenberg 2005).

32. The 2004 version of the plan called for four marine transfer stations, a larger commitment to recycling, and shipping of commercial waste through the West Side (Urbina 2004).

33. Galesi, a major Republican donor, is also involved with a controversial deal to purchase property in the South Bronx to lease to Rupert Murdoch for a paper

printing facility. This "job creation" venture cost the state $13 million. According to one critic of the plan, "If Murdoch lives up to his word, this $13 million welfare check will go to create a whopping 100 jobs between now and 2002. That's it: 25 jobs a year. That comes out to $129,000 for every new job—making this the largest handout of its kind in New York State's history" (Ledbetter 1998).

34. Cost estimates for plant construction ballooned from $400 million to $700 million due to rising bond interest rates and the volatile recycling paper market. According to Hershkowitz (2002), the chief factors for the project's demise were the loss of confidence by New York State after corruption by the main community partner was uncovered (the executive director of Banana Kelly used the organization's funds for private expenses and her friend obtained a $1 million consulting contract for doing no work); the inability to obtain a wastepaper contract due to political factors (chiefly, Mayor Giuliani's refusal to grant a wastepaper contract for a facility seen to benefit his political rival, Bronx borough president Fernando Ferrer); and the burden of litigation by construction firms.

35. On August 25, 2000, Administrative Judge Helene Goldberger ordered that truck traffic be limited and that "it would appear imperative in light of the scientific evidence regarding the health effects of this pollutant to prepare an analysis of the potential effects of the emission of PM2.5 from this facility." In DEC's interim decision of February 14, 2001, the commissioner argued that the science on PM 2.5 was inadequate.

36. In February 2002, in the wake of the largest budget deficit in history, Mayor Bloomberg proposed suspension of metal, glass, and plastic recycling, (MGP), which constitutes about 9 percent of the city's recycling rate of about 20 percent. Bloomberg cited high costs of disposal (about 40 percent of recycled goods were ultimately landfilled) for the "temporary" eighteen-month suspension of the program, even though such a suspension violated city and state laws on recycling. Critics of the proposal countered that turning a program off and on led to confusion in the general public and criticized the cost argument in that all materials that are not recycled must also be exported as trash. Also, the city was set to renegotiate contracts for the handling of its MGP program in June 2002 (the contracts negotiated in 1993 for $58 per ton were set to rise to $100 per ton because of the changing recycling market). Recycling advocates argue that the problems with cost are actually more complicated, because if the recycling rate increased, the cost per ton collection would drop. Environmental groups and the city council lobbied Mayor Bloomberg to restore metal recycling, which was profitable (Truini 2002). Certain types of plastics recycling resumed in July 2003 as a result of budget negotiations. For a detailed description of the suspension and the difficulty in calculating recycling costs and savings and how these calculations are shaped by particular ideologies, see Hsieh (2005).

37. Elliot Spitzer, the New York attorney general, launched a recycling initiative in 2000. The Recycling Reinforcement Act clarifies current law to prohibit waste haulers from dumping recyclables at landfills and incinerators. The Bottle Bill Expansion Act sought to add noncarbonated beverages, such as teas, bottled water, and fruit juices, to the state's existing container deposit law. Almost 20 percent of New York City's exported waste is recyclable. Twenty percent of the

city's exported waste is compostable food and yard waste, and 8 percent of exported waste is reusable or recyclable textiles or plastics. New York City has a particularly weak record in organic recyclables. In a comparison with the eight other largest cities in the United States, New York City captures 1.3 percent of such materials, contrasting with 73 percent in San Diego (the high), Los Angeles at 49.3 percent in the middle, and Phoenix at 11 percent at the next to lowest (Biddle 2001). San Francisco increased its total trash diversion rate of 46 percent in 2000 to more than 56 percent by 2003, in large part due to its successful food waste diversion program (Swartz 2002). New York City counts construction and debris material, citing a 34.7 percent recycling rate. In 2002, the city chose to defer $20 million already allocated for composting facilities in 2003 to 2010.

38. Under wartime conditions, the U.S. government prohibited the manufacture of nearly 600 consumer products in order to conserve raw materials. Sacrifice and deprivation were deemed necessary to preserve the American way of life. In wartime, recycling was also racialized through "Let's Junk the Jap" campaigns and scrap drives (Pellow 2002).

39. Rather than take a simplistic pro- or anti-recycling approach, other analysts point to the contradictions of waste and recycling politics. In their analysis of recycling as a case study of sustainable community development, Weinberg, Pellow, and Schnaiberg (2000) find that the rhetoric of recycling as an unalloyed good that promised benefits in the "three E's: environmental, economic and equity terms" was in fact a much more complicated reality. Their book is an attempt to understand "our disillusionment and anguish over the path of modern recycling" (201). By focusing on the political economy rather than the internal logic of recycling itself, they argue that recycling is a "canary in the mine" for those of us who would like to see sustainable community development become a reality. The rhetoric behind early recycling programs promised to address aspects of the urban crisis and deindustrialization: air and water pollution, open space and landfills, the energy crisis, and greenhouse gas emissions. The reality and disillusionment with recycling is tied to the larger political economic barriers to truly sustainable community development: the difficulties in measuring costs and benefits and the fact that recycling was undermined by political interests. The reality is that recycling is not "something for nothing." It does not turn a feel-good religion to industry. Rather, the waste industry understood recycling as providing feedstock and raw materials for their industry. Large firms understood recycling as both a threat and an opportunity. Ecological gains are often quite modest, as other pollution and toxic chemical exposure are not addressed. Equity issues are often dismissed since jobs are poor quality, and sustaining even the best programs is often politically unfeasible (Weinberg, Pellow, Schnaiberg, 8–9).

40. Gandy's account of New York City's recycling history in *Recycling and the Politics of Urban Waste* (1994) has been superseded by recent events. In Gandy's account of urban recycling in London, New York, and Hamburg, he falters in his prediction of the politics of New York City's recycling program. He states: "Financial concerns have not led to pressures for privatization and there are concerns that any loss of City control of operations would lead to greater

inefficiencies, loss of data, increased involvement of organized crime in waste haulage and loss of accountability" (82). In actuality, the direct opposite occurred, in large part, but not exclusively, due to the privatization agenda of Mayor Giuliani. He continues: "What is clear is that the 1990s have seen recycling take a key place in the overall waste management strategy of the city . . . as an integral component of public policy with positive social and environmental aims" (83). In fact, the recycling in New York City took several steps backward, vulnerable to budget cuts, and lacking political capital to withstand attacks.

41. It now reaches 100 percent of its residents, far exceeding the rates of other major cities. It diverted (before the 2002 cuts in glass and plastic recycling, which I discuss below) approximately 22 percent of the waste, with only 9 percent of the DOS budget (Outerbridge 2000).

42. DOS's attitude toward recycling and its institutional culture can be seen in a DOS report published in 2001: *New York City Recycling in Context* and *New York City's Public Education Campaign for Recycling*. In it, the DOS explains how New York City's recycling rate is calculated and how the city is exceptional. The DOS begins with recycling rates as reported by *Waste News* in February 2001, where New York City, at 19.7 percent, ranked nationally in seventeenth place. It then proceeds to explain that the true calculation of recycling rates would show (factoring in commercial-residential discrepancies, yard waste, "other waste," and adjustments if returned beverage containers were counted) that New York City would rank ninth in the country.

43. For example, the city's haulers deliver recyclables to processing plants, where recyclables are sorted, baled, and shipped to market. The facilities report that the city's recyclables are contaminated because of collection techniques (up to 60 percent of the materials are unusable).

44. City council Speaker A. Gifford Miller engineered a council rejection of Bloomberg's plan that endorsed borough equity through the approval of four marine waste transfer sites, including in his district, on June 9, 2005. A couple of weeks later, the mayor rejected the council veto of his plan, and Miller backed down because he did not have enough votes to override the veto. The broader political context is mayoral: Miller at the time was a candidate running against Bloomberg (Confessore 2005).

## Chapter 5

1. In 2002, the board had five members: the president of New York State Energy Research and Development Authority; the commissioners of the State Department of Transportation, Environmental Conservation, and Economic Development; and the chair of the Public Service Commission.

2. In the past, Yeampierre worked with incarcerated mothers at the Center for Constitutional Rights, the Puerto Rican Legal Defense and Education Fund, and the American Indian Law Alliance.

3. Scholars and activists have documented the impact of nuclear power as an example of environmental injustice against Native Americans. Over 60 percent

of all known U.S. domestic deposits of uranium are found on Native lands, with most on the southern edge of the Colorado Plateau (including large sections of Arizona, Colorado, New Mexico, Utah, and Wyoming). Over the decades, these mines have produced over 95 percent of the nation's uranium for weapons production and nuclear power plants. The nuclear industry has left in its wake thousands of abandoned mines, unprotected and unsecured mine waste, and millions of gallons of liquid waste in largely untreated mill tailing ponds. The long-term burdens are numerous, as evidenced by the polluted bodies of Navajo miners, toxic groundwater, and widespread wildlife contamination. Not surprisingly, nuclear issues have been a focus of Native environmental justice activism. This is because Native lands are sites where uranium is extracted, nuclear weapons are tested, and spent nuclear fuel is buried. In terms of oil refinery pollution, "Cancer Alley" in Louisiana is the heart of environmental justice activism on the issue. Louisiana is "afloat in oil" from offshore drilling in the Gulf of Mexico, and oil companies are a key contributor to the "toxic soup" that comprises Cancer Alley (Roberts and Toffolon-Weiss 2001). The oil refinery problem is not limited to the southeastern United States. California is the third biggest state for petroleum refining, after Louisiana and Texas. The city of Richmond, California, is home to the Chevron/Texaco oil refinery and scores of petrochemical plants and related industries, many of which have experienced major accidents over the past thirty years. From extraction to processing, the burdens of environmental pollution in the oil industry have been unequally distributed. In the face of this extreme pollution, there are numerous environmental justice activists and community groups confronting these issues. On Richmond in particular, see Tai (1999). For an overview of Asian and Asian Immigrant environmental justice issues, see Sze (2004).

4. An interesting example of how a coal lobby group attempts to divide economy and the environment particularly in regard to race can be found in a 2002 study conducted by the Center for Energy and Economic Development (CEED). The group funded a $40,000 study criticizing the Kyoto Protocol for the harmful impact it would have on blacks and Hispanics. The report, *Refusing to Repeat Past Mistakes: How the Kyoto Climate Change Protocol Would Disproportionately Threaten the Economic Well-Being of Blacks and Hispanics in the United States*, was released with the support of several minority business and labor organizations such as the A. Phillip Randolph Institute, Labor Council for Latin American Advancement, the National Black Chamber of Commerce, the National Institute for Latino Development, and the U.S. Chamber of Commerce, retrievable at <http://www.ceednet.org/newsletter/06_21_00b.htm>.

5. Various briefings and alternative summits were held in addition to the formal climate negotiations occurring under the sixth Conference of Parties (COP6). For example, the Oakland, California–based Redefining Progress group held the Environmental Justice and Climate Change Forum on November 17, 2000, and several hundred grassroots activists participated in the two-day (November 19–20) Climate Justice Summit held in The Hague. The leaders are committed to the principles of clean production, sustainable development, and fair, just, and equitable plans that would rein in global climate change.

6. Retrievable at <http://www.ejcc.org/>.

7. These are: transition to an industrialized society of wood and coal (1820–1914), the emergence of the U.S. reliance on oil (1914–1945), the United States as a global power (1945–1970), and the onset of postindustrialism and the post–oil crisis years (1973–today). The overarching narrative in the twentieth century is of rising consumption of natural resources for energy. In the first decade of the century, coal represented more than 75 percent of the total energy consumption in the country (Melosi 1985). The two main shifts in energy sources are from wood and waterpower to coal (renewable to nonrenewable) in the midnineteenth century and from coal to petroleum and natural gas in the early twentieth century. After 1920, two new, oil and natural gas, sources rapidly replaced coal. Between 1949 and 1971, the world's energy consumption more than tripled.

8. During this period, more than 4,000 businesses combined into 257 corporations. By 1904, just 1 percent of American companies controlled 45 percent of manufactured products (Hirsh 1999).

9. The House of Insull, a giant utility holding company, was controlled by Samuel Insull. In 1932, the fall of the House of Insull cost investors $1 billion in the largest corporate failure in history until the savings and loans scandal in the 1980s. Insull was indicted for mail fraud, bankruptcy, and embezzlement and fled the country. Eventually he returned and was put on trial and acquitted. The courts ruled that a holding company could not be held responsible for the acts of the companies it controlled (McDonald 1962).

10. The mining and extraction of coal, gas, and oil are notoriously dirty industrial processes, causing severe air, water, and land pollution and human damage. (Merchant 1980, Davis 2002, Freese 2003).

11. In 1994, retail electricity sales (not including wholesale electricity to large industrial consumers) topped $200 billion, more than was spent on cars, telecommunications, and higher education as separate sectors (Brennan et al. 1996).

12. In power generation, some form of energy is expended to drive a turbine, which drives a generator that produces an electric current. Most comes from steam or boilers, which burn coal, natural gas, or oil to drive a turbine, which then drives a generator. Older forms of electricity generation required large-scale production (300 to 600 megawatts); now, that number can dip to as little as a 100 megawatts. Long-distance transmission is the process of conducting the flow of electricity at high voltages from points of generator to locations of groups, such as neighborhoods, industrial parks, or commercial centers. Local distribution transforms electricity from high to low voltage and controls the physical delivery. This function also includes retail sale and marketing.

13. It depended on direct current (DC) electricity, located within one mile of the plant. Alternating current (AC) transformers overcame the physical limit of direct current. The AC system won out over the DC system (Nye 1998).

14. Melosi (1985) shows that municipal electricity most often developed in cities where no profits were possible from existing systems (the major exception being Chicago). Municipal ownership did not win universal support because of fears of corruption from the public sector (Hirsh 1999).

15. Regulatory battles were especially pitched in Pennsylvania and New York State, where they became major gubernatorial campaign issues. Energy was a key issue in Franklin Delano Roosevelt's election as governor of New York in 1928 and these battles ultimately influenced the contours of his New Deal policy, particularly through the development of the Tennessee Valley Authority (Tobey 1996). Roosevelt expanded rural electrification as a national policy, which he believed would never happen in private hands because the profit margins were too low.

16. The utility consensus meant that the electricity system became, in his words, "closed." Hirsh (1999) suggests that closure occurs when humans act successfully to control feedback between system performance and institutional structure.

17. By 1935, thirty-seven states and the District of Columbia had established state regulatory commissions (Jacobson 2000).

18. Regulators assigned specific obligations and rights to power companies, also known as investor-owned utilities, including the right to eminent domain and to reasonable rates (eminent domain is the right to develop facilities and acquire land for the public interest, and "reasonable rates" are those rates determined by state regulatory agencies to guarantee a profit). Another right was the rate of return regulation, another name for the process by which utilities calculated rates on the basis of their company's assets rather than on the price electricity would fetch on the free market.

19. One review of Klinenberg's *Heat Wave* (2002) tells the substory of energy efficiency ratings in air conditioners and draws connections between the energy efficiency debate and heat wave deaths. Inefficient air-conditioner use and extra power demand lead to outages in critical times such as heat waves. The strain on the grid led to power outages and air-conditioning failures in Chicago during the 1995 heat wave. The difference between the demand that the utility was prepared to handle and the demand during the heat wave was the same as if Chicago was full of more energy-efficient air conditioners (Gladwell 2002).

20. The energy crisis played out in distinct stages. American oil production could no longer keep pace with rising demand, and natural gas was also in short supply. In 1972, oil prices began to climb as result of shortages and price hikes imposed by OPEC. In 1979, Iran cut off its oil to the United States, and the U.S. economy suffered through inflation and stagnation, which normally do not occur together. OPEC was unable to keep its members from overproducing. New oil fields were also being developed in Alaska, the North Sea, and Southeast Asia.

21. In the 1970s, the number of reactors online increased from fifteen to seventy-four, further fueling the demand for uranium, which is extracted primarily from Native communities in the West and Southwest United States.

22. Activist organizations such as the Silicon Valley Toxics Coalition have emerged as industry watchdogs, focusing on these environmental and occupational justice issues.

23. In particular, Section 210 opened the electricity generation market to independent electricity power companies and ended the monopoly control enjoyed by regulated utilities. Section 210 stemmed from President Carter's desire to increase the amount of electricity production from unconventional sources such as cogeneration facilities, in the context of the Mideast oil crisis and the OPEC embargo in 1973–1974. In these plants, boilers heat water until it becomes steam, which passes through turbines connected to electricity generators. President Carter hoped to increase the amount produced by allowing these facilities to sell power to utilities under favorable conditions.

24. *Qualifying facilities* (QF) is the general name given to classes of independent producers. PURPA defined a qualifying power production facility as a producer of electricity that used biomass, waste, or renewable resources as a primary energy source. The law prevented regulated utility companies from using their monopoly positions and financial resources to dominate the market of nonutility producers. Thus, qualifying facilities received special privileges under Section 210, such as a guaranteed market for their electricity. The Federal Energy Regulatory Commission (FERC) decided to provide QF with the maximum incentives. FERC also allowed QF to sell their entire output to utilities while purchasing supplemental and backup power at normal retail rates. QF could buy at a discount the same commodity they sold at a premium price. Utility managers began losing control of the system. For example, utilities were obliged to honor the contracts even if prices fell and energy was not needed (Hirsh 1999).

25. For example, new technology known as cogeneration equipment produced cheap power without the need for large plants. Cogeneration is a highly efficient means of generating heat and electric power simultaneously from the same energy source. It displaces fossil fuel combustion with heat that normally would be wasted in the process of power generation, thus achieving efficiencies far superior to conventional power generation. For example, gas turbines from jet engine technology (using natural gas, which was then cheap) were a major technological innovation. These turbines were installed on stationary platforms and connected to electricity generators, thereby increasing efficiency. It became the most popular source of nonutility power, increasing fourfold from 1979 to 1992.

26. The growth of conservation measures emerged in the 1980s as a result of the environmental movement. Demand-side management and integrated resource planning traded conserved electricity as the functional equivalent of generated power.

27. The act exempted independent power producers from the provision of the Public Utilities Holding Company Act that governed the corporate structure of regulated power companies. But as a political compromise, it affected only wholesale transactions, not retail wheeling (also known as customer choice).

28. The question of why—that is, the primacy of race or class and whether there is direct targeting of communities of color—is an important topic in environmental justice research. This chapter does not attempt to answer this question, which is outside its scope.

29. This report attempts to contextualize power plant pollution within global climate change. For example, it cites a study of the fifteen largest U.S. cities where climate change would increase heat related deaths in the inner city. Due to demographics and social factors, people of color are more likely to die in a heat wave and suffer more from heat-related stress and illness. For an illustration of this phenomenon, see Klinenberg (2002).

30. The Electricity Resource Plan by San Francisco's Environment Department and Public Utilities Commission proposed speeding up the closure of the existing Potrero and Hunters Point power plants without the power company's plan for a new 540 megawatt power plant at its existing Potrero plant. San Francisco's alternative energy plan proposes 150 megawatts of midsized power plants in the city by 2004 while ramping up about 480 megawatts of electricity efficiency, solar, wind power, cogeneration, fuel cell, and other alternative technologies at many locations in and around the city by 2012. It seeks to phase out fossil fuel burning for the city's electricity over twenty to thirty years. ("Electricity Resource Plan," retrievable at <http://www.sfgov.org/sfenvironment/aboutus/energy/policy.htm>).

31. It runs the state's power grid and administers the deregulated wholesale market, much like the New York Stock Exchange works. It provides a marketplace where power is bought or sold and sets the rules. There are two separate markets: a day-ahead market and a spot market that sells power an hour before it is needed (Bautista 2001).

32. New York State's path to energy deregulation was largely ignored in the mainstream press, tracked primarily in the business press in venues such as *Crains New York Business*. The major papers began to report on the issue in 1997 and 1998 only after the contours of deregulation were largely in place.

33. Governor Pataki cut $286 million in energy efficiency programs in 1992, an amount that fell to $73 million in 1996 (Gupta 2001). In 1995, Pataki shut down the New York State Energy Office, which was supposed to develop an annual energy plan to assess energy supplies and sources, administer energy and environmental efficiency programs, and direct energy-related emergency response. Pataki eliminated this office in preparation for his deregulation efforts.

34. In 2000, a number of problems occurred in the system. There was a price spike, and five companies demanded $65 million in reimbursements for overcharges for energy reserves. The costs increased in part because the reserve market was poorly designed and there was flawed software (as reported by Lentz in a, b, c in 2000).

35. It was founded in 1931 by Governor Franklin Delano Roosevelt, who passed legislation for this public power enterprise. NYPA served as a model for the Tennessee Valley Authority and national New Deal energy policy and was set up as a nonprofit public benefit corporation Construction was financed through bond sales to private investors, and bondholders are paid with proceeds from NYPA operations. NYPA sells power to government agencies, community-owned electric systems and rural electric cooperatives, private companies, private utilities for resale, and neighboring states.

36. Turbines are based on a relatively inefficient technology, producing only one-tenth of the energy of a midsize plant, but they are smaller and relatively cheaper to construct and operate.

37. These include mainstream environmental groups like the Natural Resources Defense Council, New York Public Interest Research Group, and local community groups that are not primarily representing people of color. Other groups included the East River Environmental Coalition, which was very active on the Con Ed plant on the Lower East Side, fighting for the elimination of diesel fuel. As a result, Con Ed agreed to provide $3.7 million to address air pollution concerns stemming from plans to increase output at the Fourteenth Street plant, and to set aside $2.75 million to use natural gas instead of oil, $500,000 to convert housing developments from oil to steam, and $500,000 to raise stacks. Also, the Coalition Helping to Organize a Kleaner Environment in Queens was very active.

38. CURE member organizations are: in Brooklyn: Greenpoint Waterfront Association for Parks and Planning, Stop the Barge, UPROSE, Williamsburg Watch, Neighbors Against Garbage, and El Puente; in South Bronx: The Point, Nos Quedamos, Sustainable South Bronx, Bronx Environmental Action Coalition, 426 East 149th St. HDFC; in Manhattan: East Midtown Coalition, East River Environmental Coalition; and in Queens: CHOKE.

39. Article X was enacted in 1992 to replace the more stringent Article VIII (which had more strict demands for public participation and needs requirement). In August 1999, the PSC ruled in a declatory ruling that if a private company is willing to build a power plant, it contributes to competition. The PSC considers contributing to competition to be an approved procurement process and thus requires no analysis of need for increased megawatts. Article X applications are ruled on by the state board on electric generation siting and the environment and two additional members named by the governor after an application is filed: one from the judicial district and one from the county where the facility is proposed to be located. Article X reform was also an issue that CURE lobbied on, joining with other public interest, environmental, and health organizations like the American Lung Association in producing "public interest principles for power plant siting."

40. The siting board reviews every proposal for a new power plant; it has seven members—five permanent members and two public members named by the governor, chosen from the affected neighborhoods. To obtain a certificate for a new power plant, the applicant needs to file a preliminary scoping statement, that is, a "stipulation" on the scope of the environmental impact statement; complete an application; undergo a process in front of an administrative law judge and public and evidentiary hearings; and be reviewed by the State Department of Environmental Conservation, after which the siting board makes its decision.

41. There was also a second lawsuit, *Silvercup v. NYPA*, this one over the site in Astoria, Queens, where *The Sopranos* and *Sex and the City* were filmed. The judge in that case threatened to halt construction of the Astoria turbine, charging that no serious consideration had been given to alternative sites. According to the judge, "The Court finds . . . that NYPA acted under a self imposed dead-

line and therefore only sought the most minimal of public input and comment." In his decision, he used Natural Resource Defense Council energy analyst Ashok Gupta's analysis of the estimated versus actual energy production needs. The peak load estimate for summer 2001 was 10,535 megawatts, of which New York City has 13,000 megawatts. Using the 80 percent rule of in-city generation, the city needs 8,428 megawatts, of which (preturbines), it has 8,306, leaving it 122 megawatts short. Con Ed, state agencies, and NYPA pledged $200 million in energy efficiency designed to save 271 megawatts, but the state did not use these savings in its numbers. In the *Silvercup* case, Judge Golia granted an injunction to stop construction but demanded that the studio come up with $5 million as bond in case the court ultimately decided in favor of NYPA. Silvercup refused. (Why Is Rudy in Power Plant Fray? 2001). Judge Golia ruled that New York State violated its own environmental laws and must halt work on the project in Queens (Perez-Peña 2001).

42. See Gordon and Harley (2005) and Cole and Foster (2001) for a discussion of the limits of the law in addressing environmental racism grievances.

43. Local intermediaries, such as the Pratt Center for Community and Environmental Development, also helped make this case through its geographic information system mapping of electric power sites and poverty.

45. PM 2.5 comes from fuel combustion in diesel engines, power plants, industrial facilities, and wood stoves. The burning of natural gas and diesel fuel produces PM 2.5; it is also formed in the atmosphere from sulfur dioxide, nitrogen oxides, and volatile organic compounds. It is linked to high rates of health problems, especially respiratory, and is particularly dangerous for the elderly, the young, asthmatics, and those with preexisting heart and lung conditions.

45. For a detailed description of the Sunset Energy facility and critiques of its application, see Bautista (2001). On September 22, 2000, NYSDEC advised the chair of the siting board that Sunset's applications for air and water were incomplete. The chair determined on September 25, 2000, that the application was deficient. The applicant submitted a revision to the application on December 27, 2002, which was approved in 2003.

*NISA Williamsburg Barge*: A community group, Stop the Barge, was successful at delaying construction for this proposal for two years with court proceedings. In October 2002, it won a partial legal victory in *Stop the Barge v. John P. Cahill of the Appellate Division* that would permit another court case to be brought. In December 2000, Stop the Barge filed a lawsuit requesting that a state court judge order the New York City Department of Environmental Protection (DEP) to reexamine its factual findings and DEC to rescind the permit. In August 2001, the judge agreed with DEP and DEC and dismissed the suit. Stop the Barge appealed to the appellate court for the region and won a partial victory on October 31, 2002. The appellate division held that community groups should have been allowed to contest the permit but not the DEP's factual findings (called a negative declaration on city environmental quality review). The Con Edison East River expansion has been approved under Article X, although the community group on the Lower East Side did win some concessions from Con Edison, including $3.7 million to address air pollution concerns, $2.75 million to use natural gas instead of oil, $0.5 million to convert a nearby housing development from oil to steam, and $0.5 million to raise the stacks higher from ground level in an attempt to lessen the air pollution.

46. E. Gail Suchman, CURE testimony to the city council, February 13, 2004, retrievable at <http://www.nylpi.org/pub/GailCityCouncilET.pdf>.

## Chapter 6

1. Fischer (2000) describes the antecedents to participatory inquiry in the action research methodology pioneered by Lewin in the 1940s and advocacy research of the 1960s.

2. In a review of community-based research in the field of public health, the authors identify key principles and characteristics of this research (Israel et al. 1998). Chief among the challenges facing the field are the differential power relationships between competing constituencies—academic researchers and community members. In examples where there are issues with lack of trust and control, there is significant potential for resource conflicts over funding and monetary issues, as well as conflicts over control of the knowledge and research. See also Baker et al. (1999).

3. Two important exceptions are the Deep South Center for Environmental Justice at Xavier University (led by Beverly Wright) and the Clark Atlanta University Center for Environmental Justice (led by Robert Bullard).

4. The environmental justice critique of risk is similar to but somewhat different from Ulrich Beck's influential critique of risk in *Risk Society* (1993). Beck argues that risk is created; it benefits some and hurts all, though this experience of risk is stratified by class and status. Beck asks how and why people from different social or racial groups face differential exposure to environmental risk. In a risk society, risk positions are centered on the interlocking of quality of life and production of knowledge in ways that are not central in industrial society. He refuses the distinction between "real" and "perceived" risk, which he views as false. Risks are defined as "risks in knowledge." The concept of risk is central to environmental justice, theoretically and practically. The idea that risks are risks in knowledge points to why knowledge through community-based research is central to environmental justice and why such research projects are proliferating.

5. Risk assessment takes place in four stages: hazard identification, dose response assessment, exposure assessment, and risk characterization. Some of the main problems are in the problems of extrapolation—from animal to human, from high to low. Also, the size of the sample and statistical significance are extremely high and are not necessarily the same as public health significance. Much risk assessment looks at cancer, although more recent work focuses on endocrine disrupters (Tesh 2000).

6. Sociologist Phil Brown's groundbreaking work on popular epidemiology was based in Woburn, Massachusetts, where residents suspected that toxic contami-

nation from old industrial wells (as popularized in the book and movie *A Civil Action*) led to a large number of children dying from leukemia (Brown and Mikkelson 1990). This belief led to the research study done by Woburn residents with the Harvard School of Public Health.

7. "Normal science" refers to Thomas Kuhn's argument in *The Structure of Scientific Revolutions* (1962), in which he argued against the idea of a steady accretion of scientific knowledge. He suggested that typical scientists are individuals who accept what they have been taught and apply their knowledge to solving the problems that their theories dictate and that normal science progresses because members of a mature scientific community work from a single paradigm. Kuhn argued that science is a series of peaceful interludes punctuated by intellectually violent revolutions or paradigm shifts, "the tradition-shattering complements to the tradition-bound activity of normal science." After such revolutions, "one conceptual world view is replaced by another."

8. In their discussion of the research process, the Awkwesasne (Mohawk Nation) Task Force on the Environment (ATFE) argues that engagement with research itself is a "push" factor for research. That is, experiences with nonparticipatory or nondemocratic research, and with researchers who did not emphasize an open process, or with using the research to community benefit, forced the Awkwesasne to undergo a different type of research. As a result of negative experiences with researchers, the ATFE developed a widely distributed model of research protocols and a framework for research partnerships and partnership studies that guides the specific methods. For example, the Awkwesasne research was framed with a tribal audience in mind. From the discussion on study design to the sensitivity to ownership of data issues, the history of the Awkwesasne formed the backdrop of the research. The style of communication in the research study was explicitly dialogue oriented, and data collectors came from the community itself. The studies on polychlorinated biphenyls on Mohawk youth are structured around developing long-term skills of local residents through the studies (Awkwesasne Task Force on the Environment Research Advisory Committee 1997, Santiago-Rivera et al. 1998, Schell and Tarbell 1998).

9. In North Carolina, community-based environmental justice has emphasized past research failures in structuring the contours of empowering research. Like the ATFE, the main community group involved, the South-east Halifax Environmental Awakening, emphasizes the ethical component of research, which is "a special issue in African American communities." This organization's programs promoted a multifaceted design, including community health surveys, workshops, medical care provider seminars, festivals, health consultations, outreach, data analysis and reporting, and speakers' bureaus (Wing et al. 1996).

10. The legitimacy of CBERJ is changing. As an example of its prominence and respect in the field of environmental health research, WEACT guest-edited a special issue of *Environmental Health Perspectives* on community-based research (Shepard et al. 2002). EHP is the leading journal in environmental health and published by the National Institute for Environmental Health Sciences.

11. Stevenson and Burke (1992) illustrate the problems with the rhetoric of empowerment. They argue that state-based health movements have adopted the rhetoric of new social movements and made illusory claims about improving research on health. They contribute a cautionary take on the practical limits of such research and the possibility of co-optation.

12. See Corburn for a description of Williamsburg and El Puente's asthma work. El Puente's multiyear asthma and health survey research in Williamsburg among Latino residents was conducted in cooperation with CIET, an international group of professionals from a variety of disciplines, including epidemiology, medicine, planning, communications, and other social sciences, who bring scientific research methods to community levels. It is also an academic center, based at the Universidad Autónoma de Guerrero in Mexico. The acronym comes from the name of the research center in Mexico where the organization began in 1985: Centro de Investigación de Enfermedades Tropicales (Tropical Disease Research Center). In New York, the name became "Community Information and Epidemiological Technologies," reflecting the broader application of epidemiological methods to research areas beyond the health field. More recently, in South Africa and Europe, CIET has come to stand for "Community Information, Empowerment and Transparency." In the first phase of the research in 1995, fifty high school students associated with El Puente Academy, along with five teachers and five staff members, interviewed community residents door to door, reaching 280 households and 1,065 individuals. Their survey revealed that residents felt that there were serious air pollution and respiratory disease problems in their community. The majority of problems identified were vehicle related, followed by those related to factories. After this survey, from November 1995 to January 1996, El Puente staff, with CIET's assistance, used personal monitoring equipment to measure respirable dust concentrations inside and outside its building at the foot of the Williamsburg Bridge connecting North Brooklyn and Manhattan. El Puente students did the electronic weighing of the samples at a university laboratory and calculated the results. Asthma Mastery in Action was the name of a program launched at El Puente, with support from the Childhood Asthma Initiative of the New York City Department of Public Health. The goal of the program was to improve knowledge about asthma and asthma management in the community. A group of community health workers—youth and adults who lived in the neighborhood—were the backbone of the program. Health promoters gave asthma workshops to churches and other community organizations and staffed asthma booths at community events. TV and radio spots were designed by youth for youth to talk about asthma triggers and asthma management. The theme of asthma was used to provide focus for a process of community reflection and community learning, beginning with people's own perceptions of the problem. A mural, designed and painted by El Puente youth, depicted asthma's effects on the community and how people are responding to it. It covered the exposed wall of a three-story-high corner building in the heart of the community.

13. Retrievable at <http://www.weact.org/gis/samplemaps.html>.

14. Local Law 39 required that city departments shall refer to the community boards all matters requiring public hearings by furnishing their calendars or

notices of meeting to the board chair; note in their records the recommendations of community boards made at public hearings and the failure of community boards to make recommendations; and notify the community boards of actions taken subsequent to public hearings and give the community boards information necessary for their work.

15. For a full update of the status of the plans and types of plans submitted, see Municipal Arts Society (2004) or consult the Municipal Arts Society at www.mas.org. A selected number of plans sponsored by community boards and one by a borough president have been adopted. Others have been approved, but action has been stymied by lack of funds.

There are several types of plans: comprehensive community revitalization (six plans); waterfront development plans (nine); transportation (two); open space and recreation (two); 197A (eighteen); comprehensive community plans (five); zoning (six); brownfield redevelopment (one); and housing revitalization (two). Professional consultants, either privately hired or through an institution, often provided crucial technical assistance. For example, the Pratt Institute Center for Community and Environmental Development (PICCED) has served as technical assistants on four 197A plans: Sunset Park, Bedford-Stuyvesant, Williamsburg, and Greenpoint. PICCED (renamed the Pratt Center for Community Development) is the oldest university-based advocacy planning organization in the country. Its mission is to "enhance the capacity of low- and moderate-income communities to develop innovative solutions to the physical, social, and economic challenges facing them."

16. *Williamsburg 197A Plan*: The Williamsburg 197A plan made recommendations in eight areas: zoning and land use, waterfront access and open space, environmental protection, economic development, housing, transportation, historic preservation, and community facilities. It addressed the need to promote the preservation and expansion of clean light manufacturing in order to manage growth, while promoting gentrification. It asked for a moratorium on all new noxious facilities, including power plants and waste transfer stations (this provision was taken out of the final approved version). The partners in this planning process included over twelve organizations, among them the original coalition partners in the campaign against the Brooklyn Navy Yard incinerator. The plan, submitted formally in 1998, was modified and approved by the city planning commission on December 5, 2001, and approved by the city council on January 25, 2002.

*Red Hook 197A Plan*: The Red Hook 197A planning process began in 1992, initiated by Community Board 6. The coalition working on the plan included a number of community organizations and political representatives, and over fifty public meetings were held over a decade. The goals of the plan were to improve housing and social services (especially for youth) and expand the residential community. There were over twenty-eight specific recommendations on how to meet community goals and concrete steps for implementation. These included housing development, rezoning proposals, rehabilitation of specific city-owned properties, the upgrading of the marine terminal, redevelopment of specific sites for maritime use, improving public access to the waterfront, and no new waste facilities. The plan was approved and adopted by the New York City Council in 1996, although significant modifications were made to the plan by the city planning commission. For example, the Red Hook moratorium on waste transfer stations and truck routes was eliminated as unrealistic and contrary to the larger citywide needs as defined by the DCP (Bressi 2000).

*Hunts Point 197A Plan*: This plan addressed land use and development strategies in the Hunts Point area of the South Bronx. It was organized first by the Point Community Development Corporation and coordinated by Sustainable South Bronx/the Point Community Development Corporation. The Fulton Fish Market moved to Hunts Point in 2005 from Lower Manhattan. The recommendations of the 197A plan were to develop cleaner transportation in the area of the fish market; promote public transportation by renovating the Hunts Point Station; create a South Bronx bike and pedestrian greenway; and create environmentally sustainable economic development on the waterfront through the creation of Rivermarket (a retail as opposed to a commercial food market), and the Factory Boathouse/Ecology Center. The plan was submitted formally in 2000, but the city has not acted on it thus far.

17. The rise of the China trade has led to a surge of the port—65 percent since 1998. See Lipton (2004). Although the plan has not been formalized, as of 2006, pieces of the plan have received endorsement by the Deputy Mayor's office, the Bronx Borough President, and the Hunts Points Market. See http://www.mas.org/ContentLibrary/Version_4.0_updated.pdf

18. In 1991 there were over 550 firms and 15,000 employees in the Sunset Park industrial area, with most jobs located in the apparel, industrial, and manufacturing trades.

19. For example, the Cross Harbor railroad is regulated by the federal government. The city wants to evict the company, charging in a civil suit that the company buried pesticides, petroleum waste, and old railroad ties. It is suing to get back the $750,000 it used to clean up the site. The city is punishing the company by witholding access to a new and unused $20 million rail float loading dock at Bush Terminal (Jamieson 2003).

20. The plan for a tunnel is not a new idea. The Port Authority of New York and New Jersey was originally established in 1921 with a mandate to construct such a tunnel. U.S. Representative Jerrold Nadler of the Eighth Congressional District spearheaded a campaign to build a container port at Sunset Park that would dramatically alter the waterfront area. Creating a container port would require filling out piers to the bulkhead line to create a continuous pier area. Fill would be obtained from routine dredging of the harbor. Although the fill would be toxic, it would be rendered harmless if topped with concrete. Nadler's interest in the project lay in keeping the waterfront as competitive as possible and retaining jobs for his district. He estimated that the proposed container port could generate 53,000 jobs in five years. In order to work, the plan would depend on additional changes to the regional infrastructure, which could add up to over $1 billion. The EDC initiated a two-year, $20 million environmental impact statement process in June 2001 for the Cross-Harbor Freight Movement Project. This

EIS examined the feasibility of constructing a rail freight tunnel to connect Brooklyn to the national rail system.

21. In June 2003, a coalition of labor, environmental, think tank, and civic activists announced that they had formed a coalition to lobby for federal money for the project. These organizations include 1199, Environmental Defense, the Regional Plan Association, and the Brooklyn Chamber of Commerce. This coalition did not outreach to UPROSE and local entities (Scott 2003).

22. Community Board 7 began to work on the plan in 1996, along with the Metro Chapter of the American Planning Association. A two-day community planning and design workshop was held in 1997, cosponsored with the Municipal Arts Society. The Community Board 197A committee was a key institutional player in developing the Sunset Park Waterfront Development Principles, signed by local elected officials in November 2000. The Southwest Brooklyn Industrial Development Corporation and UPROSE sponsored a competition in 2000 for the design of Third Avenue without the Gowanus Expressway.

## Conclusion

1. For copies of the strategic plan draft, see <http://www.epa.gov/compliance/resources/publications/data/planning/strategicplan/ej/>.

# References

Abu-Lughod, J. (Ed.). (1994). *From Urban Village to East Village: The Battle for New York's Lower East Side.* Oxford: Blackwell.

Ackerman, F., and Mirza, S. (2001). Waste in the Inner City: Asset or Assault? *Local Environment,* 6 (2), 113–120.

Allen, B. (2003). *Uneasy Alchemy: Citizens and Experts in Louisiana's Chemical Corridor Disputes.* Cambridge: MIT Press.

American Lung Association, Epidemiology and Statistics Unit. (2003 March). Trends in Asthma Morbidity and Mortality. Retrievable at http://www.lungusa.org/data/asthma/asthma1.pdf

Alpert, M. (1999). The Invisible Epidemic: Asthma Is on the Rise, Especially in Poor Urban Areas, and Scientists Don't Know Why. *Science,* 155 (11), 19–20.

Anderson, B. (1983). *Imagined Communities: Reflections on the Origin and Spread of Nationalism.* London: Verso.

Anderson, N. (1994). The Visible Spectrum. *Fordham Urban Law Journal,* 21 (3), 723–738.

Angotti, T., and Handhardt, E. (2001). Problems and Prospects for Healthy Mixed-Use Communities in New York City. *Planning Practice and Research,* 16 (2), 145–154.

Awkwesasne Task Force on the Environment Research Advisory Committee. (1997). A Case Study of Environmental Injustice. *International Journal of Contemporary Sociology,* 34 (2), 267–290.

Avila, E. (2004). *Popular Culture in the Age of White Flight: Fear and Fantasy in Suburban Los Angeles.* Berkeley: University of California Press.

Babcock, R., and Bosselman, F. (1973). *Exclusionary Zoning: Land Use Regulation and Housing in the 1970's.* New York: Praeger Publishers.

Baker, E. A., Homan, S., Schonhoff, R., and Kreuter, M. (1999). Principles of Practice for Academic/Practice/Community Research Partnerships. *American Journal of Preventative Medicine,* 16 (Suppl. 3), 86–93.

Barrett, W. (2002, October 23–29). Bad Policy, Big Bucks. *Village Voice.*

Barrett, W. (2003, August 20–26). New York's Prince of Darkness. *Village Voice.*

Bautista, E. (1998). Garbage Wars: The Struggle for Waterfront Justice. *Journal of Community Advocacy and Activism,* 3 (1), 17–28.

Bautista, E. (2001). *Energy and Environmental Justice: Power Plant Sitings in New York City.* Unpublished master's thesis, Pratt Institute Graduate Center for Planning and the Environment, New York.

Beck, U. (1993). *Risk Society: Towards a New Modernity* (Ritter, Trans). Thousand Oaks, CA: Sage.

Beckett, W. S., Belanger, K., Gent, J. F., Holford, T. R., and Leaderer, B. P. (1996). Asthma among Puerto Rican Hispanics: a Multi-Ethnic Comparison Study of Risk Factors. *American Journal of Respiratory and Critical Care Medicine,* 154 (4), 894–899.

Been, V., and Gupta, F. (1997). Coming to the nuisance or going to the barrios? A longitudinal analysis of environmental justice claims. *Ecology Law Quarterly,* 24 (1), 1–56.

Bennet, J. (1993, March 5). Hispanic Voters and the Politics of Sludge. *New York Times,* B1.

Berkman, L., and Kawachi, I. (Eds.). (2000). *Social Epidemiology.* New York: Oxford University Press.

Berman, M. (1982). *All That Is Solid Melts Into Air: The Experience of Modernity.* New York: Penguin.

Biddle, D. (2001 September). Comparing Recycling Programs in Major U.S. Cities. *Biocycle,* 42 (9), 34–38.

Birch, E. L. (2001). From Flames to Flowers: The Role of Planning in Re-Imaging the South Bronx. In L. Vale, and S. B. Warner (Eds.), *Imaging the City: Continuing Struggles and New Directions,* 57–93. New Brunswick, NJ: Center for Urban Policy Research.

Black Leadership Forum, Clean the Air, Georgia Coalition for the People's Agenda, the Southern Organizing Committee for Economic and Social Justice. (2002, October). *Air of Injustice.* Atlanta: Martha Keating and Felicia Davis.

Bowen, W. M. (2001). *Environmental Justice through Research Based Decision Making.* New York: Garland.

Bowen, W. M. (2002). An Analytical Review of Environmental Justice Research: What Do We Really Know? *Environmental Management,* 29 (1), 3–15.

Boyer, P. (1978). *Urban Masses and Moral Order in America, 1820–1920.* Cambridge: Harvard University Press.

Brennan, T., Palmer, K., Kopp, R., Krupnick, A., Stagliano, V., and Burtraw, D. (1996). *A Shock to the System: Restructuring America's Electricity Industry.* Washington, D.C.: Resources for the Future.

Brenner, N., and Theodore, N. (2003). *Spaces of Neoliberalism: Urban Restructuring in North America and Western Europe.* Oxford: Blackwell.

Brenner, N. (2004). *New State Spaces: Urban Government and the Rescaling of Statehood.* New York: Oxford University Press.

Bressi, T. (Ed.). (1993). *Planning and Zoning New York City: Yesterday, Today Tomorrow.* New Brunswick, NJ: Center for Urban Policy Research.

Bressi, T. (2000, March). Digging Into the Grassroots. *Planning Practice*, 660 (3), 10–13.

Brooks, A. (1989). The Office File Box–Emanations from the Battlefield. In C. Haar, and J. Kayden (Eds.), *Zoning and the American Dream: Promises Still to Keep*, 3–30. Chicago: Planners Press.

Brown, L., and Vega, W. (1996). A Protocol for Community Based Research. *American Journal of Preventative Medicine*, 12 (Suppl. 4), 4–5.

Brown, P., and Mikkelson, E. (1990). *No Safe Place: Toxic Waste, Leukemia and Community Action.* Berkeley: University of California Press.

Brown, P. (1992). Popular Epidemiology and Toxic Waste Contamination: Lay and Professional Ways of Knowing. *Journal of Health and Social Behavior*, 33 (3), 267–281.

Brown, P. (1993). Popular Epidemiology Challenges the System. *Environment*, 35 (8), 16–41.

Brown, P., Kroll-Smith, S., and Gunter, V. (2000). Knowledge, Citizens and Organizations: An Overview of Environments, Diseases and Social Conflict. In P. Brown, S. Kroll-Smith, and V. Gunter (Eds.), *Illness and the Environment: A Reader in Contested Medicine*, 9–25. New York: NYU Press.

Brown, P., Mayer, B., Zavestoski, S., Luebke, T., Mandelbaum, J., and McCormick, S. (2003). The Health Politics of Asthma: Environmental Justice and Collective Illness Experience in the United States. *Social Science and Medicine*, 57 (3), 453–464.

Brown, P., Mayer, B., Zavestoski, S., Luebke, T., Mandelbaum, J., and McCormick, S. (2005). The Health Politics of Asthma: Environmental Justice and Collective Illness Experience. In D. Pellow, and R. Brulle (Eds.), *Power, Justice, and the Environment: A Critical Appraisal of the Environmental Justice Movement*, 185–204. Cambridge: MIT Press.

Brown, R. (1937). The National Negro Health Week Movement. *Journal of Negro Education*, 6, 553–564.

Bryce, R. (1999, June 21). New York State Targets Haulers. *Crain's New York Business*, 22.

Bullard, R. (Ed.). (1994). *Unequal Protection: Environmental Justice and Communities of Color.* San Francisco: Sierra Club.

Bullard, R. (2004). Environment and Morality: Confronting Environmental Racism in the United States. New York: United Nations Research Institute for Social Development (Identities, Conflict and Cohesion Programme Paper Number 8).

Bullard, R., Johnson, G. S., and Torres, A. O. (Eds.). (2004). *Highway Robbery: Transportation, Racism, and New Routes to Equity.* Cambridge: South End Press.

Bunch, W. (1995, February 1). Smells like a Lawsuit. *Newsday*, A17.

Burger, J. (1997). A Blessing: South Bronx Coalition Jubilant over Incinerator Shutdown. *Catholic New York*, 28.

Bush, J., Moffatt, S., and Dunn, C. (2001). "Even the Birds Round Here Cough": Stigma, Air Pollution and Health in Teeside. *Health and Place*, 7 (1), 47–56.

Cardwell, D. (2000, November 16). Environmental Group Files Complaint Against M.T.A. *New York Times*, B3.

Caro, R. (1975). *The Power Broker: Robert Moses and the Fall of New York*. New York: Vintage.

Capek, S. (1993). The "Environmental Justice" Frame: A Conceptual Discussion and an Application." *Social Problems*, 40 (1), 5–24.

Carr, W., Zeitel, L., and Weiss, K. (1992). Variations in Asthma Hospitalizations and Deaths in New York City. *American Journal of Public Health*, 82 (1), 59–65.

Castells, M. (1983). *The City and the Grassroots: A Cross Cultural Theory of Urban Social Movements*. Berkeley: University of California.

Centers for Disease Control. (October 13, 2000). Measuring Childhood Asthma Prevalence Before and After the 1997 Redesign of the National Health Interview Survey—United States. *Morbidity and Mortality Weekly Report*, 49 (40), 908–911.

Century, D. (1999, March 12). Still a Contender on the Waterfront. *New York Times*, E37.

Checker, M. (2001). Like Nixon Coming to China; Finding Common Ground in a Multi-Ethnic Coalition for Environmental Justice. *Anthropological Quarterly*, 74 (3), 135–146.

Christopherson, S. (1994). The Fortress City: Privatized Spaces, Consumer Citizenship. In A. Amin (Ed.), *Post Fordism: A Reader*, 409–427. Oxford: Blackwell Publishers.

Cifuentes, L., Borja-Aburto, V., Gouveia, N., Thurston, G., and Davis, D. (2001). Assessing the Health Benefits of Urban Air Pollution Reductions Associated with Climate Change Mitigation (2000–2020): Santiago, Sao Paulo, Mexico City and New York City. *Environmental Health Perspectives*, 109 (Supplement 3), 419–425.

Citizens' Association of New York, Council of Hygiene and Public Health. (1970). *Sanitary Condition of the City: Report of the Council of Hygiene and Public Health of the Citizens' Association of New York, 1866*. (Reprinted, New York: Arno Press).

Clapp, R., and Orlando, L. (2002). The Sludge Report. *Special Issue of New Solutions: A Journal of Environmental and Occupational Health Policy*, 12 (4), 337–340.

Claudio, L., Tulton, L., Coucette, J., and Landrigan, P. J. (1999). Socioeconomic Factors and Asthma Hospitalization Rates in New York City. *Journal of Asthma*, 36 (4), 343–350.

Cohen, L. (2003). *A Consumers' Republic: The Politics of Mass Consumption in Postwar America.* New York: Knopf.

Cohen, W. A. (2005). Locating Filth. In W. A. Cohen, and R. Johnson (Eds.), *Filth: Dirt, Disgust and Modern Life,* vii–xxxvii. Minneapolis: University of Minnesota.

Colangelo, L. (2004, November 20). East Siders Dump on Mike Trash Plan. *New York Daily News.*

Cole, L., and Foster, S. (2001). *From the Ground Up: Environmental Racism and the Rise of the Environmental Justice Movement.* New York: NYU Press.

Colp, C., Pappas, J., Moran, D., and Lieberman, J. (1993). Variants of Alpha 1-Antitrypsin in Puerto Rican children with Asthma. *Chest,* 103 (3), 812–815.

Colten, C. (2004). *An Unnatural Metropolis: Wresting New Orleans from Nature.* Baton Rouge: Louisiana State University Press.

Commoner, B., et al. (2003). Airborne Dioxin Deposition in Nunavut. In D. L. Downie, and T. Fenge (Eds.), *Northern Lights Against POPs: Combatting Toxic Threats in the Arctic* (87–108). Montreal: McGill.

Confessore, N. (2005, June 23). Mayor Wins Test Over His Trash Disposal Plan as Council Drops Veto Override Vote. *New York Times,* B5.

Corburn, J. (2002). Combining Community-Based Research and Local Knowledge to Confront Asthma and Subsistence-Fishing Hazards in Greenpoint/Williamsburg, Brooklyn, New York. In P. Shepard, M. E. Northridge, S. Prakash, and G. Stover (Eds.). Community, Research, and Environmental Justice. *Environmental Health Perspectives,* 110 (Suppl. 2), 241–248.

Corburn, J. (2005). *Street Science: Community Knowledge and Environmental Health Justice.* Cambridge: MIT Press.

Corey, S. (1994). *King Garbage: A History of Solid Waste Management in New York City, 1881–1970.* Unpublished doctoral dissertation, New York University, New York.

Crain, E. F., Weiss, K. B., Bijur, P. E., Hersh, M., Westbrook, L., and Stein, R. E. (1994). An Estimate of the Prevalence of Asthma and Wheezing among Inner-City children. *Pediatrics,* 94 (3), 356–362.

Crenson, M. (1971). *The Un-Politics of Air Pollution: A Study of Non-Decision-Making in the Cities.* Baltimore: Johns Hopkins University Press.

Critchell, D. (2000, February 6). Residents Seethe as a Ruling Allows a Garbage Station. *New York Times,* 14.

Cronon, W. (1992). *Nature's Metropolis: Chicago and the Great West.* New York: Norton.

Crooks, H. (1993). *Giants of Garbage: The Rise of the Global Waste Industry and the Politics of Pollution Control.* Toronto: James Lorimer.

Curlee, T. R., Schexnayder, S., Vogt, D., Wolfe, A., Kelsay, M., and Feldman, D. (1994). *Waste to Energy in the United State: A Social and Economic Assessment.* Westport, Conn.: Quorum Books.

Davila, A. (2004). *Barrio Dreams: Puerto Ricans, Latinos, and the Neoliberal City.* Berkeley: University of California Press.

Davis, D. L. (2002). *When Smoke Ran Like Water: Tales of Environmental Deception and the Battle Against Pollution.* New York: Basic.

de La Peña, C. (2003). *The Body Electric: How Strange Machines Built the Modern American.* New York: NYU Press.

De Palo, V. A., Mayo, P. H., Friedman, P., and Rosen, M. J. (1994). Demographic Influence on Asthma hospital Admission Rates in New York City. *Chest,* 106 (2), 447–451.

Denning, M. (1996). *Cultural Front: The Laboring of American Culture in the Twentieth Century.* London: Verso.

Di Chiro, G. (1998). Environmental Justice from the Grassroots: Reflections of History, Gender and Expertise. In D. Faber (Ed.), *The Struggle for Ecological Democracy: Environmental Justice Movements in the United States,* 104–135. New York: Guilford Press.

Dockery, D. W., Pope, C. A., Xu, X., Spengler, J. D., Ware, J. H., Fay, M. E., Ferris, B. G., and Speizer, F. E. (1993). An Association between Air Pollution and Mortality in Six U.S. Cities. *New England Journal of Medicine,* 329 (24), 1753–1759.

Dowie, M. (1995). *Losing Ground: American Environmentalism at the Close of the Twentieth Century.* Cambridge: MIT Press.

Downie, D. L., and Fenge, T. (Eds.). (2003). *Northern Lights Against POPs: Combatting Toxic Threats in the Arctic.* Montreal: McGill.

Drummond, N. (2000). Quality of Life with Asthma: the Existential and the Aesthetic. *Sociology of Health and Illness,* 22 (2), 235–253.

Du Bois, W. E. B. (1899). *The Philadelphia Negro: a Social Study.* Philadelphia: University of Pennsylvania Press.

Du Bois, W. E. B. (Ed.). (1906). *The Health and Physique of the Negro American. Report of a social study Made Under the direction of Atlanta University; together with the proceedings of the eleventh Conference for the Study of the Negro Problems* held at Atlanta University, on May the 29th, 1906. Atlanta: Atlanta University Press.

Duffy, J. (1990). *The Sanitarians: A History of American Public Health.* Urbana: University of Illinois Press.

Dunlap, D. (1989, May 17). Atop a Harlem Waste Plant, a Park Grows. *The New York Times,* B1.

Egan, M. (2002). Subaltern Environmentalism in the United States: A Historiographic Review. *Environment and History,* 8 (1), 21–41.

Egbert, B. (2002, April 22). Stink over Fertilizer Plant. *Daily News (New York),* 1.

Elliot, A. (2003, August 28). Sewage Spill During Blackout Exposes a Lingering Problem. *New York Times,* A25.

English, M. (1992, December 21). Gearing Up for War; Battle over Sludge Plant. *Newsday*, 21.

Epstein, B. (1997). The Environmental Justice/Toxics Movement: Politics of Race and Gender. *Capitalism, Nature Socialism*, 8 (3), 63–87.

Epstein, H. (2003, October). Ghetto Miasma–Enough To Make You Sick? *The New York Times Magazine*, 75.

Fainstein, S. (1994). *The City Builders: Property, Politics and Planning in London and New York*. Oxford: Blackwell Books.

Farrell, B. (2003, January 7). Waterfront Park Plans put on Hold. *Daily News* (New York), Suburban, 1.

Feagin, J. (1989). Arenas of Conflict: Zoning and Land Use Reform in Critical Political-Economic Perspective. In C. Haar, and J. Kayden (Eds.), *Zoning and the American Dream: Promises Still to Keep*, 73–100. Chicago: Planners Press.

Fischer, F. (2000). *Citizens, Experts and the Environment: The Politics of Local Knowledge*. Durham: Duke University Press.

Fisher-Fishkin, S. (2005). Crossroads of Cultures: The Transnational Turn in American Studies Presidential Address to the American Studies. *American Quarterly*, 57 (1), 17–51.

Fitch, R. (1993). *The Assassination of New York*. New York: Verso.

Flanders, S. (2001, August 6). Fewer Children are Hospitalized for Asthma Since 1997 Effort. *New York Times*, B1.

Fletcher, T. (2004). *From Love Canal to Environmental Justice: The Politics of Hazardous Waste on the Canada–U.S. Border*. Peterborough, Ont: Broadview Press.

Flynn, K., Mcdonald, J., Weber, M., and Curran, T. (1991, February 19). Steisel Watched as Ex-Partners Got 468 M Deal. *Newsday*, 6.

Flynn, K., and Calderone, J. (1991, April 3). Links to Dinkins Hidden in Sludge" *Newsday*, 8.

Flynn, K., and Calderone, J. (1991, November 8). City Stink Forces Sludge Firm Out. *Newsday*, 8.

Flynn, K. (1992, April 15). Sludge Plan Probe: DA Checks Ties Between Firms and Politicians. *Newsday*, 23.

Ford, M., Edwards, G., Rodriguez, J., Gibson, R., and Tilley, B. (1996). An Empowerment-Centered, Church-Based Asthma Education Program for African American Adults. *Health and Social Work*, 21 (1), 70–75.

Freese, B. (2003). *Coal: A Human History*. Cambridge: Perseus Pub.

Freilla, O. (2004). Burying Robert Moses's Legacy in New York City. In R. Bullard, G. Johnson, and A. Torres (Eds.), *Highway Robbery: Transportation and New Routes to Equity*. Cambridge: South End Press.

Fried, J. (1992, April 30). Plan is Cut for Plants in Converting of Sludge. *The New York Times*, p. B3.

Fricker, R., and Hengartner, N. (2001). Environmental Equity and the Distribution of Toxic Release Inventory and Other Environmentally Undesirable Sites in

Metropolitan New York City. *Environmental and Ecological Statistics*, 8 (1), 33–52.

Friedman, A. (2001, November). Reprieve for Fresh Kills. *Planning Magazine*, 4–9.

Frost, L. (2005). *Never One Nation: Freaks, Savages, and Whiteness in U.S. Popular Culture, 1850–1877*. Minneapolis: University of Minnesota.

Gabbay, J. (1982). "Asthma Attacked? Tactics for the Reconstruction of a Disease Concept." In P. Wright, and A. Treacher (Eds.), *The Problem of Medical Knowledge: Examining the Social Construction of Medicine*, 23–43. Edinburgh: Edinburgh University Press.

Gamble, V. N. (Ed.). (1989). *Germs Have No Color Line: Blacks and American Medicine, 1900–1940*. New York: Garland Publishing.

Gamble, V. N. (1995). *Making a Place for Ourselves: the Black Hospital Movement, 1920–1945*. New York: Oxford University Press.

Gandy, M. (1994). *Recycling and the Politics of Urban Waste*. New York: St. Martins Press.

Gandy, M. (2002). *Concrete and Clay: Reworking Nature in New York City*. Cambridge: MIT Press.

Gandy, M. (2003). Life Without Germs: Contested Episodes in the History of Tuberculosis. In M. Gandy, and A. Zumla (Eds.), *The Return of the White Plague: Global Poverty and the "New" Tuberculosis*, 15–38. London: Verso.

Garg, A., and Landrigan, P. (2002). Children's Environmental Health. *American Annals of Political and Social Science*, 584 (1), 135–144.

Garg, R., Karpati, A., Leighton, J., Perrin. M., and Shah, M. (2003). Asthma Facts, Second Edition. New York City Department of Health and Mental Hygiene. Retrievable at http://www.ci.nyc.ny.us/html/doh/pdf/asthma/facts.pdf

Gayle, D., and Goodrich, J. (1990). *Privatization and Deregulation in Global Perspective*. New York: Quorum Books.

Gelobter, M. (1994). The Meaning of Urban Environmental Justice. *Fordham Urban Law Journal*, 21 (3), 841–856.

Gilmore, R. W. (2002). Fatal Couplings of Power and Difference: Notes on Racism and Geography. *Professional Geographer*, 54 (1), 15–24.

Gladwell, M. (2002, August 12). Political Heat: The Great Chicago Heat Wave, and Other Unnatural Disasters. *New Yorker*, 76.

Gibbs, L. (2002). Citizen Activism for Environmental Health. *American Annals of Political and Social Science*. 584 Annals 7, 97–109.

Gilliland, F., McConnell, R., Peters, J., and Gong, H. (1999). A Theoretical Basis for Investigating Ambient Air Pollution and Children's Respiratory Health. *Environmental Health Perspectives*, 107 (Suppl. 3), 403–407.

Goings, K., and Mohl, R. A. (Eds.). (1996). *The New African American Urban History*. Thousand Oaks: Sage Publications.

Gold, A. (1990, March 22). Dump Search in New York. *New York Times*, B1.

Goldstein, N., and Madtes, C. (2001, December). The State of Garbage in America. *Biocycle*, 42 (11), 42–54.

Gonzalez, J. (1992, July 22). An Arresting Example of Courage. *Daily News*.

Gordon, H., and Harley, K. (2005). Environmental Justice and the Legal System. In D. Pellow, and R. Brulle (Eds.), *Power, Justice, and the Environment: A Critical Appraisal of the Environmental Justice Movement*, 153–170. Cambridge: MIT Press.

Gottlieb, R. (1993). *Forcing the Spring: The Transformation of the American Environmental Movement*. Washington, D.C.: Island Press.

Govtrack.us. (2005). 109th Congress H.R. 553: Solid Waste Compact Act Retrievable at http://www.govtrack.us/congress/bill.xpd?bill=h109-553

Green, A. (Ed.). (1992). *Medical Waste Incineration and Pollution Prevention*. New York: Van Nostrand Reinhold.

Greenberg, D. (2000). Reconstructing Race and Protest: Environmental Justice in New York City. *Environmental History*, 5 (2), 223–250.

Greenberg, M., Poppwer, F., West, B., and Krueckeberg, D. (1994). Linking City Planning and Public Health in the United States. *Journal of Planning Literature*, 8 (3), 228–239.

Gregory, S. (1998). *Black Corona: Race and the Politics of Place in an Urban Community*. Princeton: Princeton University Press.

Gregory, R., Slovic, P., and Flynn, J. (1996). Risk Perceptions, Stigma, and Health Policy. *Health and Place*, 2 (4), 213–220.

Grover, V., and Grover, V. K. (2002, January). Globalisation and Solid Waste Indicators. *The Warmer Bulletin*, 14–15.

Gupta, A. (2001, June). Power Splurge: Why New York Doesn't Need More Power Plants. *City Limits Magazine*, 31.

Guyer, R. (2000). Breath of Life: Stories of Asthma from an Exhibition at the National Library of Medicine. *American Journal of Public Health*, 90 (6), 874–879.

Gwynn, R. C., and Thurston, G. (2001). The Burden of Air Pollution: Impacts Among Racial Minorities. *Environmental Health Perspectives*, 109 (Suppl. 4), 501–506.

Haines, M. (2001). *The Urban Mortality Transition in the United States: 1890–1940*, NBER Working Paper H0134.

Hall, P. (1988). *Cities of Tomorrow: An Intellectual History of City Planning in the Twentieth Century*. Oxford: Blackwell.

Hamilton, C. (1993). Environmental Consequences on Urban Growth and Blight. In R. Hofrichter (Ed.), *Toxic Struggles: The Theory and Practice of Environmental Justice*, 67–75. Philadelphia: New Society.

Harding, S. (1991). *Whose Science? Whose Knowledge?* Ithaca: Cornell University Press.

Harding, S. (Ed.). (1993). *The "Racial" Economy of Science: Toward a Democratic Future*. Bloomington: Indiana University Press.

Harris, L. (1995). Banana Kelly's Toughest Fight. *New Yorker*, 71 (21), 32–40.

Harrison, Ballard, and Allen. (1950). Plan for Rezoning the City of New York. New York.

Harrison, E., and Eaton, M. (2001). The Role of Municipalities in Regulating the Land Application of Sewage Sludge and Septage. *Natural Resources Journal*, 41 (1), 77–123.

Harvey, D. (1989). *The Condition of Postmodernity: An Enquiry into the Origins of Cultural Change.* Oxford: Blackwell.

Harvey, D. (1996). *Justice, Nature and the Geography of Difference.* Oxford: Blackwell.

Harvey, D. (2001). *Spaces of Capital: Towards a Critical Geography.* Edinburgh: Edinburgh University Press.

Harwood, S. (2003). Environmental Justice on the Streets: Advocacy Planning as a Tool to Contest Environmental Racism. *Journal of Planning Education and Research,* 23 (1), 24–38.

Hawthorne, M. (2001, January 18). NJ Sludge Falls Short of New Law, Critics Say. *Columbus Dispatch,* 1C.

Hearing Before the Committee on Science House of Representatives. One Hundred and Sixth Congress, Second Session. March 22, 2000. EPA's Sludge Rule: Closed Minds ♦of Open Debate. Retrievable at http://www.house.gov/science/106_hearing.htm#Energy_and_Environment

Hennelly, R. (1994, July 12). Bronx Burnout: Bankrupt Medical Waste Incinerator Goes Up in Smoke. *Village Voice,* 10–11.

Hershkowitz, A. (2002). *Bronx Ecology: Blueprint for a New Environmentalism.* Washington, D.C.: Island Press.

Higgins, R. (1994). Race, Pollution and the Mastery of Nature. *Environmental Ethics,* 16 (3), 251–263.

Hirsh, R. (1999). *Power Loss: The Origins of Deregulation and Restructuring in the American Electric Utility System.* Cambridge: MIT Press.

Hofrichter, R., (Ed.). (1993). *Toxic Struggles: The Theory and Practice of Environmental Justice.* Philadelphia: New Society.

Holusha, J. (1991, September 8). The Nation; in Some Parts, The Battle Cry is 'Don't Dump on Me. *New York Times,* 4.

Holusha, J. (1994, May 6). Pioneering Bronx Plant to Recycle City's Paper. *New York Times,* Section D., 1.

Holusha, J. (1996, June 12). State Approves Bronx Paper-Recycling Mill. *New York Times,* B3.

Hsieh, T. S. (2005). To Recycle or Not To Recycle? Analyzing the New York City's Recycling Program Suspension. *Interdisciplinary Environmental Review,* 6 (1), 82–91.

Hu, W. (2003, June 9). Albany: Fresh Kills Environmental Study" *New York Times,* B1.

Hubbard, R., and Wald, E. (1993). *Exploding the Gene Myth: How Genetic Information is Produced and Manipulated by Scientists, Physicians, Employers, Insurance Companies, Educators and Law Enforcers.* Boston: Beacon Press.

Hum, T. (2004). Immigrant Global Neighborhoods in New York City. In J. Krase, and R. Hutchison (Eds.), *Race and Ethnicity in New York City*, Research in Urban Sociology Vol. 7, 25–55. Amsterdam: Elsevier.

Hurewitz, M. (1991, August 19). Incinerator Gets 'Em Burning Mad. *New York Post*, 13.

Hurley, A. (1995). *Environmental Inequalities: Class, Race and Industrial Pollution in Gary, Indiana, 1945–1980.* Chapel Hill: University of North Carolina Press.

Independent Budget Office (2001). Overview of the Waste Stream Managed by the New York City Department of Sanitation, Retrievable at http://www.ibo.nyc.ny.us/

In Pennsylvania, Giuliani Draws Protest on Trash. (1999, February 6). *New York Times*, B5.

Israel, B. A., Schulz, A. J., Parker, E. A., and Becker, A. B. (1998). Review of Community-Based Research: Assessing Partnership Approaches to Improve Public Health. *Annual Review of Public Health*, 19, 173–202.

Jackson, K. (1985). Crabgrass Frontier: The Suburbanization of the United States. Oxford: Oxford University Press.

Jacobsen, B. (2000, April 1). New York States Sues Big Apple over Trash Export. *Waste Age.*

Jacobson, C. D. (2000). *Ties that Bind: Economic and Political Dilemmas of Urban Utility Networks, 1800–1990.* Pittsburgh: University of Pittsburgh Press.

Jamieson, W. (2003, March 2). Riding the Bounding Rails. *New York Times*, 14, 1.

Johnson, K. (2001, February 8). Critics of Power Generators Sue: Citing Threat to Environment. *New York Times*, B4.

Johnson, K. (2002, August 2). Trash Plan Alters Mix of Winners and Losers. *New York Times*, B1.

Johnson, K. (2003, February 9). Energy Consumers Playing the Field: Oh, Behave! *New York Times*, 37, 40.

Jones, A. P. (1998). Asthma and Domestic Air Quality. *Social Science and Medicine*, 47 (6), 755–764.

Jonnes, J. (1986). *We're Still Here.* Boston: Atlantic Monthly Press.

Kappstatter, B. (1997, June 27). Incinerator Plans to Close. *Daily News*, Suburban, 1.

Kay, J. H. (1998). *Asphalt Nation: How the Automobile Took over America, and How We Can Take It Back.* Berkeley: University of California Press.

Keil, R. (1995). The Environmental Problematic in World Cities. In P. Knox, and P. J. Taylor (Eds.), *World Cities in a World System*, 280–297. Cambridge: Cambridge University Press.

Keller, E. F. (1985). *Reflections in Gender and Science*. New Haven: Yale University Press.

Kelly, K. (1973). *Garbage: The History and Future of Garbage in America*. New York: Saturday Review Press.

Kelman, A. (2003). *A River and Its City: The Nature of Landscape in New Orleans*. Berkeley: University of California Press.

Kemp, R. (Ed.). *Privatization: The Provision of Public Services by the Public Sector*. Jefferson: McFarland and Company.

Kirschner, D. S. (1986). *The Paradox of Professionalism: Reform and Public Service in Urban America, 1900–1940*. Westport: Greenwood Press.

Klinenberg, E. (2002). *Heat Wave: A Social Autopsy of Disaster in Chicago*. Chicago: University of Chicago Press.

Knox, P. (1995). World Cities and the Organization of Global Space." In R. J. Johnston, P. J. Taylor, and M. J. Watts (Eds.), *Geographies of Global Change: Remapping the World*, 232–247. Oxford: Blackwell.

Koren, S. H. (1995). Associations between Criteria Air Pollutants and Asthma. *Environmental Health Perspectives*, 103 (Suppl. 6), 235–242.

Kozyriskyj, A., and O'Neil, J. (1999). The Social Construction of Childhood Asthma: Changing Explanations of the Relationship Between Socioeconomic Status and Asthma. *Critical Public Health*, 9 (3), 197–210.

Krauss, C. (1992). Women and Toxic Waste Protests: Race, Class, and Gender as Resources of Resistance. *Qualitative Sociology*, 16 (3), 247–261.

Krieger, J., Song, L., Takaro, T., and Stout, J. (2000). Asthma and the Home Environment of Low-Income Urban Children: Preliminary Findings from the Seattle-King County Health Homes Project. *Journal of Urban Health: Bulletin of the New York Academy of Medicine*, 77 (1), 50–67.

Kuhn, T. (1962). *The Structure of Scientific Revolutions*. Chicago: University of Chicago Press.

Lake, R. (1996). Volunteers, NIMBYs and Environmental Justice: Dilemmas of Democratic Practice. *Antipode*, 28 (2), 160–174.

Lauter, P. (2002). American Studies, American Politics and the Reinvention of Class. In D. Pease, and R. Wiegman (Eds.), *The Futures of American Studies*, 486–509. Durham, N.C.: Duke University Press.

Latino Issues Forum. (2001, November). *Power Against the People: Moving Beyond Crisis Planning in California*. San Francisco: Estrada, T. and DeGannes, K.

Lavelle, M., and Coyle, M. (1993). Unequal Protection: The Racial Divide in Environmental Law. In R. Hofrichter (Ed.), *Toxic Struggles: The Theory and Practice of Environmental Justice*, 136–143. Philadelphia: New Society.

Ledbetter, J. (1998, July 22–28). "Rupert's Welfare." *Village Voice*.

Ledogar, R., Penchaszadeh, A., Iglesias, C., and Garden-Acosta, L. (2000). Asthma and Latino Cultures: Different Prevalence Reported Among Groups Sharing the Same Environment. *American Journal of Public Health*, 90 (6), 929–935.

Lee, C. (1993). Beyond Toxic Wastes and Race. In R. Bullard (Ed.), *Confronting Environmental Racism: Voices from the Grassroots*, 41–52. Boston: South End Press.

Lee, F. (1989, June 24). New York Says It Will End Sea Dumping. *New York Times*, 25.

Lentz, P. (1995, November 13). Mayor Aiming at Mob Carters. *Crain's New York Business*, 3.

Lentz, P. (1999, March 15). Cartload of Mergers Brings New Firms to Trash Business. *Crain's New York Business*, 4.

Lentz, P. (1999, April 19). Electric Deregulation Juices State Power Plant Proposals. *Crain's New York Business*, 4.

Lentz, P. (1999, September 16). Deregulation, No Contest. *Crain's New York Business*, 24.

Lentz, P. (2000, April 17). Deregulation turns ugly. *Crain's New York Business*, 4.

Lentz, P. (2000, July 3). 10 New Power Projects Eyes for NYC. *Crain's New York Business*, 3.

Lentz, P. (2000, July 31). Electric Bills Jump 43%. *Crain's New York Business*, 4.

Lentz, P. (2001, November 19). City's Small Garbage Carters are Seeking Hauls of Justice. *Crain's New York Business*, 4.

Lerner, S. (2005). *Diamond: A Struggle for Environmental Justice in Louisiana's Chemical Corridor.* Cambridge: MIT Press.

Levin, S. (1999, May 27–June 2). Incinerator Re-Emerges as Issue as New Legal Action is Filed. *Bronx Press Review*.

Lewis-Jones, R., and Winkler, M. (1991). *Sludge Parasites and Other Pathogens.* New York: Ellis Horwood.

Lipsitz, G. (1998). *The Possessive Investment in Whiteness: How White People Profit from Identity Politics.* Philadelphia: Temple University Press.

Lipsitz, G. (2001). *American Studies in a Moment of Danger.* Minneapolis: University of Minnesota.

Lipton, E. (2001, March 24). City Trash Follows Long and Winding Road. *New York Times*, B1.

Lipton, E. (2001, May 28). Giuliani Calls for Tightening Controls on Electricity Rates. *New York Times*, B3.

Lipton, E. (2003, December 2). City Seeks Ideas As Trash Costs Dwarf Estimate. *New York Times*, A1.

Lipton, E. (2004, November 22). New York Port Hums Again, with Asian Trade. *New York Times*, B1.

Loh, P., and Sugerman-Brozen, J. (2002). Environmental Justice Organizing for Environmental Health. *American Annals of Political and Social Science*, 584 (1), 100–124.

Loh, P., Sugerman-Brozan, J., Wiggins, S., Noiles, D., and Archibald, C. (2002). From Asthma to AirBeat: community-driven monitoring of fine particles and black carbon in Roxbury, Massachusetts. *Environmental Health Perspectives*, 110 (Suppl. 2), 297–301.

Loka Institute. (1998, July). *Community-Based Research in the United States: An Introductory Reconnaissance, Including Twelve Organizational Case Studies and Comparison with the Dutch Science Shops and the Mainstream American Research System* (report). Washington, D.C.: R. Sclove, M. Scammell, and B. Holland.

Lueck, T. (2001, January 20). Neighbors will have a Voice in Gowanus Road Project. *New York Times*, B2.

Luo, M. (2004, February 22). M.T.A. May Back Out of Plan to Convert Diesel Bus Depot. *New York Times*, 31.

Ma, M. (2004, November 21). Nabe Fury Over Mike Trash Plan. *Daily News*.

Maantay, J. (2000). Industrial Zoning Changes and Environmental Justice in New York City: An Historical, Geographical and Cultural Analysis. Unpublished doctoral dissertation, Rutgers University.

Maantay, J. (2001). Zoning, Equity, and Public Health. *American Journal of Public Health*, 19 (7), 1033–1041.

Maeder, J. (2001, November 30). On the Beach Wash-ups, July–September 1988. *Daily News*, 93.

Mahler, J. (2005). *Ladies and Gentlemen, The Bronx Is Burning: 1977, Baseball, Politics, and the Battle for the Soul of a City.* New York: Farrar, Straus and Giroux.

Mailick, M., Holden, G., and Walther, V. (1994). Coping With Childhood Asthma: Caretakers Views. *Health and Social Work*, 19 (2), 103–111.

Makielski, S. J. (1966). *The Politics of Zoning: The New York Experience.* New York: Columbia University Press.

Marcuse, P. (1980). Housing Policy and City Planning: The Puzzling Split in the United States, 1893–1931. In G. Cherry (Ed.), *Shaping an Urban World,* 23–58. New York: St. Martin's Press.

Markel, H. (1999). *Quarantine!: East European Jewish Immigrants and the New York City Epidemics of 1892.* Baltimore: Johns Hopkins University Press.

Marteau, T., and Johnston, M. (1986). Determinants of Beliefs about Illness: A Study of Parents of Children with Diabetes, Asthma, Epilepsy, and No Chronic Illness. *Journal of Psychosomatic Research*, 20 (6), 673–683.

Martin, D., and Barry, D. (1998, December 3). Giuliani Stirs Up Border Tensions with Trash Plan. *New York Times*, A1.

Martin, D. (1999, May 6). City's Last Waste Incinerator is Torn Down. *New York Times*, B8.

May, E. T. (1996). The Radical Roots of American Studies: Presidential Address to the American Studies Association, November 9, 1995. *American Quarterly*, 48 (2), 179–200.

Mayo, D. G., and Hollander, R. D. (Eds.). (1991). *Acceptable Evidence: Science and Values in Risk Management.* New York: Oxford University Press.

McArdle, A., and Erzen, T. (2001). *Zero Tolerance: Quality of Life and the New Police Brutality in New York City*. New York: NYU Press.

McBride, D. (1991). *From TB to AIDS: Epidemics among Urban Blacks since 1900*. Albany: State University of New York Press.

McDonald, F. (1962). *Insull*. Chicago: University of Chicago Press.

McKinley, J., and Cardwell, D. (2001, April 7). Court Clears Plan to Build Power Plants. *New York Times*, B1.

McKinley, J. (1992, August 28). Plan on Garbage Backed by Council in New York City. *New York Times*, B1.

McNamara, W. (2002). *The California Energy Crisis: Lessons for a Deregulating Industry*. Tulsa, Ok.: PennWell.

Mechling, J. (1996). American Studies as a Social Movement. In M. Fishwick (Ed.), *An American Mosaic: Rethinking American Culture History*, 15–26. New York: American Heritage.

Medzon, K. M. (1992, July 23). 19 Arrested Protesting Incinerator. *The Riverdale Press*, A1.

Melosi, M. (1981). *Garbage in the Cities: Refuse, Reform, and the Environment, 1880–1980*. Texas: Texas A&M University Press.

Melosi, M. (1985). *Coping with Abundance: Energy and Environment in Industrial America*. Philadelphia: Temple University Press.

Melosi, M. (2001). *Effluent America: Cities, Industry, Energy and the Environment*. Pittsburgh: University of Pittsburgh Press.

Mele, C. (2000). *Selling the Lower East Side: Culture, Real Estate, and the Resistance in the New York City*. Minneapolis: University of Minnesota Press.

Merchant, C. (1980). *The Death of Nature: Women, Ecology, and the Scientific Revolution: A Feminist Reappraisal of the Scientific Revolution*. San Francisco: Harper and Row.

Miller, B. (2000). *Fat of the Land: Garbage in New York: The Last Two Hundred Years*. New York: Four Windows Eight Walls.

Miller, R. L. (1999). Breathing Freely: the Need for Asthma Research on Gene-Environment Interactions. *American Journal of Public Health*, 89 (6), 819–822.

Miller, V. (1994). Planning, Power and Politics: A Case Study of the Land Use and Siting history of the North River Water Pollution Control Plant. *Fordham Urban Law Journal*, 21 (3), 707–722.

Mitchell, E. A. (1991). Racial Inequalities in Childhood Asthma. *Social Science and Medicine*, 32 (7), 831–836.

Mitra, S. (1994, January). Stopping Freight. *City Limits*, 16–21.

Morello-Frosch, R., Pastor, M., and Sadd, J. (2002). Integrating Environmental Justice and the Precautionary Principle in Research and Policy-making. *American Annals of Political and Social Science*, 584 (1), 47–68.

Motley, R. S. (1993). Planning the Equitable City. In T. Bressi (Ed.), *Planning and Zoning New York City: Yesterday, Today Tomorrow* (206–223). New Brunswick, NJ: Center for Urban Policy Research.

Municipal Art Society Planning Center. (1998). *The State of 197-a Planning in New York City*. New York.

Municipal Arts Society Planning Center. (2004). *Planning for All New Yorkers: Briefing Book of Community Based Plans*. (2004). Retrievable at http://www.mas.org/PlanningCenter/#BBook

Muñiz, V. (1998). *Resisting Gentrification and Displacement: Voices of Puerto Rican Women of the Barrio*. New York: Garland Publishing.

Murphy, E. F. (1989). Euclid and the Environment. In C. Haar, and J. Kayden (Eds.), *Zoning and the American Dream: Promises Still to Keep*, 154–186. Chicago: Planners Press.

Myers, S. L. (1993, February 20). Proposal for Sludge Plant in Brooklyn is Withdrawn. *New York Times*, 23.

Natural Resources Defense Council. (1997, February). *Too Good to Throw Away: Recycling's Proven Record*. Washington, D.C.: Allen Hershkowitz.

Natural Resources Defense Council and the Coalition for Clean Air. (1998, April). *Exhausted by Diesel: How America's Dependence on Diesel Engines Threatens Our Health*. Washington, D.C.: G. Solomon, T. R. Campbell, T. Carmichael, G. R. Feuer, J. Hathaway.

Nelson, A. (2003). Black Power, Biomedicine and the Politics of Knowledge. PhD diss., New York University.

New York City Department of City Planning. (1977). *The South Bronx: A Plan for Revitalization Summary*. New York City.

New York City Department of City Planning, Community District Profiles, Retrievable at http://www.nyc.gov/html/dcp/html/lucds/cdstart.shtml

New York City Department of City Planning. (1995). *Fair Share: An Assessment of New York City's Facility Siting Process*. New York City.

New York City Department of Health and Mental Hygiene. (2003, April). *NYC Vital Signs. A Report from the New York City Community Health Survey*, 2 (4). New York City.

New York City Department of Sanitation. (2000). *D.S.N.Y. Annual Report*. Retrievable at http://www.nyc.gov/html/dsny/downloads/pdf/ar2000.pdf

New York City Department of Sanitation. (2001). *Department of Sanitation Annual Report*. New York City.

New York City Department of Sanitation. (2001). *DOS Bureau of Planning and Budget Report, Second Quarter*. New York City.

New York City Department of Sanitation. (2001). *New York City Recycling In Context*. Retrievable at http://www.nyc.gov/html/nycwasteless/downloads/pdf/recycling_context1.pdf

New York City Department of Sanitation. (2002). *D.S.N.Y. Annual Report*. Retrievable at http://www.nyc.gov/html/dsny/downloads/pdf/ar2002.pdf

New York Independent Office. (2001, February). *An Overview: The Waste Stream Managed by the NYC Department of Sanitation*. New York City.

New York Power Trip Threatens Growth. (1999, July 19). *Crain's New York Business,* p. 8.

Nocon, A., and Booth, T. (1989–1990). The Social Impact of Asthma: A Review of the Literature. *Social Work and Social Sciences Review,* 1 (3), 177–200.

Norlander, G. (2002). Public Utility Law Project of New York. (2002, November). *Electricity Deregulation in New York State 1996–2002.* New York: Retrievable at www.pulp.org.

Northridge, M. E., Prakash, S., and Stover, G. (Eds.). Community, Research, and Environmental Justice. *Environmental Health Perspectives,* 110 (Suppl.), 217–221.

Nossiter, A. (1995, September 5). Asthma Common and on the Rise in the Crowded South Bronx. *New York Times,* 1.

Nye, D. (1990). *Electrifying America: Social Meanings of a New Technology.* Cambridge: MIT Press.

Nye, D. (1998). *Consuming Power: A Social History of American Energies.* Cambridge: MIT Press.

O'Connell, K. (2001, March). The Manhattan Transfer. *Waste Age,* 182–185.

O'Connell, K. (2002, March). In and Out. *Waste Age,* 36–38.

O'Fallon, L. R., and Dearry, A. (2002). Community-Based Participatory Research as a Tool to Advance Environmental Health Sciences. *Environmental Health Perspectives,* 110 (Suppl. 2), 155–159.

Office of Lead Hazard Control, U.S. Department of Housing and Urban Development. April 1999. *The Healthy Homes Initiative: A Preliminary Plan.*

Omi, M., and Winant, H. (1986). *Racial Formation in the United States: From the 1960s to the 1980s.* New York: Routledge.

Otey, A. M. (1992, May 13). Resident's Burn over Incinerator. *Newsday,* 27.

Outerbridge, T. (2000, April). The Crisis of Closing Fresh Kills. *Biocycle,* 41 (4), 47–50.

Pastor, M., Sadd, J., and Hipp, J. (2001). Which Came First? Toxic Facilities, Minority Move-In, and Environmental Justice. *Journal of Urban Affairs,* 23 (1), 1–21.

Pellow, D. N. (2000). Environmental Inequality Formation. *American Behavioral Scientist,* 43 (4), 581–601.

Pellow, D. N. (2002). *Garbage Wars: The Struggle for Environmental Justice in Chicago.* Cambridge: MIT Press.

Pellow, D. N., and Park, L. (2003). *The Silicon Valley of Dreams: Environmental Injustice, Immigrant Workers and the High-Tech Global Economy.* New York: NYU Press.

Pellow, D., and Brulle, R. (Eds.). (2005). *Power, Justice, and the Environment: A Critical Appraisal of the Environmental Justice Movement.* Cambridge: MIT Press.

Perera, F. P., Rauh, V., Whyatt, R. M., Tsai, W. Y., Bernert, J. T., Tu, Y. H., Andrews, H., Ramirez, J., Qu, L., and Tang, D. (2003). Molecular Evidence of an Interaction Between Prenatal Environmental Exposures on Birth Outcomes in a Multiethnic Population. *Environmental Health Perspectives*, 111 (2), 201–205.

Pérez-Peña, R. (2001, March 23). Power Plants May be in Use a Bit Longer. *New York Times*, B1.

Pérez-Peña, R. (2001, April 5). Judge Stops Power Project Until Review is Conducted. *New York Times*, B1.

Pérez-Peña, R. (2001, November 21). Court Upholds Tougher Rules on Pollution. *New York Times*, D1.

Pérez-Peña, R. (2003, April 19). Study Finds Asthma In 25% of Children In Central Harlem. *New York Times*, A1.

Perris, R., and Chait, J. (1998). *Williamsburg Waterfront 197A plan: A Matter of Balance: Housing, Industry, Open Space in Community Board 1.* New York: Municipal Art Society Planning Center and the Pratt Institute Center for Community and Environmental Development.

Peterson, J. (1979). The Impact of Sanitary Reform Upon American Urban Planning, 1840–1890. *Journal of Social History*, 12 (1), 83–103.

Pinder, L. (2002). Commentary on the Kennedy Krieger Institute Lead Paint Repair and Maintenance Study. *Neurotoxicology and Teratology*, 24 (4), 477–479.

Platt, H. (1991). *The Electric City: Energy and the Growth of the Chicago Area, 1880–1930.* Chicago: University of Chicago Press.

Platt, R. (1991). *Land Use Control: Geography, Law and Public Policy.* Upper Saddle River, W.J.: Prentice Hall.

President's Task Force on Environmental Health Risks and Safety Risks to Children. Originally released January 28, 1999. Revised May 2000. *Asthma and the Environment: A Strategy to Protect Children.*

Polgreen, L. (2003, January 17). Pollution Linked to Low Birth Weights in African Americans. *New York Times*, B6.

Preston, S., and Haines, M. (1991). *Fatal Years: Child Mortality in Late Nineteenth-century America.* Princeton: Princeton University Press.

Pristin, T. (2002, June 2). Harlem Neighborhood Competes for a Stretch of Riverfront Turf. *New York Times*, B3.

Prout, A., Hayes, L., and Gelder, L. (1999). Medicines and the Maintenance of Ordinariness in the Household Management of Childhood Asthma. *Sociology of Health and Illness*, 21 (2), 137–162.

Pulido, L., and Peña, D.G. (1998). Environmentalism and Positionality: The Early Pesticide Campaign of the United Farm Workers' Organizing Committee, 1965–1971. *Race, Gender and Class*, 6 (1), 33–50.

Pulido, L. (2000) Rethinking Environmental Racism: White Privilege and Urban Development in Southern California. *Annals of the Association of American Geographers*, 90 (1), 12–40.

Purnick, J. (1989, December 6). The Foul Mystery of North River. *New York Times*, A30.

Ramirez-Valles, J. (1998). Promoting Health, Promoting Women: The Construction of Female and Professional Identities in the Discourse of Community Health Workers. *Social Science and Medicine*, 47 (11), 1749–1764.

Randall, J. (1999, March 12). Harrisburg: Give Us Trash. *Staten Island Advance*.

"Rate Reform Lacks Energy." (1998, April 24). *Daily News*, 46.

Raver, A. (1999, October 1). Up From the Ruins, Red Hook Faces a Dump. *New York Times*, F1.

Reiss, M. (1991, November 26). The Garbage Broker. *Village Voice*, 30–40.

Revell, K. (1992). Regulating the Landscape: Real Estate Values, City Planning, and the 1916 Zoning Ordinance. In D. Ward, and O. Zunz (Eds.), *The Landscape of Modernity: Essays on New York City, 1900–1940*, 19–45. New York: Russell Sage Foundation.

Riccardi, M. (2001, February 26). Judge Threatens to Halt Work on Queens Power Plants. *New York Law Journal*, 1.

Roberts, J. T., and Toffolon-Weiss, M. (2001). *Chronicles from the Environmental Justice Frontline*. Cambridge: Cambridge University Press.

Roberts, S. (2002). *Infectious Fear: Tuberculosis, Public Health and the Politics of Color and Illness in Baltimore, Maryland, 1880–1940*. PhD diss., Princeton University.

Robinson, C. M. (1908). *The Call of the City*. San Francisco and New York, P. Elder and Co.

Roig-Franzia, M. (2001, August 25). My Kids were Used as Guinea Pigs. *Washington Post*, A1, 12.

Rose, T. (1994). *Black Noise: Rap Music and Black Culture in Contemporary America*. Hanover: Wesleyan University Press.

Rosen, G. (1993). *A History of Public Health*. Baltimore: Johns Hopkins.

Rosenstreich, D. L., Eggleston, P., Kattan, M., et al. (1997). The Role of Cockroach Allergy and Exposure to Cockroach Allergen in Causing Morbidity among Inner-City Children with Asthma. *New England Journal of Medicine*, 336, 1356–1363.

Royte, E. (2005). *Garbage Land: On the Secret Trail of Trash*. New York: Little, Brown.

Ruiz, A. (2001, February 26). Why is Rudy in Power Plant Fray? *The Daily News*, Suburban, p. 4.

Rutenberg, J. (2005, October 18). The Manager as Mayor: While Aides Get a Free Hand, Bloomberg Measures Results. *New York Times*, A1.

Sandercock, L. (Ed.). (1998). *Making the Invisible Visible: A Multicultural Planning History*. Berkeley: University of California Press.

Santora, M. (2005, January 14). U.S. Praises Program in City for Children with Asthma. *New York Times*.

Savitch, H. V. (1988). *Post-Industrial Cities: Politics and Planning in New York, Paris and London*. Princeton: Princeton University Press.

Santiago-Rivera, A. L., Morse, G. S., Hunt, A., and Lickers, H. (1998). Building a Community-Based Research Partnership: Lessons from the Mohawk Nation of Akwesasne. *Journal of Community Psychology*, 26 (2), 163–174.

Saving the Sound. (1998, March 24). *New York Times*, A22.

Schell, L., and Tarbell, A. (1998). A Partnership Study of PCBs and the Health of Mohawk Youth: Lessons from Our Past and Guidelines for Our Future. *Environmental Health Perspectives*, 106 (Suppl. 3), 833–840.

Schwartz, J. (1993). *The New York Approach: Robert Moses, Urban Liberals and the Redevelopment of the Inner City*. Columbus: Ohio State University Press.

Schultz, S., and McShane, C. (1978). To Engineer the Metropolis: Sewers, Sanitation and City Planning in Late Nineteenth Century America. *Journal of American History*, 65 (2), 389–411.

Sclar, E. (2000). *You Don't Always Get What You Pay For: The Economics of Privatization*. Ithaca: Cornell University Press.

Scott, J. (2003, June 4). Coalition Adds New Support for a Harbor Freight Tunnel. *New York Times*, B4.

Severo, R. (1989, November 30). Odors from Plant Anger Many in Harlem. *New York Times*, B1.

Shaw, R. (1996). *The Activist's Handbook: A Primer for the 1990s and Beyond*. Berkeley: University of California Press.

Shell, E. (2000). Does Civilization Cause Asthma? *Atlantic Monthly*, 285 (5), 90–100.

Shepard, P. (1994). Issues of Community Empowerment. *Fordham Urban Law Journal*, 21 (3), 739–755.

Shepard, P., Northridge, M. E., Prakash, S., and Stover, G. (Eds.). (2002). Community, Research, and Environmental Justice. *Environmental Health Perspectives*, 110 (Suppl. 2).

Shrader-Frechette, K. (2002). *Environmental Justice: Creating Equality, Reclaiming Democracy*. New York: Oxford.

Shipler, D. (2004). *The Working Poor: Invisible in America*. New York: Knopf.

Silver, C. (1997). The Racial Origins of Zoning in American Cities. In J. M. Thomas, and M. Ritzdorf (Eds.), *In the Shadows: Urban Planning and the African American Community*, 23–42. Newbury Park, CA: Sage Publications.

Smith, N. (1984). *Uneven Development: Nature, Capital and the Production of Space*. Oxford: Blackwell.

Smith, N. (1996). *The New Urban Frontier: Gentrification and the Revanchist City*. London: Routledge.

Smith, M. P. (1988). *Comparative Urban and Community Research: Power, Community and the City*. New Brunswick, N.J.: Transaction Publishers.

Smith, S. (1995). *Sick and Tired of Being Sick and Tired: Black Women's Health Activism in America, 1890–1950*. Philadelphia: University of Pennsylvania Press.

Smothers, R. (2002, July 23). Company Offers to Buy Land In Linden for a Waste Station. *New York Times*, B5.

Soller, M. (2001, March 18). The New NIMBYs Are Taking Back Their Back Yards—and Their Air. *Los Angeles Times*, M6.

Spencer, J. (2000, February 4). Judge Rejects Laws Limiting Trash Hauling to Virginia. *New York Times*, B9.

Starr, P. (1990). The Limits of Privatization. In D. Gayle, and J. Goodrich (Eds.), *Privatization and Deregulation in Global Perspective* (109–126). New York: Quorum Books.

Stauber, J. C., and Rampton, S. (1995). *Toxic Sludge is Good for You: Lies, Damn Lies, and the Public Relations Industry*. Monroe, Me.: Common Courage Press.

Stein, B. (1992). Incinerator Expansion Eyed. *Riverdale Press*, A1.

Steingraber, S. (1997). *Living Downstream: An Ecologist Looks at Cancer and the Environment*. Reading, Mass: Addison-Wesley.

Stevenson, L., Garg, R., and Leighton, J. (2000). Asthma Hospitalization in New York City 1988–1997. *Journal of Urban Health: Bulletin of the New York Academy of Medicine*, 77 (1), 137–139.

Stevenson, M., and Burke, M. (1992). Bureaucratic Logic in New Social Movement Clothing: The Limits of Health Promotion Research. *Canadian Journal of Public Health*, 83 (Suppl. 1), 47–53.

Stewart, B. (2000, March 9). Bronx Loudly Opposes Waste Station Plan. *New York Times*, B4.

Stolberg, S. G. (1999, October 18). Poor People are Fighting Baffling Surge in Asthma. *New York Times*, A1.

Strickland, R. (1993). The Template of the Ideal City. In T. Bressi (Ed.), *Planning and Zoning New York City: Yesterday, Today Tomorrow* (48–60). New Brunswick, N.J.: Center for Urban Policy Research.

Strasser, S. (1999). *Waste and Want: A Social History of Trash*. New York: Metropolitan Books.

Sugarman, R. (1997, January 22). Toxic Fumes are Seen in Remission. *Daily News*, Suburban, 1.

Sugrue, T. (1996). *The Origins of the Urban Crisis: Race and Inequality in Postwar Detroit*. Princeton: Princeton University Press.

Swartz, N. (2002, April). The San Franscisco Feat. *Waste Age*, 94–99.

Sweeney, J. (2002). *The California Electricity Crisis*. Stanford: Hoover Press.

Szasz, A., and Meuser, M. (2000). Unintended, Inexorable: The Production of Environmental Inequalities in Santa Clara County, California. *American Behavioral Scientist*, 43 (4), 602–632.

Sze, J. (2002). The Literature of Environmental Justice. In J. Adamson, M. M. Evans, and R. Stein (Eds.), *The Environmental Justice Reader: Politics, Poetics and Pedagogy*, 163–180. Tucson: University of Arizona Press.

Sze, J. (2004). Asian American Activism for Environmental Justice. *Peace Review*, 16 (2), 149–156.

Sze, J. (2005). Race and Power: An Introduction to Environmental Justice Energy Activism. In D. Pellow, and R. Brulle (Eds.), *Power, Justice, and the Environment: A Critical Appraisal of the Environmental Justice Movement*, 101–115. Cambridge: MIT Press.

Tai, S. (1999). Environmental Hazards and the Richmond Laotian American Community: A Case Study in Environmental Justice. *Asian Law Journal*, 6 (1), 189–207.

Targ, N. (2005). The States' Comprehensive Approach to Environmental Justice. In D. Pellow, and R. Brulle (Eds.), *Power, Justice, and the Environment: A Critical Appraisal of the Environmental Justice Movement*, 171–184. Cambridge: MIT Press.

Tatum, J. (2000). *Muted Voices: The Recovery of Democracy in the Shaping of Technology*. Bethlehem, Pa.: Lehigh University Press.

Taylor, D. E. (2000). The Rise of the Environmental Justice Paradigm: Injustice Framing and the Social Construction of Environmental Discourses. *American Behavioral Scientist*, 43 (4), 508–580.

Taylor, D. (2002). Race, Class, Gender and American Environmentalism. United States Department of Agriculture, Forest Service (Pacific Northwest Research Station) General Technical Report. Retrievable at http://www.fs.fed.us/pnw/pubs/gtr534.pdf

Tesh, S. (1996). *Hidden Arguments: Political Ideology and Disease Prevention Policy*. New Brunswick, N.J.: Rutgers University Press.

Tesh, S. (2000). *Uncertain Hazards: Environmental Activists and Scientific Proof*. Ithaca: Cornell University Press.

The Zoning Resolution of the City of New York retrievable at http://www.nyc.gov/html/dcp/html/zoneform.html

Thomas, J. M. (1997). *Redevelopment and Race: Planning a Finer City in Postwar Detroit*. Baltimore: Johns Hopkins Press.

Thomas, J. M., and Ritzdorf, M. (Eds.). (1997). *In the Shadows: Urban Planning and the African American Community*. Newbury Park, Calif.: Sage Publications.

Tickner, J. A. (Ed). (2003). *Precaution, Environmental Science, and Preventive Public Policy*. Washington, D.C.: Island Press.

Tobey, R. (1996). *Technology as Freedom: The New Deal and the Electrical Modernization of the American Home*. Berkeley: University of California Press.

Tokar, B. (1997). *Earth For Sale: Reclaiming Ecology in the Age of Corporate Greenwash*. Boston: South End Press.

Troesken, W. (2004). *Water, Race, and Disease*. Cambridge: MIT Press.

Truini, J. (2002, February 18). New York City May Curtail Curbside Recycling Programs. *Waste News*.

The Turbine Mess. (2001, March 20). *New York Times*, 24.

Urbina, I. (2004, August 16) For Bronx Land With Spotty Past, No Lack of Plans. *New York Times*, B1.

Urbina, I. (2004, October 7). City Trash Plan Forgoes Trucks, Favoring Barges. *New York Times*, A1.

United Church of Christ, Commission for Racial Justice. (1987). *Toxic Wastes and Race in the United States: A National Report on the Racial and Socio-Economic Characteristics of Communities with Hazardous Waste Sites*. New York: United Church of Christ.

Van Natta, D. (1995). Mill Sought for Bronx is Blocked by Train Buff. *New York Times*, 31.

Wailoo, K. (2001). *Dying in the City of the Blues: Sickle Cell Anemia and the Politics of Race and Health*. Chapel Hill, N.C.: University of North Carolina Press.

Wakefield, S., Elliott, S., Cole, D., and Eyles, J. (2001). Environmental Risk and (re)action: Air Quality, Health, and Civic Involvement in an Urban Industrial Neighborhood. *Health and Place*, 7 (3), 163–177.

Waldinger, R. (1996). *Still the Promised City?: African-Americans and New Immigrants in Postindustrial New York*. Cambridge: Harvard University Press.

Waldman, A. (1999, August 24). Trash Giant Skirts Conditions Set for Bronx Station, Critics Say. *New York Times*, B1.

Wallace, D., and Wallace, R. (1999). *A Plague on Your Houses: How New York City Burned Down and National Health Crumbled*. New York: Verso.

Wallace, D., and Wallace, R. (2003). The Recent Tuberculosis Epidemic in New York City: Warnings from the De-Developing World. In M. Gandy, and A. Zumla (Eds.), *The Return of the White Plague: Global Poverty and the "New" Tuberculosis*, 125–146. London: Verso.

Wallerstein, N. (1999). Power Between Evaluation and Community: Research relationships within New Mexico's Healthier Communities. *Social Science and Medicine*, 49 (1), 39–53.

Ward, D., and Zunz, O. (Eds.). (1992). *The Landscape of Modernity: Essays on New York City, 1900–1940*. New York: Russell Sage Foundation.

Washington, S. (2005). *Packing Them In: An Archaeology of Environmental Racism in Chicago, 1865–1954*. Lanham, Md.: Lexington Books.

Weinberg, A. S., Pellow, D. N., and Schnaiberg, A. (2000). *Urban Recycling and the Search for Sustainable Community Development*. Princeton: Princeton University Press.

Weiss, K. B., and Wagener, D. K. (1990). Geographic variations in US asthma mortality: small-area analyses of excess mortality: 1981–1985. *American Journal of Epidemiology*, 132: 107–115.

Weiss, M. (1992). Density and Intervention: New York's Planning Traditions. In D. Ward, and O. Zunz (Eds.), *The Landscape of Modernity: Essays on New York City, 1900–1940*, 46–75. New York: Russell Sage Foundation.

Wilder, C. S. (2000). *Covenant With Color: Race and Social Power in Brooklyn*. New York: Columbia University Press.

Williams, L. (1996, August 23). A Blueprint for Red Hook: Plan Sees New Apartments and School. *Daily News*, Suburban, 1.

Williams, R. W. 1999. Environmental Injustice in America and its Politics of Scale. *Political Geography*, 18 (1), 49–74.

Willis, C. (1993). A 3D CBD: How the 1916 Zoning Law Shaped Manhattan's Central Business Districts. In T. Bressi (Ed.), *Planning and Zoning New York City: Yesterday, Today Tomorrow*, 3–26. New Brunswick, N.J.: Center for Urban Policy Research.

Wilson, S., Scamagas, P., Grado, J., and Norgaard, L. (1998). The Fresno Asthma Project: A Model Intervention to Control Asthma in Multi-Ethnic, Low-income, Inner-city communities. *Health Education and Behavior*, 25 (1), 79–98.

Wilson, W. J. (1987). *The Truly Disadvantaged: The Inner City, the Underclass, and Public Policy*. Chicago: University of Chicago Press.

Wing, S., Grant, G., Green, M., and Stewart, C. (1996). Community-based Collaboration for Environmental Justice: South-East Halifax Environmental Reawakening. *Environment and Urbanization*, 8 (2), 129–140.

Wing, S. (1998). Whose Epidemiology, Whose Health? *International Journal of Health Services*, 28 (2), 241–252.

Wing, S. (2000). Limits of Epidemiology. In P. Brown, S. Kroll-Smith, and V. Gunter (Eds.), *Illness and the Environment: A Reader in Contested Medicine*, 29–45. New York: NYU Press.

Winnick, L. (1990). *New People in Old Neighborhoods: The Role of New Immigrants in Rejuvenating New York's Communities*. New York: Russell Sage Foundation.

Woodruff, T., Parker, J. D., Kyle, A. D., and Schoendorf, K. C. (2003). National Disparities in Exposure to Air Pollution during Pregnancy. *Environmental Health Perspectives*, 111 (7), 942–946.

Wynne, B. (1996). May the Sheep Safely Graze? A Reflexive View of the Expert-Lay Knowledge Divide. In S. Lash, B. Szerszyniski, and B. Wynne (Eds.), 44–83. *Risk, Environment and Modernity: Toward a New Modernity*. London: Sage.

Yardley, J. (2001, July 27). New York's Sewage was a Texas Town's Gold. *New York Times*, A12.

Yeampierre, E. (1998). Uprising at Sunset. *Journal of Community Advocacy and Activism*, 3 (1), 62–65.

Young, I. (1990). *Justice and the Politics of Difference*. Princeton: Princeton University Press.

Young, I. (2000). *Inclusion and Democracy*. New York: Oxford University Press.

# Index